777365

Modern Governments

Italy–Republic Without Government?

General Editor: Max Beloff

Gladstone Professor of Government and Public Administration,
University of Oxford

Italy - Republic Without Government?

P. A. ALLUM

Lecturer in Politics at the
University of Reading

Weidenfeld and Nicolson
London

ISBN 0 297 76646 5 Cased

Printed in Great Britain by
Willmer Brothers Limited, Birkenhead

Contents

Preface xi
Map showing regions and regional capitals 18

Part I: Italian Society 1

1 Modern Italy in the Making 3
 Unification 3
 Parliamentary Politics 1860–1925 4
 The Centralized Administrative Tradition 7
 Fascism and the 'Corporate State' 11
 The Resistance 15

2 One Nation: Two Societies 20
 The Southern Question 20
 The Economic Miracle 25
 Internal Migration 33
 Class Structure 36
 Political Culture 40

Part II: Civil Society in Italy 45

3 Catholic Church: A State within Civil Society 47
 Church-State Relations 48
 The Place of the Church in Italian Society 51
 The Political Activities of the Church 58

4 Political Parties: The Politics of Patronage 62
 Parties and the Party System 62
 Party Organization 68
 Elections and the Electorate 74
 Party Finance and Power Structure 83

5 Interest Groups: The Politics of Clientela and Parentela 93
 The Groups and their Characteristics 94
 Patterns of Interest Group Activity 99
 (a) Influencing Public Opinion: The Press 99
 (b) Direct Representation in Parliament and Lobbying 101
 (c) Bureaucratic Intervention: *Clientela* and *Parentela* 104

Part III: The Italian State 109

6 Executive and Legislature: A Classic Parliamentary
Government? 111
The Role of President of the Republic 111
(a) The Functions of the Office 112
(b) The Political Influence of the President 114
The Position of the Cabinet 117
(a) Cabinet Instability but Ministerial Stability 119
(b) Cabinet Instability and its Effect on Policy-Making 121
The Power of Parliament 124
(a) Italian Parliamentarians: the Dominance of the
Middle Class 126
(b) Parliamentary Organization and Procedure 128
(c) Parliament and the Legislative Process 130
(d) Parliament and the Control of the Government 135
Executive-Legislative Relations 137

7 Public Administration and the Military: Bureaucracy,
Enterprise and Repression 139
The Italian Administrative System 140
(a) Government by Ministry 141
(b) Government by Special Agency 148
The Civil Service: Structure and Recruitment 153
The Decision-Making Process: the Administration's
relations with the Executive and Interest Groups 161
The Problems of Economic Planning and Development 167
The Military: Organization and Recruitment 172

8 The Judiciary: Archaic Laws and Judicial Confusion 180
Organization of the Courts: Dual System of Jurisdiction 182
(a) The Ordinary Courts 182
(b) The Administrative Courts 186
The Position of the Constitutional Court 191
The Judges and the Independence of the Judiciary 199
The Protection of Civil Rights 204

9 Local and Regional Government: Political Autonomy
or Regional Decentralization? 212
Local Government 213
(a) The Structure of Local Government 213
(b) The Functions of Local Government 216
(c) Control of Local Government: The Prefect 221
Regional Government 225
(a) The Structure of Regional Government 225
(b) Powers of Regional Government 228
(c) Control of Regional Government 233

viii

The Regional Debate: Political Autonomy or
Administrative Decentralization   235

Conclusion: Republic Without Government?   239
Bibliography   251
Index   259

Preface

Since the fall of Fascism in 1945, Italy has returned to a parliamentary system of government in the classical tradition of liberal democracy. The characteristics of this tradition are well-known: political power derived from popular sovereignty – government issuing from free and contested elections; the organization of the State based on the concept of political pluralism and on the belief in a certain institutional separation of powers; political power limited by law – legal protection of a certain number of political freedoms regarded as fundamental (opinion, assembly, association etc.). Given that the political institutions of the liberal democratic tradition operate within capitalist economic structures, political power derives not only from popular sovereignty but also from economic wealth. This association of capitalist economy and parliamentary institutions led the French political scientist Maurice Duverger to coin the term 'pluto-democracies'. In so doing, he focused attention on two important, if sometimes neglected, aspects of the present Italian regime. First, the economic power of certain individuals, companies and classes confers political power on them. Second, this type of regime is the preserve of wealthy nations – Italy is a member of the club of the ten richest and most industrialized nations in the world.

In his analysis of liberal democratic states, Antonio Gramsci, the Italian Marxist, distinguished between two superstructures of society on the basis of the exercise of different functions: on the one hand, *civil society*, which he defined as 'all the organizations commonly called "private" '; and which disputed the function of the intellectual and moral leadership of society; on the other hand, the *State,* which had the function of 'direct rule' or command which 'was expressed in the legal government'. In other words, the function of the organizations of civil society is to create support or consent for the present organization of society by cultural and ideological means. Thus civil society is the arena of ideological competition about how society should be organized. The function of the State is to secure acceptance of the present arrangements by coercion or threat of coercion. The two superstructures are complementary in the sense that all societies establish some sort of balance between consent and coercion. In general, it can be said that the weaker the consent of the ruled towards the present organization of society, the more the rulers will be forced to depend on the control of the state apparatus; and the weaker the coercion of the state apparatus, the more rulers will need to obtain the consent of the ruled. The limits of this balance are represented by the absolute consent of all the population (a practical impossibility) and absolute force (the denial of the liberal democratic state).

The utility of this distinction is that it enables analysis to focus on the links between a given organization of society and its political arrangements. The link is furnished by the personnel responsible for the twin functions of consent and coercion. Gramsci called this personnel 'the intellectuals' : a category that he defined in a much more extensive manner than is traditional. Intellectuals are all those people who give a social group 'its homogeneity and consciousness of its own function'; and hence, in another phrase, they are 'experts in legitimation'. The problem of political analysis for Gramsci turned on the relations between the intellectuals and the different social groups in a given society; and the manner in which they organized concretely their specific functions (i.e. the internal articulations of civil society and the State). Social groups are the expression of the economic structure of society; they create different types of intellectuals who are responsible for organizing civil society and the State. Thus civil society is the link between society and the State : it furnishes 'the ethical foundation of the State'.

Gramsci was well aware that the organic distinction between civil society and the State was never fully achieved in practice. Coercion was found in civil society and consent was pursued actively by the State, but he believed that liberal democratic states came nearest to achieving it. It has also to be noted that liberal democratic states have come to play a much more important and direct role in civil society than they did when Gramsci wrote. Be that as it may, it remains true that the dominant function of the associations and organized groups in civil society is the organization of consent, and hence, civil society is the arena of ideological competition, while the dominant function of the state institutions is the organization of coercion, and, hence, the State is the arena of power conflict. Moreover, it is as well to remember that this distinction enabled Gramsci to identify the factors distinguishing the politics of the advanced industrial nations from the politics of rural backward ones in relation to the level of development of civil society. This made him more sensitive to the possible deformations of the proletarian revolution in non-industrial societies, which he baptized 'statolatria' (state-worship), than any of his Marxist contemporaries.

This study has been organized into three parts: Italian society, Italian civil society, and the Italian State. Given its intention of being a text describing the institutional mechanisms of the state system and their operation (*phénoménologie*), much more space has been devoted to the organizational and political (in the restricted sense) aspects of the superstructures and less to their ideological articulation and reciprocal relations than Gramsci would ever have given. Thus the two chapters of Part I outline what the French geographer Jean Gottmann has felicitously called, in another context, the 'iconography' of the political situation (i.e. the historical, economic, social and cultural background of postwar Italy) and which he opposed to 'movement' (i.e. of men and ideas) as the basis of social change. Parts II and III treat in detail the structures and mode of operation of the major institutional components of civil society and the State. In consequence, the three chapters of Part II are devoted to the Catholic Church, political parties and interest groups, while the four chapters of Part III examine the various institutions of the state system (Executive and Legislature, Public Administration and the Military, the Judiciary, Regional and Local Government). Particular attention has been paid throughout to the activity of the personnel in all institutions in view of the importance accorded to the function of intellectual organization in the framework that we have utilized. After all, Marx was not alone in believing that 'men make their own history, but', he was quick to add, 'they do not make it just as they please.'

I would like to thank Professors Max Beloff and Peter Campbell for reading the manuscript in draft, and for their suggestions and criticisms. Of course they are in no way responsible for the views expressed. Since some of the latter will not be to everyone's taste, I should, perhaps, stress that responsibility for what appears hereafter is mine alone.

Reading and Sanary-sur-Mer (Var) 1972   P.A.A.

Part I
Italian Society

'C'est le gouvernement des deux derniers siècles qui a donné à un peuple très fin ces funestes maximes de conduite'

Stendhal

1 Modern Italy in the Making

Italian politics has been permanently affected by the manner in which national unification was achieved. First, the fact that unification was, paraphrasing Benedetto Croce, the heroic work of a minority, has meant the domination of Italian political life by a tiny oligarchy. Secondly, it ensured the establishment of a strongly centralized state as the only means by which the victors of 1860 believed that they could forge Metternich's 'geographical expression' into a modern nation state. Thirdly, unification provoked a compromise between the ruling classes of North and South which was responsible for the dual development of the country that has persisted down to the present time.

Unification

The unification of Italy was a compromise imposed by Cavour's diplomacy. The structure of the new state was determined by the outcome of the complicated chain of events set in motion by Garibaldi's legendary expedition of 1860. The landing at Marsala in Sicily and the triumphal march of the 'Thousand' over the mainland to Naples was the signal for a general rising of the peasantry to satisfy age-old land hunger. The southern gentry deserted the Bourbons to save its property; and Cavour intervened to forestall the social revolution which he was convinced Garibaldi was busily fermenting. In consequence, the southern gentry rallied to Cavour and the House of Savoy, and Piedmontese troops were called into the South to put down that bloody civil war which the new Italian authorities euphemistically called 'Southern brigandage'. As one of the Piedmontese representatives in Naples in 1861 wrote to the Minister of the Interior: 'the landowners feel that without our army they would

3

be slaughtered by brigands . . .' For this reason they were quite prepared to let Cavour impose his solution for national unity on the new nation. This consisted, according to one of his adversaries, of 'imposing one state (Piedmont) on all the other states of Italy'. The Piedmontese constitutional charter, the celebrated *Statuto albertino* of 1848, was merely extended to all the other states without any concession to their institutions or traditions. The Parliament in Turin was enlarged to seat the members of the other regions. The head of state was the King of Piedmont, Victor Emanuel II, who refused, on assuming the crown of Italy, to change his title to Victor Emanuel I. The administrative system adopted was the centralized French-style Prefectoral system introduced into Piedmont by Napoleon.

The liberal historian Rosario Romeo clearly delineated the significance of these events when he wrote 'if the Risorgimento in the North was the social revolution of a bourgeoisie active in the development of capitalism against the old landowning classes, in the South and Sicily, on the other hand, it was the old landowning classes and their allies which fought the battles of the Risorgimento with notorious consequences for the structure of the ruling classes of united Italy . . .' Unification created in fact, that division of labour between political forces which governed pre-fascist Italy and which Gramsci made famous in the concept of *blocco storico*, the historical alliance between northern capital and southern land. Moreover, the key to the operation of the pre-Fascist Italian political system is manifest in Romeo's statement: the northern bourgeoisie were already organized as a social class whereas the southern gentry remained disorganized. Hence the former organized the new nation while the latter enjoyed local supremacy thanks to Piedmontese protection. Furthermore, the former could always count on the latter's support so long as it did not touch the latter's local privileges. For more than ninety years it did not.

Parliamentary Politics 1860–1925

The *Statuto albertino* established a constitutional monarchy based on a parliamentary system of government in Piedmont, which was extended to the rest of the peninsula in 1861. The new constitution was a direct copy of the French Constitution of

1830. Governmental power ceased to be the monopoly of the Crown and passed into the hands of the Council of Ministers responsible to the elected representative assembly, the Chamber of Deputies. The monarch and the old ruling class continued to exercise considerable influence through the royally appointed Senate, which was granted an equal share of the legislative power with the Chamber. Nonetheless, although the landed gentry and professional bourgeoisie gained access to power for the first time, the manner of unification ensured the domination of Italian political life by a tiny oligarchy. It must always be borne in mind that Italian politics of the pre-Fascist period was a parliamentary battle between a very restricted class of factions. In 1861, the national electorate was less than 2 per cent of the population, and although successfully enlarged it was still less than 25 per cent after Giolitti's introduction of so-called universal male suffrage in 1913. Turnout in this period averaged only 50 per cent. Women, moreover, did not receive the vote until 1945. In this, it must be remembered that Italy differed little from many other European countries. But there was one significant difference: the loss of his temporal power led the Pope to decree the abstention of Catholics from participation in the public life of the new nation which deprived the country of an important section of the population, eligible in other respects.

The parties or factions were recruited, as elsewhere in Europe at the time, from the landowning gentry and professional bourgeoisie. Cavour's party, or *destra storica* as it was known, which brought to the government of the new nation the Hegelian concept of the function of the State, was organized around the Piedmontese bourgeoisie and the large landed and professional classes. On the other hand, the *sinistra storica,* as the opposition party was known, was based, insofar as it had a coherent social basis, on the smaller gentry and educated urban classes. Many of its members were those whose ambitions had been disappointed in the distribution of patronage in the years following unification. Thus it is correct to state that the political differences were in methods and not ideas. Indeed the liberal historian, Federico Chabod, has written that 'in pre-1914 Italy the parties had virtually no policy – policy lay with Parliament and Members of Parliament . . .' Nonetheless a regional division between *destra* (North) and *sinistra* (South) grew during the first decade of unity

5

as a result of what was considered to be the excessive 'Piedmontization' of the new state (by which was meant the imposition of Piedmontese rules and personnel on the other regions, and particularly the South) and a certain softness in handling southern brigandage. These factors eventually alienated the southern gentry from the *destra* and brought about the fall of Cavour's party from office on 18 March 1876. Thereafter even the differences in methods between the two parties became blurred because the new Prime Minister, Depretis, perfected the system of *trasformismo* to ensure a permanent government majority in Parliament whoever was in office. *Trasformismo* was a system based on the practice of Members of Parliament supporting and opposing different governments without any reference to their policy or programmes. This was made possible because majorities in the Italian parliament were created by governments, not governments by Parliamentary majorities. This in turn was due to the breach which existed between elector and Member of Parliament and which enhanced the power of patronage in a system of very restricted suffrage. It must be remembered that Parliamentarians were local notables: the landlords and entrepreneurs with a taste for politics, the shabby lawyers and professional men with all their hangers-on. It was natural, therefore, that they should become the agents of local interests and Parliament the market place for the distribution of the spoils of government.

The last decade of the century saw the rise of the first real political party in Italy, the Socialist Party. It played only a small part in the Italian parliament before the First World War because the restricted suffrage limited its representation. Moreover its policy of keeping faith with Marxist revolutionary principles (as it understood them) excluded active participation in a bourgeois government. This policy was maintained, in contrast to what happened to other European Socialist Parties, throughout the 1914–18 war. In January 1919 a second real political party appeared with the aim of being an organized party and not just a collection of Members of Parliament. This was the Popular or Catholic Party. Its advent represented the official return of Catholics into Italian public life and they returned not as individuals but as a compact organized mass with a programme of their own. In the General Elections of 1919, the two organized parties won more than half the seats in the Chamber of Deputies, and the old parliamentary groups found themselves in a position where they could not govern without previous agreement with either of these two parties. Thus the political struggle became a genuinely inter-party affair for the first time. Giolitti and the old style parliamentary leaders could not understand that matters of state had henceforth to be discussed with party leaders who might not sit in Parliament. This misunderstanding of the new direction of politics ushered in by the war, the failure of the Socialist Party to accept the rules of the parliamentary system and the burden the Popular Party imposed as allies proved too much for the leaders of the old parliamentary groups. Italian parliamentary politics had taken a new turning and the old remedies no longer sufficed.

It was into this turmoil that the Fascist Party, organized along military lines from 1919–20, was able by a combination of terror-ism and ruse to conquer power. The March on Rome was, as Chabod has observed, 'not a revolution, but a parade' because the old parliamentary leaders were prepared to negotiate with the Fascists where they had failed with the Socialists and Catholics. In the early years Mussolini was prepared to rule through Parliament, but after the Acerbo Majority Electoral Law of 1924, the Matteotti murder and the Aventine secession of 1924, the pretence of parliamentary government was abandoned. The year 1926 was crucial for the creation of the dictatorship: the first move was the prohibition of all political parties except the Fascist Party: it was followed by the introduction of the so-called 'Corporate State'; in 1928 the single national list was introduced for election to the Chamber of Deputies and in 1929 Mussolini made peace with the Church in the Lateran Pacts. The 1930s saw the high summer of the 'Corporate State' in which even the Chamber of Deputies was replaced by a Chamber of Corporations whose members, called National Councillors, were appointed by the government.

The Centralized Administrative Tradition

On unification, the founding fathers of modern Italy provision-ally established a strong centralized state. This became a perma-nent acquisition because they came to believe that it was the only way of forging the states and petty principalities that constituted

7

the new country into a nation. The creation of a centralized state was, in some ways, a surprise because not only was there an important minority which opposed it in the name of federalism, but because the majority of the *destra storica*, led by Cavour himself, were admirers of the English system of local government with its widespread local autonomy. However unification was carried out by a small oligarchy (the progressive bourgeoisie) and there were many powerful groups which opposed it or were indifferent to it. Four can be named: (1) The ruling classes of the former states (the legitimists); (2) the clergy who feared for the overthrow of the Pope's temporal power and the extension of anti-clericalism; (3) the peasantry whose age-old land-hunger was being severely repressed; and (4) the dissident democrats and republicans. Hence the new liberals who constituted the progressive bourgeoisie became afraid that any form of decentralized power would permit the dissident groups to destroy the new political regime; and this they were determined to prevent.

Two factors were decisive in ensuring that the hurried adoption of the Napoleonic prefectoral system in 1861 became permanent. First, a positive evaluation of Bonapartism by the Piedmontese liberals in the decade after 1848; and second, the North's brutal contact with the social reality of the South. The fear of revolution was one of the things that haunted the liberal bourgeoisie which founded modern Italy; and in 1861 the Second Empire seemed to have exorcized the spectre of revolution. If this was so as many Italian liberals believed, then some credit must go to the Napoleonic system of administration. Senator Cadorna, a typical Piedmontese liberal, spoke for many when he declared in the Senate during the debate on local government organization in 1866:

the organization of the administration in France is a genuine model, and I believe that France owes to the force, vitality and goodness of its administration its having passed unharmed through its hundred revolutions. . . .

Contact between North and South aroused all those fears and suspicions which were later to be canalized into what was to become known as the 'Southern Question'. It is well known that Piedmontese liberals were dismayed at the great disparities in conditions between the two regions of Italy which they found when they went south in 1861. Farini spoke for all of them when he wrote to Cavour on his arrival in the former Kingdom of Naples as Governor, after its liberation by Garibaldi: 'This is not Italy! This is Africa: the bedouins are the flower of civic virtue besides these country bumpkins . . .' This duality in economic conditions, social structure and political conduct between the two halves of Italy convinced the Northern liberals that the majority of Italians were incapable of governing themselves because of centuries of absolutism and foreign domination. Moreover the Piedmontese bourgeoisie quickly realized that the southern gentry with whom they had allied themselves in the process of unification to prevent Garibaldi from carrying out a democratic revolution, were too weak to defend the new regime either against Bourbon reaction or against peasant revolution without the strong protecting hand of the state. The radical historian Gaetano Salvemini has summed up the situation in his usual forthright manner:

> In the South the small nuclei of bourgeois and petty bourgeois, mainly intellectuals, who formed the basis of the liberal and national anti-bourbon party, felt themselves incapable of holding the country with their own forces alone against the peasants' revolt. . . . Administrative centralization was for the Southern liberals then the only form in which they could conceive national unity.

Finally, many liberals, and probably Cavour himself, believed that continued toleration of the new state and non-intervention by the major European powers was conditional upon the ability of the new state to ensure law and order at home.

What then did the administrative system adopted entail? First, that all governmental power was allocated to the central government; second, that it had intensive control over the lesser units of government (Provinces and Communes); third, that this power was exercised by the agent of the central government in the provinces, the Prefect. The decentralized units of government like the communes (which gained only towards the end of the century the right to elect their mayors and a similar electorate to that of Parliament) were given a number of important functions to perform in such varied fields as education, sanitation and poor relief, public works and taxation. But their ability to exercise these functions was greatly hampered by strict Prefectoral supervision. Indeed prefectoral control of local administration provided the national government with a large share of the kinds of administrative satisfactions and penalties that could be bartered for legislative support and that the deputies could translate into electoral support. This meant inevitably that the Prefect, in addition to being the State's representative in the Province, became the agent of the particular governments in office.

By imposing the strait-jacket of Piedmontese 'normative integration', necessary for the development of the North, on all the other regions of Italy, the rulers of the new nation exasperated the differences between the developed and backward regions. National monetary credit, fiscal and commercial policies were concerned with the needs of the industrializing regions of the country; the rest, like the South, had to depend on occasional programmes of public works and other temporary forms of assistance administered by the Prefect. In this way, the question of administrative decentralization and regional autonomy became inextricably linked with what was to become the major question of Italian political life, the 'Southern Question'.

Since the policy pursued by the national state, which was responsible for worsening the regional differences, was dictated by the mutual interests of the ruling alliance of northern capital and southern land, it was natural that opposition to administrative centralization should take the form of proposals for regional autonomy and should come from opposition groups backed by popular movements of protest. This was the case in 1896–1905, 1919 26 and 1943–8, the three periods when regionalization was seriously canvassed as a political issue. On the first occasion, the government created a Civil Commissioner for Sicily to placate the *fasci siciliani*; and it was to him that the Palermo Socialists addressed their famous Memorandum demanding the right of regional autonomy for the island. On the second occasion the Sardinian Action Party put forward the same demand for its island; and the Sicilian Catholic leader, Luigi Sturzo, made 'administrative decentralization, local autonomy and the construction of the regions' a central plank of the Popular Party programme. On the third occasion, the principle of regional autonomy was won. Similarly, the ruling classes resisted these demands on every occasion because they believed that a centralized state provided the best defence of their interests. Thus the most that they were prepared to concede before the fall of Fascism was a small measure of bureaucratic deconcentration; the field services of the various ministries, customs, postal, telegraph, tax, educational services etc., were removed from the Prefect's control and placed under provincial directors.

These latter tendencies were, in any case, obstructed by the general economic and technical developments of the later nineteenth century. Rising industrialization led to the entrusting to the government of new functions. Thus existing ministries extended their sphere of activity and created new agencies; the Ministry of the Treasury dates from 1877, and the Ministry of Agriculture, Industry and Commerce from the following year; 1880 saw the establishment of the Ministry of Posts and 1902 the Advisory Council of Labour which was to become the Ministry of Labour. The same period saw the beginning of the state programmes in the field of social insurance (1898), nationalization of the railways (1905), telephone services (1907), etc. In consequence, on the eve of the First World War, the Italian administrative system was characterized by the scale and scope of its intervention in economic and social life and its high degree of centralization. The scope of intervention was wider than that of any comparable European country and covered both welfare programmes and direct entrepreneurial activity. The latter worked hand in glove with private interests. The high degree of centralization meant the concentration of bureaucratic activity in Rome and not in the provinces, coupled with a lack of autonomy for local government which was tightly supervised from the centre.

Fascism and the 'Corporate State'

In 1922, in the wake of the troubled post-war years, the Italian ruling class resorted to its own special brand of Bonapartism to defend its privileges from would-be subversion. The Bolshevik peril was made the justification for handing power over to Mussolini. What actually constituted the Bolshevik peril depended, as a student of Italian Fascism observed, 'partly upon the facts of the situation, but at least as much upon what people feared. The large Socialist votes in the national and municipal elections, the great economic organizations over which the Socialists ruled, were, of course, the special peril of the people who did not like them . . .' The failure of the occupation of the factories in 1920 had demonstrated that the fear of a real Bolshevik Revolution was unfounded. If ever there was a time for revolution, that was it, but the Socialists preferred talk of revolution to taking revolutionary action. And yet the demonstrations and agitation were sufficiently frightening to cause the wealthy and the middle classes to look for a saviour. Mussolini was the man that they chose. Previously they had believed that the constitutional authorities were the defenders of the established order and private property, but after the occupation of the factories men of property came to the conclusion that the authorities could not be trusted to answer their call. After all, the factories had been occupied and the government had done nothing. As the Fascist historian and apologist, Chiurco, proclaimed: 'The bourgeoisie must know how to be the governing class and wish to be the governing class and, with resolution, act as a governing class . . .' This it manifestly had not done.

How did the Fascists react? By creating a personal dictatorship; and the so-called 'Corporate State'. The personal dictatorship required the subordination of all the institutions of the state system to the dictator; and the suppression of all opposition. The first necessitated no formal change in the *Statuto albertino*; simply the transformation of the whole state machine (Crown, Council of Ministers, Parliament, Administration, Military and Judiciary) into instruments of the dictator. Alongside, or replacing them, new institutions were created: the Fascist Grand Council, the Militia, the Fascist Party and the Special Tribunal for the Defence of the State. The second was achieved by outlawing all 'parties, groups and political organizations' under the Law of Associations of 26 November 1926, on the pretext that they were Freemasons! At the same time the opposition press was swept away – all publications had forthwith to be vetted by the Minister of the Interior – and the so-called independent journals were badgered into submission, either by accepting dictation from the Ministry of Propaganda or by selling out to Fascist interests. Similarly, radio and cinema were taken over and supervised by the appropriate Fascist authorities.

The nature of the 'Corporate State' is more difficult to outline. Mussolini described its purpose in a typical piece of rhetoric in a speech at the end of the discussion on the new law on corporations before the Fascist Assembly in December 1933 :

Three conditions are necessary for the full, complete, integral and revolutionary fulfilment of the Corporate State : a single party, by means of which there shall be effectuated political control as well as economic control, and which shall be, above the competing interests, a bond which unites all in a common faith. Nor is that enough. We must have, as well as a single party, the totalitarian state, that is to say, the State which absorbs itself, to transform and make them effective, all the energy, all the interests, and all the hope of the people. And even that is not enough. The third, and ultimate, and the most important condition, is to live in a period of the highest ideal tension. We are now living in this period of the highest ideal tension.

As a result of his analysis of the 'Corporate State' in the 1930s, Salvemini was forced to conclude that it was 'the greatest humbug of the twentieth century' :

Mussolini has solved the problem of the relations between capital and labour [he wrote] by the same methods which Marinetti used to create a new art, a new literature, and a new cuisine. Marinetti invented the word 'futurism', organized a diabolical outcry around the word, and finally succeeded in making people believe in the existence of futurism. Mussolini took over a nebulous term 'corporation', organized around the war-cry an uproar still more diabolical than the example given by Marinetti, and succeeded in persuading many people that the salvation of the world lay in the corporation. All the categories of the traditional economic system remained intact : profit, interest and wages. But profit becomes the corporative salary of the employer; interest becomes the corporative salary of the capitalist; wages becomes the corporative profit and interest of the worker. The worker is no longer a worker, but has become 'a civil servant in the broadest sense of the term'. Don Quixote attacked windmills as if they were real monsters; Mussolini deals with real monsters as if they were windmills.

Although the 'Corporate State' system was introduced by Law of 3 April 1926, it was not fully implemented until the constitution of the twenty-two corporations in 1934 by decree because they had failed to come into action spontaneously. They were institutions in which labour and capital were expected to collaborate for the achievement of common ends under state supervision. The idea was the employers and workers would be members of one of the corporations and the institutions of a series of labour courts within the judicial system would regulate collective and individual labour disputes. Since all labour disputes that could not be conciliated would be settled by these courts, strikes, lockouts and other forms of economic warfare were outlawed, the country would be free from the threat of economic strife. In point of fact the corporative system became a cover for increased state centralization in the interests of capital. On the same day as the Corporative State was instituted, the Prefects were given a stranglehold over local government; they became the direct emanations of the Head of the Government in the provinces; everything became subordinated to them. Through them the Fascist State extended its control over all aspects of Italian life and conducted its battles to form a *homo fascistimus*. It was the Prefect who directed the press and enforced political conformity, repressed agitation and administered summary political justice, propagandized the regime's achievements and distributed sustenance to the ruling middle and upper classes.

The creation of the corporations, furthermore, together with the numerous economic agencies that increased state centralization and intervention required, resulted in thousands of additional soft jobs for deserving Fascists. This was not a negligible factor in a relatively poor country like Italy, where unemployment among the intelligentsia has always been rife. Indeed it was responsible for a major occupational change among the southern intelligentsia from landholding and local politics to employment in the national bureaucracy. Government intervention in the economy increased enormously in the thirties when the depression set in and the State had to come to the rescue of the Banks. As a result it suddenly found itself in control of the larger concerns of key sectors of the economy. It created IRI (*Istituto per la ricostruzione industriale*) to meet this situation, and operated it as a special kind of investment bank (i.e. it kept the stock it bought instead of selling it to the public). Eventually it not only acquired a controlling interest in the largest and most important enterprises but obtained a virtual monopoly in many sectors of the Italian economy, including steel, shipbuilding and banking. It had been the government's intention to dispose of these assets when the crisis was over, but the onset of the

Ethiopian War led to a change of thinking. The State retained its interests and these were one of the few economic assets Fascism bequeathed to its successors.

I have stressed the ambiguity which surrounded the nature of the 'Corporate State' because it was more than an academic question : Herman Finer observed in 1935 that one of the questions which divided the Italian ruling oligarchy was whether the system included the Fascist system as a whole, or whether it had only a narrower meaning, i.e. only the regulation of the economic relations between workers and employers and between the various branches of production. Did it include militarism, the dictatorship and all the rest, or just the problem of economic production? Did it imply a theory of just economic distribution? There were people who wanted the one without the other and vice versa. What needs to be emphasized is that neither was possible without the other. Both were necessary if a tiny oligarchy was to defend a highly privileged economic and social position against the mass of the nation.

Finally, the Fascist interlude was responsible for one major development with immeasurable repercussions on postwar Italian politics. This was the reintegration of the Catholic Church into Italian national life. The Lateran Pacts (which were later written into the Republican Constitution of 1948) were very favourable to the Church which was given control of education. Mussolini's desire to legitimize his regime encouraged him to give the Church a position of leadership, particularly in local life. The autonomy which the pacts accorded to its organizations, notably Catholic Action enabled it to train a whole generation of leaders on the margin of, if not outside, the regime. Thus Fascism indirectly placed the Catholics in a privileged position to take control of the State when the regime fell.

The Resistance

It is often claimed that the Resistance introduced a new dimension into postwar politics : the people as protagonists. If it is recognized that defeat by the Allies in the Second World War was the root cause of the overthrow of Fascism, it is still maintained that the Resistance was a truly mass movement, the first in Italian national history. However it is clear that not only

15

did the Palace coup of 23 July 1945, which saw the King dismiss Mussolini and replace him by Marshal Badoglio, catch the anti-Fascist groups unawares and leave the initiative with the Royal government by placing it in a strong position with the Allies as the government in office, but also that the political consciousness acquired in the eighteen months' partisan struggle, which was responsible for the novelties in the postwar situation, was only skin deep. First, the partisan struggle was geographically restricted to the northern and central regions, north of the Arno. Second, its numbers were small: at the time of the national insurrection of 25 April 1945, the partisan bands had enrolled some 250,000 men, an exiguous minority in a population of 45 million people. Third, it was socially limited: the majority of its members came, as so often in Italian history, from the intellectual strata of the bourgeoisie and petty bourgeoisie, but also, for the first time, from the working class. It was this latter element which raised so many contemporary hopes.

Unfortunately the peasantry, which still formed the mass of the population in 1945, adopted its traditional attitude of 'wait and see'. In addition, conservative politicians in the Liberal and Christian Democratic parties furnished an important element of the personnel of the Committee of National Liberation (CLN – the Resistance's political organization), particularly in the early liberated regions of Rome and the South. Thus while it is largely true that the partisans enjoyed the support of the populations of both town and country in the guerrilla war of liberation against Nazi-German occupation, it is also true that the great majority of the population did not see in the Resistance and its political organization, the CLN, a political movement capable of reconstructing the State on an entirely new basis. In fact, a few months were all that were necessary for the conservatives, led by De Gasperi, to liquidate the Resistance's revolutionary *élan*.

In these circumstances, what were the Resistance's achievements, if any? First, it was instrumental in the overthrow of the monarchy and the creation of the Republic. Second, it ensured the introduction of universal suffrage by the extension of the vote to women (on Togliatti's initiative). Third, it was responsible for the most original aspects of the Republican Constitution of 1948. This fact was reflected not only in its social content, in ideas such as that 'Italy is a democratic republic founded on work', but in institutions like the Constitutional Court, popular legislative initiative and Referendum, etc., as well as the wide degree of regional autonomy envisaged. Some sections of the CLN, led by the Action Party, had originally taken the view that the CLN should form the regional basis for a new structure of government, but this was shattered by the decision of the CLNAI (responsible for northern Italy) in 1944 not to proclaim itself a provisional government at the moment of liberation for fear of provoking a new civil war and Allied military intervention. It was a clear indication that the Resistance leaders realized that they only represented a minority. Thus, despite the overthrow of the monarchy, the essential continuity of the major institutions of the state system (the administration and the military) was preserved; a capitalist market economy was accepted almost without dispute; and the institutional innovations of the Constitution were ignored for many years.

In the context of this study, the significance of the formative events outlined is to stress the narrowness of the Italian political tradition. Not only has the country been governed by a restricted oligarchy, but the latter has preferred to keep the instruments of government under its close central supervision. The Resistance breached this rigid structure in one or two places but it was still sufficiently strong to determine most, if not all, of postwar Italian politics. In fact it is no paradox to say that the economic developments of the last decade have introduced more mobility into Italian society than all the events of the previous century of national history.

Piedmont	Brescia	La Spezia
Alessandria	Como	Savona
Asti	Cremona	
Cuneo	Mantova	*Trento-Alto Adige*
Novara	Milano	Bolzano
Torino	Pavia	Trento
Vercelli	Sondrio	
Val d'Aosta	Varese	*Venetia*
Aosta		Belluno
	Liguria	Padova
Lombardy	Genova	Rovigo
Bergamo	Imperia	Treviso
		Venezia

Verona
Vicenza

Friuli-Venezia Giulia
Gorizia
Trieste
Udine
Pordenone

Emilia-Romagna
Bologna
Ferrara
Forli
Modena
Parma
Piacenza
Ravenna
Reggio-Emilia

Tuscany
Arezzo
Firenze
Grosseto
Livorno
Lucca
Massa Carrara
Pisa
Pistoia
Siena

The Marches
Ancona

Ascoli Piceno
Macerata
Pesaro

Umbria
Perugia
Terni

Latium
Frosinone
Latina
Rieti
Roma
Viterbo

Molise
Campobasso

Abruzzi
Chieti
L'Aquila
Pescara
Teramo

Campania
Avellino
Benevento
Caserta
Napoli
Salerno

Apulia
Bari
Brindisi
Foggia
Lecce
Taranto

Basilicata
Matera
Potenza

Calabria
Catanzaro
Cosenza
Reggio-Calabria

Sicily
Agrigento
Caltanissetta
Catania
Enna
Messina
Palermo
Ragusa
Siracusa
Trapani

Sardinai
Cagliari
Nuoro
Sassari

N.B.

Italy breaks down into a number of geographical divisions. Mention of geographical areas in the text refers to one or other of these groupings.

1. *North and South:*
    North (Piedmont, Val'd'Aosta, Lombardy, Liguria, Trento-Alto Adige, Venetia, Friuli-Venezia Giulia, Emilia-Romagna, The Marches, Tuscany, Umbria, and Latium).
    South (Molise, Abruzzi, Campania, Apulia, Basilicata, Calabria, Sicily and Sardinia)

2. *North, Centre, South and Islands:*
    North (Piedmont, Val d'Aosta, Lombardy, Trento-Alto Adige, Liguria, Venetia, Friuli-Venezia Giulia)
    Centre (Emilia-Romagna, Tuscany, The Marches, Umbria, Latium)
    South (Campania, Apulia, Molise, Abruzzi, Basilicata and Calabria)
    Islands (Sicily and Sardinia)

3. *Industrial triangle, NE Italy (or 'White' provinces), Centre (or 'Red' provinces), Mainland South and Islands.*
    Industrial triangle (Piedmont, Val d'Aosta, Liguria and Provinces of Milan and Pavia from Lombardy)
    NE Italy or 'White' provinces (Trento-Alto Adige, Venetia, Friuli-Venezia Giulia and provinces of Como, Bergamo, Brescia, Sondrio and Varese from Lombardy)
    Centre or 'Red' provinces (Emilia-Romagna, Tuscany, The Marches, Umbria, and the provinces of Cremona and Mantova from Lombardy, and Rieti from Latium)
    Mainland South (Campania, Apulia, Basilicata, Calabria and provinces of Frosinone, Latina, Roma and Viterbo from Latium), (Sicily and Sardinia).

2 One Nation: Two Societies

Italian patriots have always contested Metternich's claim that Italy was a geographical expression and not a true nation. Unification certainly convinced the Piedmontese administrators and politicians who went South in 1860–1 that the new state comprised two societies, if not two nations, the two Italies – North and South. It was to be some years, however, before the full implications of this discovery became apparent. Then, around 1875, it became clear that if the northern part of the country was economically dynamic and socially flourishing, the southern half, by contrast, was economically stagnant and socially disintegrating: that if the one was resolutely European, the other had a distinctly oriental flavour. The South's plight became known as 'the Southern Question'; and it has remained to plague successive Italian governments for more than a hundred years. It still remains to plague the government today.

The Southern Question

It is not easy to explain fully such a complex phenomenon as the differences between North and South Italy. If the long-term factors resulting from centuries of separate history are put aside and attention is focused on those which accompanied the industrial revolutions of northern Europe, three causes can be advanced for the slow progress of the southern economy since unification. The first derived from the unfavourable natural conditions: poverty of the soil, adverse climate, water shortage and the lack of mineral resources. In addition, the remoteness from the rich markets of northern Europe at a time when transport costs were of paramount importance in the location of industry must not be overlooked.

The second cause lay in the South's geographical setting. The northern regions were close to the countries where the industrial revolution started and developed, and so enjoyed a favourable stimulus to industrialization. The familiar cumulative effects of every growth process operating through external economies, commercial credit, financial organization and the like stimulated industry in the North, and made it more difficult for other regions to develop competitive activities. The cumulative effect worked also in the social field; the higher standard of living offered wider opportunities for education and vocational training; it also created wider opportunities and incentives for scientific research linked to industrial objectives which, in turn, widened the basis for pure research. At the same time, it improved both private and public organization, and developed participation in public life, both national and local. A higher general intellectual level, moreover, enlarged social relations, spread the means of communications, eased relations between town and country, village and village, etc., and eliminated resistance to change. From this bare description, it is clear that the priority of the North in the process of industrialization helped to increase the gap, not only in the standard of living compared with the South, but also in the potentiality for industrial development, because the South remained an agrarian 'communal' type of society, organized round the family and the primary group, ruled by simple feeling, with village life regulated by custom and tradition, etc.

The third reason was the most important single cause : unification and its economic consequences. Unification provoked a compromise between the ruling classes of North and South, in which the Piedmontese bourgeoisie won the leadership of the movement for unification – Cavour's policies triumphed in 1861 thanks to the support of the southern gentry. The Piedmontese had no hesitation in imposing their economic policy on the new nation. The Catholic economist, Pasquale Saraceno, has called it 'normative integration'; and succinctly described it as follows : '... the principal objective of the policy of state intervention was that of unifying the framework within which the entrepreneur in the different regions had to operate ...' Its significance is clear when we recall that it was an unquestioned article of faith of the classical economic doctrine to which the Piedmontese bourgeoisie subscribed, that, by eliminating the obstacles to the free movement of goods, capital and people between different economies, beneficial effects were to be expected in all regions, both backward and advanced. No liberal economist accepts this view today. Indeed they are prepared to agree with Marx that uncontrolled communications between advanced and backward regions, far from benefiting the latter, will actually harm them. This is what happened to the South during the first half-century of unification. The national monetary, credit, fiscal and commercial policies were concerned with the needs of the industrializing parts of the country. The South had to depend on occasional programmes of public works and other temporary forms of assistance.

These developments prompt the question : why was so little done to alleviate the South's conditions? The short answer is that its ruling class (the southern gentry) benefited from them. It was part of the compromise by which Cavour outwitted Garibaldi and achieved his own form of unification; he ensured them control of the land in return for support of his policies in the new nation-state. This was the basis of the *blocco storico* – the ruling alliance between northern capital and southern land – which conditioned the whole development of Italian politics. It can be seen clearly for example, in the contrast in political organization and activity between the two major areas of the country.

The development of capitalism and the class struggle in the North meant that political activity and organization became based on economic and social groupings. In fact northern politics was the continuous struggle of organized and organizing class and group interests. Stunted capitalist development in the South and the fragmentation of the class struggle meant, on the other hand, that such political organization as it knew was built on the *clientela*. Southern politics were no more than the trading of favours down the hierarchical chains of personal acquaintances. In these circumstances, it was easy for northern capitalist interests to dominate post-Risorgimento politics. Little was done for the South because it was part of the bargain struck that southern politicians should be left free to enjoy their local privileges. On this condition they busied themselves in local government for patronage and provided national governments with the required parliamentary majorities. The reactions of the southern peasantry to these events and their consequences were born of desperation. They took two significant forms : emigration and *jacqueries*. Southern emigration rose massively in the late nineteenth century as the landless labourers departed *en masse* for the New World, and has continued down to the present time in one form or another. It is estimated that six million people have left the South in the past twenty-five years, 2.2 million in the sixties. The history of the South since unification is studded with *jacqueries*; and the 1970 riots in Reggio di Calabria are sure to join the *fasci siciliani* and *moti* of '98 as among the most celebrated.

It was to meet the political danger inherent in this situation that the government implemented a limited programme of land reform and created the *Cassa per il Mezzogiorno* (Southern Development Fund) in 1950 with authority to spend a billion lire in ten years. Once again, economic and political support was forthcoming only for a massive programme of social welfare; industrialization would have meant competition for northern industry which its leaders were not prepared to contemplate in 1950. The public works programme which was introduced to buy political support was legitimized under the title of 'pre-industrialization'. Thus, for the first decade of the fifties, the *Cassa*'s brief was to provide the infrastructure – roads, water, electricity and other services – which was claimed to be essential for economic development. In this period the chief beneficiary of the government's southern policy in addition to southern placemen and their *clientela* was northern industry, because it supplied the equipment. The policy's lack of success in promoting a higher growth rate in the South than in the North led to a shift in priorities in the sixties to grandiose industrial projects (like the Taranto steel works and the Alfasud car factory near Naples) in the hope that they would attract small and medium industry in their wake. They so rarely achieved this result that they became white elephants (*cattedrali nel deserto*) of little local benefit. Nonetheless *per capita* income, investment and consumption levels did begin to rise, although this was due more to two spontaneous factors than to government policy. First, the massive rural exodus from the South, which led to a second factor : the choking of northern cities and the total submerging of their social amenities. The latter is responsible for the growing interest of northern businessmen in the South. In recent years the big names of industry, like Fiat, Montedison, Pirelli, SIR, and the companies of the state-holdings, IRI and ENI, have found it advantageous to locate new plant in the South where they enjoy financial incentives in addition to avoiding the labour and housing shortages and stricter union practices of the North.

In 1971 the government initiated a new drive on the southern problem by reorganizing the *Cassa* and authorizing it to spend 7200 billion lire in two years, which is more than the total it has spent in its twenty-two years of existence. The law of 6 October 1971 for the South lays down that the development of the South is henceforth to be treated as the central problem of economic planning. At the same time, it became necessary to overhaul the existing mechanisms of southern development because the new system of regional government was to become fully operative in spring 1972, and the regions had authority to tackle local development problems. Thus the Interministerial Committee for the South was dissolved and southern policy was made the responsibility of CIPE (Interministerial Committee for Economic Planning), aided by a committee of regional chairmen. As a result, the regions will undertake their own local problems co-ordinated by CIPE. The function of the *Cassa* will change on the completion of its present projects: it will become a planning and advisory body concentrating on special projects, particularly those affecting more than one region, or covering new industrial zones, the expansion of metropolitan areas and the safeguarding of natural resources. Furthermore, the new law authorizes the establishment of a new, special, southern finance corporation with a capital of 200 million lire in the first instance, in addition to the existing specialist financial institutions (ISVEIMER, IRFIS, CIS, INSUD, ESPI, SFRIS etc.) which provide loans and take equity participations. Finally, the state-holding corporations are directed to locate 80 per cent of their future capital investment in the South; and private firms of a certain size are required to submit their investment plans to CIPE to ensure that they conform with the national plan and, as far as possible, benefit the South. Whether this policy will be more than a panacea depends to a large extent on the substance of EEC regional policies, because pressure for the continued rapid integration of Italian industry into Europe will almost certainly confirm the economic marginality of the

South unless co-ordinated action is taken at the supra-national level. In any event, success can only be relative, since, as the Budget Minister, Antonio Giolitti, estimated in 1971, it would require an investment of 45,000 billion lire and the creation of a million new jobs in the South by 1980 to close the gap with the North. And it is unrealistic to expect the North to stand still to let the South catch up.

The Economic Miracle

The development of the Italian economy in the postwar period has been one of the country's most notable achievements. It has consistently had one of the highest growth rates of any industrial country in this period. Indeed its growth rate of almost 6 per cent annually in the two decades 1951–71 has been exceeded by Japan alone among the major capitalist countries. Its GNP doubled in twelve years (1950–62) and it appeared well on the way to repeating the performance before the recession of 1971–2. The single most important factor in this achievement was Italy's integration into the capitalist world economic system. This was accomplished with American assistance in the postwar 'reconstruction' of the late forties.

The prodigious economic expansion of the USA during the Second World War completely transformed the capitalist world's economic situation by creating a new industrial productive system dominated by America. In consequence, from the end of the war, the USA has pursued a policy of promoting world trade and stabilizing the economic cycle. Hence, starting at Bretton Woods in July 1944, where it took on the burden of the monetary regulation of world trade, it promoted the creation of a whole series of institutions (GATT, OEEC (later OECD), World Bank, IMF, etc.) whose object was to harmonize world monetary and commercial policy. The extent to which the USA has been successful (world trade has expanded without precedence in the twenty-five postwar years), has been a permanent condition of Italian economic growth. The links between the Italian economy and that of the USA have been so close that the dictum 'everytime the USA sneezes, Italy catches a cold' has been true. The bad years for the Italian economy have been those of American recessions (1952, 1957, 1963, 1969, etc.). Finally, American help was not limited to providing the framework for Italian economic growth; it supplied the necessary foreign exchange for 'reconstruction' in the immediate postwar years. Italy obtained an essential $3.5 billion in aid via UNRRA and the Marshall Plan between 1945 and 1950.

Important as the international framework has been, Italy's competitive integration in the capitalist world economic system would not have been achieved without a number of internal decisions taken during the 'reconstruction' period. Fundamental in these was the economic policy, known as the 'Einaudi line', inaugurated by the liberal economist, Luigi Einaudi, when he became Vice-Prime Minister and Minister of the Budget in summer 1947. The key elements in the 'Einaudi line' were hard money and the manipulation of credit. While Governor of the Bank of Italy, before becoming Minister, Einaudi had already made a census of Italian industry, dividing firms into categories on the basis of their productive and competitive potential. Thus while instituting a hard money policy to combat runaway inflation, credit was made selective (i.e. it was made available to firms with competitive possibilities while the others were left to sell out or go bankrupt). Credit became a weapon for rationalizing Italian industry which, in turn, favoured the concentration of capital. The mechanism used was to make the Bank of Italy responsible for the commercial banks' liquidity, a power which the Bank had enjoyed until 1936 when the Fascist government had arrogated it to itself. Skilfully using the economic crisis of 1947, the fourth De Gasperi government pushed through a package of reforms that enabled the Bank of Italy to impose reserve requirements on the commercial banks, maintain close surveillance over them and oversee the bond market and new issues.

The 'Einaudi line' was conducive to a number of economic decisions which turned Italian entrepreneurial attitudes upside down. The first was the attack on Montecatini's traditional monopoly in the chemical engineering sector by the electrical monopoly Edison in 1948. It was followed by the discovery of natural gas in the Po Valley which led to the creation of ENI (National Hydrocarbons Corporation) in 1953. The struggle between three of Italy's major industrial groups destroyed the existing static equilibrium in the chemical engineering and petrochemical sectors, and spread over into other industries, putting an end to the corporative phase of the Italian economy that had prevailed hitherto. As a result, within fifteen years Italy had a modern mass chemical engineering industry led by firms of international dimensions. The second decision was the Sinigaglia plan: the reorganization of the IRI steel plants on a rational basis which furnished Italy with a major steel industry operating at world prices for the first time. It was an essential technical pre-requisite for economic growth.

The third had probably the most far-reaching consequences on the general public: it was Fiat's decision to manufacture the '600' in 1953. It marked a change of scale in the Italian economy from the manufacturing of luxury goods for a limited clientele to the manufacturing of consumer goods for a mass market. The initial investment in the '600' in 1953 was 300 billion lire in the new plant at Mirafiore; by 1962 this had become 700 billion lire. Similarly, the annual number of cars registered in Italy was 122,000 in 1953; by 1968 it had passed the million mark. The place this jump gave Fiat in the national economy has been described by the radical journalist, Eugenio Scalfari:

When Fiat decides on another investment, another jump in productivity, the effects on the rest of the economy are immediate. They are immediate on Pirelli, on Marelli, on Italsider, on AGIP, on the state budget. More tyres for Fiat, more upholstered seats for Fiat, more steel for Fiat, more petrol for Fiat, more roads for Fiat; in the space of a few months a gigantic mechanism is set in motion that accumulates around the car policy decided on by Fiat a volume of investments which is certainly not less than 20 per cent of the entire investments of the country. Who can resist a wave of these dimensions? Who claims that Italy is not a planned economy? Only it is planning put out to tender. It is not undertaken by the Minister of the Budget and Economic Planning, but by Fiat.

These decisions all had a common function: economic rationalization and the creation of market capacity. In fact so successful was the use of monetary policy in the postwar years, that, allied to the political weakness of coalition governments, it has enabled the Bank of Italy, in conjunction with the major financial holding groups, to dominate Italian economic policy-making ever since.

The growth of world trade, American aid, a successful monetary policy and the decisions that it evoked were not of themselves

27

sufficient to bring about the Italian economic miracle. They were vital preconditions, but as *The Economist* remarked in 1972, 'what mattered was the quality, supply and price of its labour, combined with a high level of capital formation'. Certainly Italy was favoured by a combination of circumstances. First, a plentiful supply of reasonably skilled labour at low wage rates was available, which was able to meet the rising needs of the industrial and service sectors. Moreover when the labour surplus of the urban zones began to dry up, it was replaced by a massive rural exodus. Second, rapid growth in productivity: given the relative technical backwardness of Italian industry at the end of the war, investment in the most up-to-date equipment induced bigger improvements in productivity (i.e. economies of scale) than was the case in other, more advanced industrial societies. Third, the drop in the price of raw materials due to favourable terms of trade with raw material-producing countries. Fourth, capital formation which grew very rapidly. It was aided, in addition to the factors mentioned, by the decision taken in 1951 to free imports, and a policy of freer trade. Although Italian tariffs remained among the highest of the OECD countries in the fifties, and Italy was recalcitrant about implementing some of its common Market obligations in the sixties, industrial competition stimulated Italian industry to embark on an export-led boom. Fifth, the archaic tax system was so easy to circumvent that no self-respecting firm of businessman ever paid on profits anything like what he should have done.

Last but not least was the cold war and specific political action: the Christian Democrats and Liberals not only expelled the Communists and Socialists from the government in May 1947, but just as important, they succeeded in splitting the trade-union movement in July 1948. Such action led to two developments. On the one hand, the elimination of the working-class parties from the government necessitated generating new sources of support for it. This explains an ambiguity in the 'Einaudi line': alongside the measures promoting economic rationalization, the government used subsidies and patronage to favour the growth of a parasitic stratum in agriculture, urban speculation, small commerce, the liberal professions and the bureaucracy (see Table 2.iii). Tied to the State, this stratum furnished the government with much needed electoral support throughout the next two decades. The government's very cautious southern policy (modest land reform and the *Cassa per il Mezzogiorno*) followed the same logic (rationalization of agriculture and support of parasitic groups). These middlemen have had a political influence in the postwar period out of all proportion to their economic importance.

On the other hand, government pressure on the trade union movement was maintained throughout the fifties, when strike action was tarred with the political brush, industrial areas flooded with cheap labour, and labour leaders and militants suffered constant police harassing. The consequences of this activity were low wages and high profits. Mr Edward Denison of Brookings Institute, author of one of the most intensive studies of Italian growth between 1950 and 1962, calculated that the availability of cheap labour accounted for about 40 per cent of Italian economic expansion; another 12 per cent could be imputed to capital formation; and a further 20 per cent to economies of scale. These figures are only indications, but they provide a useful clue to the factors behind the postwar Italian economic miracle.

Wage restraint was at its height in the 1950s; and it was possible for the economy of those years to guarantee a high rate of expansion without worrying about the need to stabilize the trade cycle. In the sixties, the situation changed : it was no longer easy to maintain high profit margins in the face of international competition stimulated by the Common Market and the Kennedy Round. At the same time, the level of employment had risen sharply as a result of migration from the South. Near full employment increased trade-union bargaining power and in consequence workers' wage demands and trade-union activity revived with a violence unknown for a decade. Not surprisingly, Italian industry was unable to maintain a united front. The giant corporations, both public and private (IRI and ENI, Fiat and Pirelli, etc.), whose complex productive processes require high capital overheads (see Table 2.i) and are now integrated at an intercontinental level, were much more prepared to make wage concessions because it was essential to them to avoid closures and disruption wherever possible. Hence they were in the van in according high wage increases, in the early and late sixties (14 per cent in 1962; 15 per cent in 1969 and 17 per cent in 1970). The small and medium industrialists, on the other hand, who had done so well out of the boom years (1958–62), could not afford such increases and they reacted to them with panic measures (flight of capital abroad, slump in investment) which brought on an economic depression in 1963–4). It is only fair to add that they were stampeded into these reactions by the so-called 'electricity barons' who were among the oldest and most powerful of Italian industrialists. Having enjoyed control of a fundamental public service under monopoly conditions, they had developed a parasitic attitude to business and an interventionist policy in politics. In the early sixties they dominated *Confindustria* and forced it into an investment strike to blackmail the politicians against the 'opening to the left'. The upshot of their campaign was the nationalization of the electrical supply industry, but also an economic crisis. Moreover, the rise in wages won by the workers to gain a decent living wage meant zero profits for the small entrepreneurs overburdened with high social overheads (social security etc. of the giant inefficient parasitic tertiary sector); and zero profits are not conducive to private investment.

Table 2. i
Largest Italian Industrial Companies in 1969 (in millions of dollars)

Rank outside USA	Company	Sector	Sales	Assets	Net profits	Invested capital	Employees
8	Montedison	Chemicals	2315·7	4561·3	66·2	1873·9	142,326
13	Fiat	Cars	2135·7	1608·9	55·1	516·9	158,445
28	ENI	Oil	1444·0	4026·0	6·2	1295·2	59,960
54	Pirelli	Tyres	949·9	993·3	25·0	213·5	69,285
64	Italsider (IRI)	Steel	886·7	2649·2	22·0	478·7	37,427
101	Olivetti	Typewriters	592·8	332·4	11·6	111·6	60,681
135	Snia-Viscosa	Art. Fibres	441·6	432·0	13·6	145·1	29,500
185	Alfa-Romeo (IRI)	Cars	316·5	286·4	9·6	117·8	17,858

Source: F. R. Willis, *Italy Chooses Europe* (New York, 1971), p. 190

Although the Italian economy responded to the government's deflationary measures in 1964 by increasing productivity and increased government investment (from 20 per cent to 80 per cent of total investment in three years), which made many consider that Italy had at last become an advanced industrial nation, lack of private investment (and hence no growth in investment in absolute terms) coupled with the international monetary crisis since 1968 led to a further depression (1971–3) which revealed the fragility of the Italian industrial structure.

These developments indicate that while the themes of Italian political economy are those of advanced countries – planning and tax reforms to rationalize the economy, incomes policy and trade union legislation to control the growing power of organized labour – its real problems lie elsewhere. Despite the dominance of a limited number of giant corporations (only eight Italian firms figure in the Fortune list of the leading 200 non-American firms [see Table 2.i]), the roots of Italian industry are still the small, family-owned firms generally run by the entrepreneur who is often of artisan origin and who knows how to make something, but who runs into trouble when his firm grows beyond a certain size or passes to the second generation (Innocenti, the motor firm acquired by British Leyland in 1972 is a classic example). Furthermore, even the giant corporations are low on technology, research and management. This situation has had two consequences. First, the big corporations have responded to the economic crisis by searching for higher levels of productivity, reducing labour needs and concentrating labour requirements on the central age-groups of the labour force. This has led them into mergers, associations and consortia with large foreign companies to acquire the necessary management and technological skills. At the same time, it has given them wider access to international financial and credit facilities. In this way they have been able not only to face keener foreign competition, but have also adopted a more international or European than purely Italian viewpoint. Hence, in many areas they can act individually or in alliances, with a considerable degree of autonomy from the government.

Second, every time there is a recession, the government has been forced to intervene to bale out the small- and medium-sized firms in financial difficulties, either by making funds available to existing state-holding companies or creating new ones (EFIM, GESPI, etc.). Such practices work naturally in favour of the concentration of capital and the compression of the work force. Those small firms which have survived have rationalized by adopting the opposite strategy to the large firms: they have decentralized the work process by abandoning the factory system and returning to the cottage system. In this way, they employ the marginal groups of the labour force (women and the aged), whom they can exploit on low hourly piece-rates (and so gain extra profitability), and cut out trade-union problems. This form of production which was still in operation in the clothing, shoe-making and skin-making sectors, has recently been extended to hosiery, manufacturing and light engineering. In this way, the small firms are once again able to meet foreign competition. This kind of structural development has only been possible because of the length of the depression (almost a decade) which Italian industry has suffered. Moreover, it not only tends to perpetuate the geographical duality of the country's economy, but creates a further structural one.

In conclusion some things are fairly clear. The qualitative jump in Italy's economic system in the postwar period from a capitalist to a neocapitalist one, which can be dated from the miracle (1958–62) was the result of external factors, and principally the favourable situation accruing to Italy from its insertion in the world economic system. This explains not only the miracle itself but why it occurred without other decisive changes like the size of the home market, relations between North and South, or composition of the ruling class. Further, it was an incomplete jump. In fact, Michele Selvati has talked of 'precocious maturity', claiming that Italy had reached the neocapitalist stage with an incomplete industrial base, poorly distributed and with large reserves of labour in the low productivity sectors. The country's problem at the moment is to relaunch investment which has been at zero level since 1963. This requires a recovery in capital accumulation. It can be achieved in one of two ways: either squeezing the real wages of the working class to the levels of the 1950s; or attacking middle class privileges. The one brings the government into a head-on clash with organized labour; the other stimulates neo-fascist terrorism. So far the strength of organized labour has been sufficient to block effectively a recovery in capital accumulation, while the parasitic strata have used their strength in strategic places in the governmental machine to paralyse rationalization plans they oppose. Finally, the permanent condition of postwar growth, the continued expansion of world trade, has been thrown into doubt by the international monetary crisis. Hence the present crisis, to which there does not appear to be an easy or immediate solution. One is bound to say, however, that the situation constitutes more of a threat to organized labour than to the parasitic groups, which is always the case when the employment situation deteriorates.

Internal Migration

The impact of the 'economic miracle' is visible in all aspects of Italian life. Any visitor to the North or Centre will be struck by the manner in which the Italians have embraced the consumer philosophy of the West.

Of course not all Italians have benefited from rising prosperity. Foremost among these are the population of the depressed areas of the South. However many southerners have tried to benefit and have ended up in squalid shanty towns in the North. All observers agree that massive internal migration is the most important social phenomenon that has occurred in Italy since the war. Indeed alongside the economic miracle that was its cause, it has dominated postwar Italian economic and social life.

Emigration has been a permanent feature of Italian society since unification, but it is only in the last two decades that geographical mobility has reached a mass dimension. For example, in the decade 1956–65, 15.8 million people changed residence (10.5 million in North and Centre as against 5.3 million in South and Islands). Thus while foreign emigration has continued unabated (1.3 million people quit the national territory between 1954 and 1964, mainly for European and *not* transoceanic destinations), it has been overshadowed by the exodus from the countryside to the city (2.6 million fewer people were employed on the land in the twelve years, 1952–63, while the provincial capitals grew by nearly three million people in the same period); and from the South and Islands towards the North (1.9 million of the 5.3 million Southerners who changed residence went North as against 0.6 of the 10.5 million in the Centre-North who went south).

The nature of internal migration can best be seen from Table 2.ii. It indicates that while migrational movement was all in one direction from the rural areas to the industrial triangle (the only other regions to have a positive migrational balance were Lazio and Tuscany, the sites of Rome and Florence respectively), it was insufficient to prevent the population density rising in the

33

departure regions, above all in the mainland South and the Islands. The only regions with a declining overall population were the Three Venetias, The Marches and Umbria. The significance of this situation is clear when it is realized that at the end of the first decade of the so-called new Southern policy, the number of persons employed in industry in the South had risen by only 46,000 as against 928,000 in the North and Centre, while the labour force in the two regions grew by 2.2 and 1.8 million respectively.

Table 2. ii
Population Movement by Major Regions 1951–66 (in thousands)

Region	Natural increase	Migration	Overall situation
Industrial triangle	+ 775·4	+1,957·7	+2,733·1
White provinces (N.E. Italy)	+ 717·3	− 524·4	+ 192·9
Red provinces (Centre)	+ 655·7	− 242·5	+ 413·2
Mainland south	+3,302·3	−1,394·1	+1,908·2
Islands	+1,271·3	− 745·2	+ 526·1
ITALY	+6,725·0	− 948·9	+5,776·1

Sources: elaborated from ISTAT data reproduced in *Annuario Politico Italiano* (*1964, 1965 and 1967*)

The reasons for this mass internal migration are to be found in the 'economic miracle', Southerners are attracted by higher incomes (wage-rates in the agricultural sector are often only half that of the industrial and service sectors); regular employment; shorter hours and better working conditions for the higher wage (the growth of the economy has been such as to permit the peasant the choice of an alternative employment for the first time); and adequate social security benefits. To these economic reasons must be added social ones arising from the conditions of rural life (lack of public services, primitive living conditions and the lack of amenities, etc.) that the mass media have shown do not measure up to the possibilities of city life.

In spite of these aspirations for a better life, the situation in which the migrants have had to seek it have been most unsatisfactory. Often they ended up in utterly miserable conditions, as Visconti's artistic treatment of emigrants' problems in Milan in his film *Rocco e i suoi fratelli* portrayed them : discrimination in housing, employment and remuneration; and apathy, when not open hostility, on the part of the local authorities. Indeed it was only the rise of an anti-Southerner racialist movement in Piedmont in 1956–7, the Movement for the Regional Autonomy of Piedmont (MARP), and the electoral success of its campaign to limit the number of southern immigrants in Turin, that drew Italian commentators' attention to the problem in the late fifties. A typical example of the government's apathy, moreover, was the fact that the Fascist law of 1930 on residence certificates and the Republican law of 1949 banning employment registration except in the commune of legal residence were not repealed until 1961. This legislation was responsible for the exploitation of hundreds of thousands of 'clandestine' migrant workers because without a residence permit they could not apply for official vacancies at local labour exchanges.

The consequences of this mass migration have been far-reaching. First, it has contributed to the cultural homogenization of the Italian people. The increased contact between people of different regional origins can only lead to greater understanding and awareness of the problems of other regions and their mutual solidarity as Italians and Europeans. Of course, this is a slow process and hence a long-term trend : in the sixties three out of four Italian marriages were between partners born in the same province. More important in the short run, and this provides a second point, is the rapid recruitment of rural workers in northern industry which has interrupted the process of progressive individualistic integration of the traditional working class, which is now heavily outnumbered on the shop floor. This new blood has reignited working-class consciousness and combativeness when it was on the wane; and it furnished the vanguard of the 'Hot Autumn' of 1969. Third, migration has tended to deprive the regions of departure of the most active and entrepreneurial members of all classes. And while it is true that the regions have benefited from 'remittances' sent home by migrants, this is nothing to the benefit that they would have gained if the migrants had been employed in their native regions. Fourthly, since the migrations have been uncontrolled and unplanned, they have disturbed the population equilibrium between

35

regions as well as upsetting the population distribution over the national territory. The abandonment of the southern countryside risks letting it become a desert, while the choking of northern cities and the consequent submersion of their local amenities only stresses the inadequacy of the postwar Southern policy after two decades. Paradoxically enough, the social cost of migration and its destruction of the environment could force the northern industrialists to invest in the South on the scale necessary to achieve the real break-through in its economic and social development. It has not done so yet, but as Sylos-Labini has indicated recently, a critical juncture has been reached when either southern development will be accelerated and become self-sustaining or it will abort with disastrous repercussions for the country as a whole.

Class Structure

In considering class structure, it is necessary to remember that class is a relationship and consequently classes define themselves in relation to other classes. Furthermore, the particular class relations of a society will depend on the particular societal system or social formation with which it is associated. Social formations relate to certain basic types of economic organization in a historical period. For example, the so-called traditional or feudal social formation is associated with an agrarian society based on agricultural property and production. Similarly, the so-called modern or capitalist social formation is associated with a free market, industrializing society. Finally, it has been suggested that a so-called contemporary or neo-capitalist social formation relating to an oligopolistic postindustrial society can be discerned in Western Europe and North America. The peculiar feature of Italian society at the present time is that two, and even three, of these social formations coexist within the national boundaries.

Once the major social formations have been located, it is further necessary to distinguish the principal classes, or social groupings active in them. Five seem significant: (1) the large and medium bourgeoisie (landowners, entrepreneurs, managers and professional men); (2) the new (salaried) middle classes (private and public white-collar workers); (3) the old (self-employed) middle classes (small farmers, shopkeepers and artisans);

(4) the working class (industrial and agricultural proletariat); and (5) the subproletariat (the big city poor and landless labourers). The relations of the principal classes vary between social formations, but their global strengths are set out in Table 2.iii.

Table 2. iii
Major Social Classes *1881–1971* (in thousands of persons)

	1881	*1901*	*1921*	*1936*	*1951*	*1961*	*1971*
1 Large and medium							
bourgeoisie	340	300	350	330	400	500	500
landowners/entrepreneurs/managers	200		200	220	250	200	200
professional men	140		150	110	150	200	300
2a Non-productive middle							
class (new middle class)	350	450	520	940	1,800	2,200	3,100
private employees	100	150	160	340	800	1,000	1,800
public employees	250	300	360	600	1,000	1,200	1,300
shopkeepers	450	700	1,000	1,010	1,100	1,340	1,800
2b Productive middle class							
(old middle class)	6,650	6,800	7,600	7,210	7,300	6,200	5,600
peasant farmers	4,600	5,000	5,500	5,000	4,800	3,500	2,400
artisans	1,300	900	1,000	1,000	1,100	1,000	1,100
Self-employed in services	300	200	200	200	300	300	400
2c Special groups	660	650	730	720	800	900	800
military	160	200	360	300	290	330	350
clergy	130	130	120	120	120	120	150
others (domestic)	370	320	250	300	390	450	300
3 Working class	7,400	8,100	8,400	8,500	9,500	9,900	9,500
agricultural	3,200	3,900	4,000	3,000	2,700	2,100	1,200
industrial	2,500	2,800	3,300	3,900	4,100	4,300	4,300
building	500	600	700	800	1,300	2,000	1,700
trade	100	100	100	200	600	600	700
transport/services	300	300	400	600	800	900	1,600
Total active population	15,400	16,300	17,600	17,700	19,800	10,600	19,500
Total population	29,300	33,400	37,400	41,200	47,200	49,000	54,000
Percentage active	51.7	48.0	46.5	42.8	41.7	39.1	35.5

Source: P. Sylos-Labini, 'Sviluppo economico e classi sociali in Italia' in *Quaderni di Sociologia* (Nov.-Dec. 1972), p. 429.

The traditional or feudal social formation is characterized by the landowner-peasant relationship. The large landowner has property rights over vast estates which he neither exploits nor works himself, but from which he collects the rents of his dependent peasants. Where the large estates are broken up and independent peasant smallholders acquire the land, a fragmented class situation tends to develop because the various groups (landowners, tenants, peasant smallholders and landless labourers) belong to different sectors of the rural economy. Finally, the middle classes, mainly independent professional men and artisans, are only partially differentiated. They tend to link themselves with one or other of the two principal classes in conflict according to the particular historical situation, but normally they side with the dominant class of landowners. In this social formation, class position is largely based on birth and wealth, with rigid class boundaries and little mobility. Social relations tend to be ascriptive and are founded on primary groups (family, godparenthood, neighbourhood and friendship), which embrace most aspects of the individual's life.

The modern or capitalist social formation is based on the dichotomy between entrepreneurs and workers. The entrepreneurs form a homogenous upper class with a limited landowning component facing a rapidly growing and organizing industrial proletariat and a still substantial peasantry. Organizations of both workers and peasants tend to be functional, but are still sectorial and corporative rather than general. Differences of skill and political culture separate the craft skills from the mass of manual workers. The middle classes are on the increase; and are a ragbag of old and new roles, of ascending and descending groups and individuals which comprise a most composite configuration. In general, professional men are at the zenith of their power acting as mediators between the entrepreneurs and the State, while white-collar workers, although quite numerous, are without much power, prestige or importance, Social relations are increasingly based on personal achievements, in consequence, birth plays a less important role in class position, and wealth and power a more important one. Secondary associations (parties, industrial companies, professional groups and cultural associations) come to rival primary groups in fashioning social relations.

The contemporary or neo-capitalist social formation is characterized by a decline in agricultural occupations, a stabilization in industrial expansion, and a rapid development of the service sector. A deep dichotomy in class situation, exists, but it is more easily seen at the organizational level. At the top we find a ruling class composed of the intellectual and technical elites, financial, managerial, political and military. At the other pole is the mass of white-collar (salaried) and blue-collar (wage-earning) workers whose life styles, standards and control over their work do not differ substantially. The middle classes, professional men, technical and specialist intellectuals, are much more integrated than in earlier social formations. The basis of social stratification is wealth, achievement and power, above all power; class boundaries are not over-rigid and social mobility is based on technical skills, and what one group of researchers have called 'political ability'. This applies as much to the lower classes as to the dominant elite, where birth could still represent an important factor in determining the nature of social relations.

The traditional social relation prevailed in Italy at the time of unification, but the modern social formation had already made its appearance in Piedmont and became dominant in the North in the late nineteenth century (see Table 2.iii), with the rationalization of agriculture and industrialization. The contemporary social formation was heralded into Italy by the 'economic miracle', probably led by a few dozen managers working in the giant public and private corporations. Thus the traditional social formation is typical of the South, the Islands and parts of the Centre and North-East; the modern formation has spread out of the industrial triangle and now has enclaves in larger and smaller zones over the whole country in industrial urban areas, but more in the Centre and North-East than in the South and the Islands. The contemporary formation is almost entirely confined to the industrial triangle because of the great concentration of Italian big industry.

What is the meaning of this intermingling of social formations for the class structure of contemporary Italy? First, class structures tend nationally to be fragmented and unstable – certainly more than would be the case if one social formation was dominant in a pure form – and power is subject to alliances. Second, the dominant group, nationally, is the elite of business or corporation managers (the so-called 'technocrats'), but it is not hegemonic; the independent entrepreneurs and businessmen, linked to a large part of the service class of professional men and white-collar workers (the new, salaried middle classes are the only social group to have known an enormous, continued expansion in numbers in recent years) by a strong network of class interests, are still powerful. Indeed, Sylos-Labini has remarked that the growth of the new type of middle class is as much due to political patronage as to technological progress. He states quite categorically that these 'salaries are nothing but hidden unemployment subsidies . . . the consequences of a specific policy of political and social stabilization.' Third, the landed proprietors have virtually disappeared as an influential and autonomous class. In those regions where the traditional social formation is still entrenched, they have been replaced by a bureaucratic power structure based on a parasitic intermediary stratum which, allied to the declining of the old middle class, has frustrated all attempts at modernization. Fourth, despite the growth in class consciousness due to the urbanization of both rural and industrial workers in all social formations, labour organizations remained weak everywhere until comparatively recently. Although industrial organizations made great strides in the sixties, particularly in the modern and contemporary social formations, and the trade unions are at present among the most important political organizations in the country, the industrial working class remains weak : less than one fifth of workers form an industrial proletariat in the true sense (i.e. work in factories of more than a hundred workers). Finally, the working population has declined from 50 per cent to 36 per cent in the last ninety years. Originally due to the decline of traditional activities, it is now the result of the fact that employment is not keeping pace with population growth. It means, of course, a growing reservoir of big city and rural poor in the traditional zones which provides the local potentates with troops and so a powerful bargaining counter.

Political Culture

In view of the fragmentation and discontinuity of class structures, it is hardly surprising that the predominant cultural pattern in Italy is one of fragmentation and isolation. The heterogeneity is compounded by the diverse historical experiences of the different regions of Italy both before unification and after. Even the Resistance was a regional experience, as demonstrated by the expression 'the wind from the North' to which it gave rise. Hence the very idea of the nation as the primary political community of all social groups has been a source of conflict; this is one of the aspects, and not the least important, of the 'Southern Question'. For example, the fact that Italy on unification was constituted from political communities of widely differing levels of economic and social development was incomprehensible to the mass of northerners. They believed that the country had been united on the basis of equality, so that if the South did not make the same progress as the North it must be due to the racial inferiority of the southerners, and hence was congenital. Given the utility of this widely held commonplace to the pre-Fascist ruling class, it was natural that it should be given a so-called scientific basis by a generation of positivist sociologists at the turn of the century. Of course all the sociologists did was to furnish a theoretical justification for the existing relationship between North and South, based on northern political hegemony. Nonetheless, however false these received views and however bogus the theory that supported them, they were responsible for much of the hostility displayed towards southern migrants, despised as *cafoni* (country bumpkins), in the postwar period.

The insistence of the post-Risorgimento rulers of Italy on the principle of the nation as the basic unit of the political community had further cultural consequences. The wish to treat all regions equally naturally led to an attempt to impose a uniformity of custom and tradition on the populations of all regions. This merely accentuated their differences and stressed the contradiction between the concrete identity of the region or city and the abstract identity of the State and its institutions; between them ('those in Rome') and us ('the last wheel of the wagon', 'good only for military service and as canon fodder'). It was responsible for two particularly important developments: on the one hand, the estrangement of large sections of the population from the State; and on the other, the institutionalization of regional subcultures.

The imposition of parliamentary institutions in regions where the socio-economic structures and values to support such institutions had not developed, led to practices which undermined their very legitimacy. The most obvious example was the South, where the imposition of popular sovereignty (with its implication of political authority derived from below) on a patriarchal or traditional agrarian society (which hallowed political authority de-

rived from above) led to a complete transformation of the democratic process.

Politics became, and have remained, encapsulated in a clientelist or patronage polity which has become institutionalized as
a subculture in the South and the Islands. It can be considered
as a regional variant of what has been called the culture of
poverty. Its components were compounded of parasitism and riot.
It was the duty of the ruler and wealthy to provide a livelihood
for the people. So long as they did so, they received its enthusias-
tic support. But if they did not, the people rioted until they did.

For historical reasons, Italy divides into five coherent regions
(see Map) and each has developed a distinctive subculture which
has institutionalized the social conflicts in it. We have already
outlined the clientelist subculture which dominates the South and
the Islands. In the White and Red provinces, the conflictual
element in the social structure has become instutionalized into a
good-evil dichotomy, the former within the Catholic tradition
and the latter within a Marxist framework. In the White provinces the positive pole is constituted by the Church in both its
spiritual and sociological expressions (hierarchy, Catholic organizations and activity), and the negative pole by its enemies, the
atheists and Marxists who promote the otherthrow of its most
sacred traditional values. In the Red provinces, the positive
pole is the proletariat (and often just the people), the party and
all its associations, while the negative pole is furnished by the
established elements in society, particularly the Church (seen in
its concrete structure), the Vatican, with the big monopolies, the
judiciary and the police, etc.

The reasons for the predominance of the Catholic and Marxist
subcultures in these regions are simple : the White provinces
are those where, under the Austrian Empire before unification,
the local clergy led and defended Italian nationality against the
foreign ruler. Conversely, the Red provinces formed part of the
Papal States : the Church played the role of oppressive ruler and
unification took the form of a virulent anti-clericalism which the
nascent Socialist movement infused with an ideological and
institutional backing at the turn of the century. After the war,
the Communists, through their leading role in the Resistance,
acceded to the Socialist institutional inheritance. Moreover the
impulse to the institutionalization of these cultural patterns was

provided by the fact that both Catholics and Socialists were excluded from participation in the political life of the new nation which issued from the Risorgimento. Finally, although they were not backward regions, their change from agrarian to industrializing ones has been gradual and steady – with few discontinuities if we except Fascism in the Red provinces – and so conducive to the *enracinement* of subcultures.

The industrial triangle is culturally the most complex and open region in Italy. It has known rapid change since the war and considerable internal dislocation. At present, modern and contemporary social formations cohabit within the area, but it is dominated by the latter, which is characterized by what Wright-Mills has called 'middle class culture'. The increasing bureaucratization of corporation life stresses the consumer and status aspects of different occupational groupings, thereby hoping to blur the dichotomy between managers and salaried and wage-earning employees. But it remains and has been compounded by the rationalization in production methods imposed on Italian industry to enable it to remain competitive in international markets; and the influx of rural immigrants to the factories, who are totally unprepared for the draconian discipline of modern industrial methods. This has been responsible for a heightening of working-class consciousness in an area where the rapid growth in prosperity had led orthodox liberal sociologists to predict a progressive *embourgeoisement* of the Italian working class.

The various aspects of Italian society which we have discussed in this chapter emphasize duality and discontinuity. Their importance is perhaps most easily grasped if the basic elements are outlined in the form of sociological models : a simple pre-capitalist agrarian one and an advanced capitalist or post-capitalist. The significant areas of contrast are the extent of the division of labour, type of role, social relations and values predominant in both types of society. Simple societies have little division of labour and so of role specialization; in contrast complex industrial societies have developed an extensive division of labour and role specialization. Conflict in both types of society takes a different form. In the former, social relations are ascriptive; and are founded on primary groups which embrace all aspects of an individual's life, while secondary associations are almost unknown. In consequence, the social hierarchy is founded on status, deference and tradition; it is largely a static society with conflict centred on control of the land. On the other hand, social relations in the latter are achieved; and are fashioned as much by secondary associations as by primary groups. Conflict which is founded on economic resources and knowledge is mediated by organizations. As a result, the social hierarchy is more functional; and characterized by social mobility, because the market situation is a fundamental feature.

Table 2. iv
Some Simple Indices of the Development of Civil Society by National Area in 1960

	North	Centre	South	Islands	Italy
Party membership (per 1,000)*	69·4	99·7	74·2	79·2	83·2
Unionization (per 1,000)†	682	641	312	371	584
Newspaper distribution (1,000)	148	160	25	34	105
TV sets (per 1,000)	17·7	17·4	7·2	5·1	13·4
Radio sets (per 1,000)	172·2	142·8	84·8	89·2	133·9
Cinema (per 1,000)	0·262	0·233	0·138	0·161	0·211

(* = for DC, PCI, PSI and PSDI only; † = for CGIL and CISL only)
Sources: elaborated for Cattaneo Institute data and Weiss I., *Politica dell'Informazione* (Milan, 1960), p. 48

Thus we should expect the more advanced regions of the country (primarily the North) to score higher on indices of the development of civil society (party membership, unionization, newspaper readership, TV sets, radio sets and cinema attendance) than the backward regions (primarily the South). This is the general pattern, as Table 2.iv shows.

In conclusion, however, the fundamental point is the general poverty of Italian civil society. On almost all national indices of the development of civil society, Italy scores lower than the other nine most wealthy and industrialized nations. Professor Sylos-Labini has called the Italians 'a semi-literate people' because over seventy per cent of the work force has only a primary school leaving certificate (i.e. can do little more than read and write). It explains, he claims, the arrogance of petty civil servants, the low level of Italian political life and the 'mandarin' attitude of the petty bourgeoisie. This cultural poverty is a fact of major importance to remember in the discussion of the various institutions in subsequent chapters.

Part II
Civil Society
in Italy

Ho notato altra volta che in una determinata società nessuno è disorganizzato e senza partito, purché si intendono organizzazione e partito in senso largo e non formale. In questa molteplicità di società particolari, di carattere duplice – naturale e contrattuale o volontario – una o più prevalgono relativamente o assolutamente, costituendo l'apparato egemonico di un gruppo sociale sul resto della popolazione (o società civile), base dello Stato inteso strettamente come apparato governativo – coercitivo.

Gramsci

(I have noted elsewhere that in a given society nobody is disorganized and without a party, as long as organization and party are understood in a broad and not formal sense. In this multitude of particular associations of a dual character – natural and contractual or voluntary – one or two prevail relatively or absolutely, constituting the hegemonic apparatus of a social group over the rest of the population (or civil society), foundation of the State understood in the restricted sense as the coercive-governmental apparatus.)

3 The Catholic Church: A State within Civil Society

'And if a man consider the origin of this great ecclesiastical
dominion, he will easily perceive that the Papacy is no other than
the ghost of the deceased Roman Empire sitting crowned upon
the grave thereof. For so did the Papacy start up on a sudden
out of the ruins of that great heathen power.' So Thomas Hobbes
claimed at the conclusion of *The Leviathan*. Since the Emperor
Constantine made Christianity the official religion of the Roman
Empire in AD 313 and left the Pope to fend for himself, the
Catholic Church has been identified with Imperial Rome, and
has had a political role. Indeed for many centuries it conceived
its mission as that of preserving the imperial ideal : the unity of
Western Christendom was nothing less than the preservation of
civilization. Furthermore, from the early Middle Ages, when the
Popes acquired a principality for themselves, they have had
temporal as well as spiritual interests to defend. With the loss of
the principality in 1870, the justification of the Catholic
Church's political activity rests on the idea that Christianity cannot be practised in isolation; the Church may not be of this world
but for the moment it is in it. Spiritual authority, to be effective,
requires participation in men's temporal affairs. Pope Pius XI
described the Catholic Church's attitude very succinctly when
he declared, on 14 May 1929, that 'where there is a question of
saving souls or preventing harm to souls, We feel the courage to
treat with the devil in person.'

The Papacy's particular interests in contemporary Italian
politics derive clearly from the geo-historical position of the Holy
See. Rome as the site of the martyrdom of St Peter has not only
been the home of the Papacy from the earliest Christian times,
but all Popes since the sixteenth century have been Italians. In
consequence, the Popes have always regarded themselves as hav-

ing a special interest in the Italian peninsula. This interest has increased as a result of the official recognition of the privileged position of the Roman Church and its titular head in Italian life in the Lateran Pacts of 1929. The influence of the Catholic Church in Italian politics is determined by a second series of factors, of which the most important is undoubtedly its ability to mobilize a large proportion of the Italian people. It is hardly surprising that the Church is a powerful institution in a country which is nominally 99 per cent Catholic. To appreciate the nature of the interest and the kind of power which the Roman Church exercises in Italian affairs, it is necessary to examine first Church-State relations in the postwar period, then the place of the Church in Italian society, and finally, the political activity of the Church.

Church-State Relations

The present relations between the Church and the Italian State are based on the Lateran Pacts of 1929, negotiated between Cardinal Gasparri and Mussolini, which put an end to the sixty-year conflict between them. The conflict had been occasioned by the entry of Italian troops into Rome on 20 September 1870, and the subsequent withdrawal of the Pope from public life as a voluntary 'prisoner in the Vatican' in protest at the usurpation of his temporal power. Pope Pius IX rejected the Law of Guarantees of 13 May 1871, by which the Italian State attempted to resolve the 'Roman Question' (it deprived him of his old sovereign rights, leaving him possession of the Vatican and Lateran Palaces and the summer residence of Castelgandolfo, but accorded him all the honours due to a sovereign, his own diplomatic corps, telegraph office and diplomatic bag, and gave him an annual allowance of 3,225,000 lire [about £150,000 at the time]) and so its application remained unilateral and he refused to allow Catholics to take part in Italian political and public life.

The Lateran Pacts comprised three documents – a treaty, a financial convention and a concordat – which collectively: (1) reasserted the sovereignty of the Holy Father and his complete jurisdiction over the territory of the Vatican, expressly converted into a sovereign, independent State; (2) established Roman Catholicism as the sole religion of the Italian State; (3) gave the

Church sole jurisdiction in matrimonial causes; (4) stipulated Catholic religious instruction in all State schools; (5) barred former priests and those under ecclesiastical sanction from State employment (and so public office); and (6) gave the Holy See a financial settlement of some 1500 million lire (about £20 million in 1929) which is reputed to have been shrewdly invested. In return, the Catholic Church recognized the Italian State as the legal and moral embodiment of the Italian people; acknowledging Rome as the State capital; and, although asserting that ecclesiastical appointments were a responsibility of the Holy See, agreed that before appointment names should be communicated to the Italian government to ascertain their suitability, and established a secret procedure for resolving deadlock. Finally, the Pacts committed the Church to observing a strict neutrality in party politics. Article 43 of the Concordat conferred State recognition on Catholic Action organizations, on condition that they remained under the direct control of the Church hierarchy and had no party political affiliations; it also expressly forbade ecclesiastics to join political parties or be active in them.

The Lateran Pacts were very favourable to the Catholic Church. In fact they were so favourable that many (including D. A. Binchy, who wrote the standard work on the Church under Fascism) forecast that the Church would pay dearly for them on the fall of Fascism. In point of fact, as the former Communist Angelo Tasca was one of the few to prophesy, the contrary occurred: the Lateran Pacts were not only not rescinded, they were written into Article 7 of the Republican Constitution of 1948. The problem of the Lateran Pacts, as far as the Constituent Assembly was concerned, was not whether to denounce or renegotiate them, but whether to include them in the Constitution or not. Nobody was anxious to reopen the 'Roman Question'. The Christian Democrats were, however, determined to write them into the Constitution, and they succeeded thanks to the support of the Communists, who wanted to preserve religious peace at all costs. The Communist Party believed that the Treaty and the Concordat were the 'twin pillars' of that peace. Hence Article 7 of the Constitution reads as follows: 'The State and the Catholic Church are, each in its own sphere, independent and sovereign. Their relations are regulated by the

49

Lateran Pacts. Modifications of the Pacts, mutually agreed upon, do not require the procedure necessary for the amendment of the Constitution.'

The Church, therefore, managed to ensure the retention of an extremely favourable framework – one which is more appropriate to a confessional State than to a modern liberal democratic one. Pius xii did not hesitate to take advantage of it to make the Church's presence felt in all areas of Italian life in the postwar years. Moreover, the Vatican's position in the nation's political life was strengthened by two further developments. First, the fall of the monarchy left it as the only traditional hierarchic institution at the centre of Italian political life. Second, the political triumph of Christian Democracy, which had been prepared under Fascism by the protected position secured for Catholic Action in the Concordat, brought the Papacy to the controlling centre of state power in Italy.

In view of this situation, and despite the new orientation of the Papacy under John xxiii, there is considerable strength of opinion in favour of a change in Church-State relations in Italy. No political group seeks to reopen the 'Roman Question', and in so far as the Lateran Treaty was simply a settlement of the international status of the Holy See, no political group seeks its denunciation. The controversial matters are the Concordat, and the clauses in it which conflict with the 'bill of Rights' section of the Republican Constitution. In 1970, the Italian Parliament passed a Divorce Bill which is in direct breach of the Church's matrimonial jurisdiction in the Concordat, to which the Church has responded by inspiring Catholics to initiate the procedure for a popular referendum to repeal the Act under Article 75 of the Constitution. This was to have been held in June 1972, but the premature dissolution of Parliament has had the effect of delaying it until summer 1974. It was not so much the principle of the indissolubility of the marriage vows but the pre-eminence of the ecclesiastical tribunals that the Vatican was concerned to defend. Since the Divorce Bill became law, the ecclesiastical tribunals have cut delays in procedure and lowered the costs of annulments. In the meantime, rumours circulate that secret negotiations are going on between the Italian government and the Holy See with a view to modifying the Concordat. If the rumours are well-founded, the negotiations are bound to be long and arduous.

The Place of the Church in Italian Society

The place of the Church in Italian society derives ultimately from two factors. On the one hand, its institutional structure, and on the other, its ability to mobilize large numbers of Italians. Its institutional structure is hierarchical and has two major components. First, what one might call the state structure of the Holy See, e.g. the Curia with its various Congregations (or Departments), Offices and Tribunals, etc.; and second, its grass-roots organization, e.g. the national ecclesiastical structure of

Table 3. i : Organization of the Roman Curia since 1967

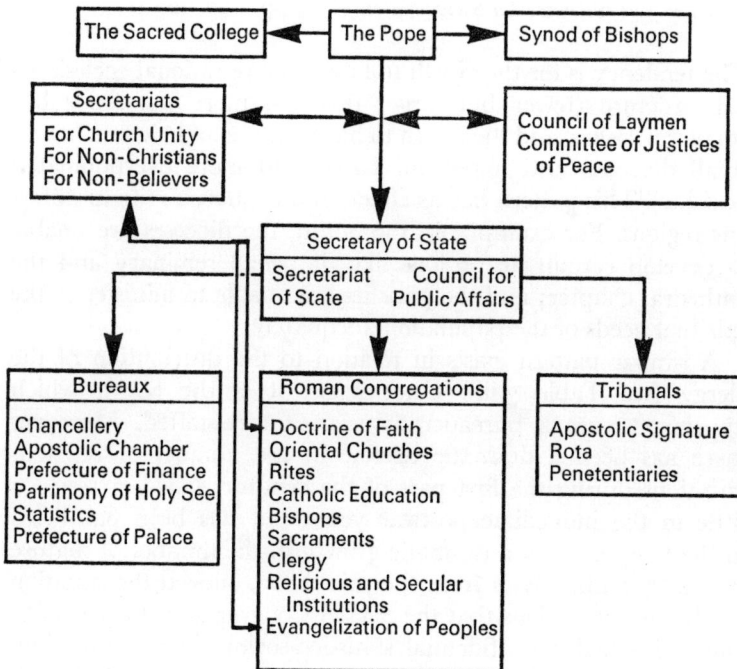

| The Sacred College | ← | The Pope | → | Synod of Bishops |

| Secretariats | Council of Laymen |
| For Church Unity / For Non-Christians / For Non-Believers | Committee of Justices of Peace |

Secretary of State

| Secretariat of State | Council for Public Affairs |

Bureaux	Roman Congregations	Tribunals
Chancellery	Doctrine of Faith	Apostolic Signature
Apostolic Chamber	Oriental Churches	Rota
Prefecture of Finance	Rites	Penetentiaries
Patrimony of Holy See	Catholic Education	
Statistics	Bishops	
Prefecture of Palace	Sacraments	
	Clergy	
	Religious and Secular Institutions	
	Evangelization of Peoples	

Source:
P. Milza, and S. Berstein, *L'Italie, La Papauté, 1870-1970* (Paris, 1970), p. 171

dioceses and parishes, etc. No mention need be made of the former, unless it be that it provides the Church with the machinery for imperative co-ordination right at the centre of Italian political life (for organization see table 3.i). As regards the latter, Italy is divided into 18 Conciliar regions which comprise some 282 dioceses and some 25,128 parishes. However the institutions are not spread equally over the country, as is clear from Table 3.ii

Table 3. ii
Ecclesiastical Structure by National Area in 1960

	Dioceses	Pop./Diocese	Parishes	Pop./Parish
North	68	311,215	12,331	1,716
Centre	94	112,517	7,268	1,422
South & Islands	120	156,146	5,529	2,895
Italy	282	176,306	25,128	1,890

Source: J. Labbens, *La Sociologia religiosa,* pp. 199–200

The tendency is for the North to have a more rational ecclesiastical structure (fewer but larger dioceses, more numerous but smaller parishes) and the South to have a more archaic one (many small dioceses, and fewer but larger and more overpopulated parishes). This pattern has its effect on the Church's life in different regions. For example, in the South, the dioceses are unable to develop certain institutions like the small seminary and the cathedral chapter; and the parishes are unable to minister to the spiritual needs of the population adequately.

A similar pattern exists in relation to the distribution of the clergy (see Table 3.iii). Once again it is the South which appears, to use a bureaucratic term, under-staffed. Moreover there has been a dramatic decline in the number of religious vocations during the first part of the century; it was arrested a little in the immediate postwar years, but has been paralleled in the late sixties by a dramatic growth in the number of mature voluntary withdrawals from the priesthood. Indeed the situation has become so serious that the Sacred Congregation for Doctrine and Faith had a confidential statistico-sociological inquiry into 'Defections from the Holy Ministry' prepared in 1971. It calculated that while 190 priests only had asked to be released from their sacerdotal functions in the twenty-five years between 1939 and 1963, the number had risen to 754 in the next five years (1964–8 inclusive). The report noted, moreover, that the motives were above all ideological : the proportion who wished to break their vows because of celibacy remained unchanged, but those who refused ecclesiastical discipline and the traditional role of the priest had increased alarmingly from 1 per cent to 42 per cent.

Table 3. iii
Distribution of Clergy by National Area in 1960

	Clergy	Pop./ Priest	Semin- arists	Monks & Nuns	Total Eccles.	Pop./ Eccles.
North	33,477	672	4,209	95,262	132,948	166
Centre	13,778	751	1,568	45,053	60,399	175
Islands & South	16,679	958	2,893	31,708	50,708	326
Italy	63,936	743	8,670	172,024	244,192	204

Source: J. Labbens, *op. cit.*, pp. 200–1

In assessing the situation in Italy, we must bear in mind that it is still more favourable to the Catholic Church than elsewhere. For example, there are only 150 French bishops against 360 Italians; and 100,000 Frenchmen in holy orders compared with almost a quarter of a million Italians. Hence it is hardly surprising that church-going is greater in Italy than in France. A French survey of 1958 showed that 33 per cent of the respondents were regular church-goers against 43 per cent who were not (the remainder were non-Catholics), while in an Italian survey carried out in 1962, 53 per cent of those interviewed claimed that they had been to mass the previous Sunday. Don Silvano Burgalassi's studies suggest that 40 per cent of regular church-goers is a truer national figure.

Moreover, there is no relationship between ecclesiastical structure, distribution of the clergy and church-going (see Tables 3.i–3.iv). This fact raises the interesting question of the Church's capacity to mobilize the Italian people and its determinants.

The Church's ability to mobilize its supporters can be measured in a series of figures : nominally Catholic (i.e. baptized) 99 per cent; practising Catholics (i.e. regular church-goers) 40 per cent; Catholic voters (i.e. voting DC) 35–40 per cent; Active Catholics (i.e. membership of Catholic Action) 5 per cent. The most important Catholic organization is Catholic Action, which is an organization of Catholic laymen associated with, and supervised by, the ecclesiastical hierarchy in its apostolic mission. It was founded after 1898 as a reaction to the triumph of liberalism and the threat to the Church's temporal power, and has acted as a kind of para-political party defending the interests of the Church in civil affairs. Hence religious and political motivations became inextricably intertwined in its action. The key role it played under Fascism in preparing Catholic leaders and providing an organizational structure within the regime led to it playing a more directly political role in the immediate postwar years, despite the formal prohibition in the Lateran Pacts. The organization of the Civic Committees for the 1948 General Elections, the supervision of DC lists and continued political proselytism certainly exceeded the purely religious role its leaders claimed for it. Pope John XXIII and Vatican II endeavoured to turn it away from politics back to its apostolic role, that of the religious training of the laity. It is generally agreed that its political influence has declined during the sixties.

Table 3. iv
Mass Appeal of Church by National Area

	Church-going	Catholic vote	Active Catholic (Member AC)
North	51%	38%	7%
Centre	26%	30%	5%
South	30%	40%	3%
Italy	40%	38%	5%

Sources: Data elaborated from S. Burgalassi, *Il comportamento religioso degli italiani*, Chap. 2

Before the War Catholic Action consisted of four separate groups: men, women, young men, and young women. In 1946 the Holy See issued new statutes establishing within it, in addition, the University Students' Movement (FUCI), the University Graduates' Movement, and the School Teachers' Movement.

At the same time, it was active in promoting or supporting a whole series of organizations (*opere*): 'some of which are of modest dimensions while others are truly mass movements having a notable influence on the economic and social life of the country (for example, Civic Committees, Italian Association of Christian Workers (ACLI), *Coldiretti*, and Catholic Union of Italian Secondary School Teachers (UCI IM).' These supporting organizations are of three types: 'dependent' (i.e. promoted by AC); 'co-ordinated' (i.e. part promoted, part recognized); and 'adherent' (i.e. recognized membership) (see Table 3.v). According to papal directives, each of the four branches and move-

Table 3. v
Organized Activity of Italian Catholic Action

Branches:	Movements:	Central Secretariats:
Uomini Cattolici	FUCI	Istituto Cattolico di Attività Soc.
Donne Cattoliche	Movimento Laureati	Ente dello Spettacolo
Gioventù maschile	Movimento Maestri	Centro Catt. Cinematografico
Gioventù femminile		Centro Catt. Teatrale
		Centro Catt. Radio-diff.
		Centro Catt. TV.
		Ist. Catt. dell'Educazione
		Seg. Moralità
		Centro Catto. Stampa

Opere:

Dipendenti:	*Coordinate:*
Centro Naz. Attività Catechistiche	Comitati Civici
Centro Sportivo Italiano	ACLI
Centro Turistico Giovanile	Centro Italiano Femminile
Fed. Attività Ricreative	Assoc. Scoutistica Ital.
Unione Catt. Italiana Ostetriche	Assoc. Guide Ital.
Assoc. Infermiere Prof. ed Asst. Sanitarie	
Convegni Maria Cristina	
Assoc. Italiana Maestri Catt.	*Aderenti:*
Comitato Docenti Universitari	Confed. Cooperative Ital.
Unione Catt. Ital. Insegnanti Medi	Centro Naz. Artigiano
Assoc. Medici Catt. Ital.	Unione Cristiana Imprenditori Dirigenti
Unione Catt. Ital. Technici	Unione Catt. Ital. Commercianti
Unione Catt. Artisti Ital.	Fronte della Famiglia
Unione Catt. Ital. Farmicisti	Unione Catt. Infermiere
Unione Catt. Giuristi Ital.	Assoc. Catt. Escercenti Cinema
	Giunta Catt. dell'Emigrazione
	Unione Editori Catt. Ital.
	Assoc. Famiglie Numerose
	Assoc. Ex-Alunni di Istituti Religiosi
	Confederazione Coltivatori Diretti.

Source: I. Weiss, *Politica dell'Informazione* (Milan, 1961), pp. 236–8

ments was to have a national organization in every diocese and parish. At the national level, an executive organ, the General Presidency, and a deliberative organ, the Central Junta were created. All the offices of the General Presidency as well as of all the national executive organs are appointed by the ecclesiastical authorities. At the diocesan level the organizational structure is identical except that the diocesan president and branch presidents are chosen by the local bishops. The same structure is used in the parishes, where the local priests choose the leaders. Although all leaders are laymen, each level has an ecclesiastical assistant representing the hierarchy. In short, the hierarchy and the clergy maintain a tight control over Catholic Action, which is the Church's devoted army and instrument.

During the postwar period, Catholic Action has counted well over three million members in some 80,000 associations, which, together with the membership of the various dependent organizations, makes 'Catholic Action effectively the largest organization numerically in the country'. Moreover it is not the only organization of Catholic laymen: there are also the lay orders (*terz'ordini*) which depend on the medieval religious orders which promoted them; and there are the Marian Congregations dependent on the Society of Jesus: 'religious associations whose task is that of educating chosen persons from any class or condition who are prepared to dedicate themselves to their own sanctification, to the apostolic mission and defence of the Church, specifically by means of special devotion to Our Lady.' Significantly, the slogan of these congregations is: 'educate the chosen for the masses and reach the masses through the chosen.'

Catholic Action's organization by diocese, on the basis of the existing ecclesiastical structure, provided it with a framework and an initial strength after the Liberation which other organizations founded on the fall of Fascism lacked. In this sense, it is easy to see why Christian Democracy triumphed politically in the postwar period. According to Galli and Prandi, Catholic Action 'reflects the level of political development of the Catholics more clearly than the Catholic oriented party. In the central and northern regions it is Catholic Action and not the Christian Democrat party that is the mass political and social organization of Italian Catholics.' Where it is strong, the Church's capacity for mobilization is strong. It is particularly strong in the White provinces of the North East, moderately strong in the industrial triangle and 'Red belt' of the Centre, and weak in the South. And yet the Catholic Church's capacity to mobilize its supporters exceeds the organizational strength of both its own ecclesiastical structure and that of Catholic Action. Why?

There are a number of obvious reasons. First, there are what one might call indirect institutional structures. The Church influences, if not controls, the Italian educational system. Although the state-school system is nationwide in scope, it suffers from considerable backwardness: class-based recruitment, unqualified teachers, and severe lack of amenities. Not surprisingly, religious instruction is a compulsory part of the syllabus in primary schools. In addition to the state system there are private schools, but these are overwhelmingly Church operated (although state subsidized) and their diplomas are recognized by the State. Finally, the Catholic Church has its own University for lay students, the Catholic University of the Sacred Heart in Milan, founded by Father Gemelli in 1929.

The Church still has control of many private welfare and charitable organizations (hospitals, nursing homes, orphanages and old folks' homes, etc.) which ensures that it plays a role in the lives of many sections of the population, especially of the needy. An example of its solicitude has been the attention which it has devoted to emigration.

Second, there are what one can call cultural factors. The strength of Catholic organizations and their consequent mass appeal in the White provinces derive from the Catholic subculture in that region, as does its relative weakness in the Red belt from the strength of the Marxist subculture there. As regards the appeal of Catholicism in the industrial triangle, where dechristianization is rife, it would seem to have its roots in the ability of the Church to recruit clergy from all social classes including the working class (see Table 10.i below).

Thus the Church has managed to keep contact with all areas of Italian society. Such explanations, however, do nothing to explain the Church's ability to mobilize the populations of the depressed South and Islands. There the ecclesiastical structure and Catholic organizations are weak, yet church-going and the Catholic vote are relatively high. The explanation would seem to lie in the nature of southern society. Ecclesiastical structure and Catholic organizations are weak, but civil society is weaker. Indeed, one can even formulate the hypothesis that the Church is stronger than the State in parts of these regions. Peter Nichols has written that:

> Its organization in Italy runs through all levels of life: schools, parish halls (which still have an important place in Italian life), hospitals, professional associations, newspapers; and everywhere there is the presence and influence of priests. A priest is often in the best position to help in any one of the highly varied set of circumstances – or not to help. In many places for instance, particularly when unemployment was at its height, it would have been impossible for a man to find a job without the goodwill of the priest. As far as the employer was concerned, a recommendation from a priest would mean that the man was not likely to be an agitator, that he would have voted for the governing party and taken notice of the reminders in the confession boxes about the serious consequences of voting for the extreme left or belonging to its organizations. A contractor in Rome would not expect his tender to be accepted unless accompanied by a letter from a cardinal. Such things were the commonplaces of Italian life. . . .

In such circumstances, it can be no surprise that the Church's place in Italian life is of the first importance.

The Political Activities of the Church

The existence of a strong Communist Party in Italy has meant that the Vatican believed, despite the contrary evidence furnished by the Communist Party itself on numerous occasions, that it would take the first opportunity which arose to overthrow the existing social order and destroy the Church as an institution. (It is worth noting, in this connection, that the Holy See has substantial capital investments in building, banking, insurance, public services and large-scale public works' projects, on the profits of which it pays the Italian State no taxes.) Furthermore the Vatican was naturally anxious to preserve the privileged position that the Church had won under Fascism, and so it was omnipresent on the political scene throughout the Allied military occupation, co-operating with the Allied Military Government. In August 1945, the Holy Consistorial Congregation issued a circular to bishops laying down the following instructions:

1 In consideration of the dangers to which religion and the public well-being are exposed and whose gravity requires the unanimous collaboration of all honest men, all those who have the right to vote, of every condition, sex and age, with no exceptions are, in conscience, strictly obliged to avail themselves of that right.

2 Catholics may give their vote only to those candidates or those lists of candidates of whom one has the certainty that they will respect and defend the observance of the divine law and the rights of religion and the Church in private and public life. The more the programme and practical activity of single candidates or lists of candidates justifies and supports the certainty, the greater the peace of mind Catholics can have in freely voting in their favour.

These instructions were the basis of those which the Italian bishops inserted in their pastoral letters at each General and Municipal Election from 1946 to 1963–4. In addition, the Conference of the Italian Episcopacy(CEI) issued appeals in successive election campaigns which quickly became a traditional landmark in the campaign. Thus in the elections for the Constituent Assembly in 1945, Catholics were admonished to vote together 'to ensure to present and future generations the blessings of a fundamental law of the nation which is not opposed to sound religious and moral principles, but rather takes from them vigorous inspiration, proclaims them and wisely follows their lofty ends.' In 1963, the appeal to vote together contained the reminder that Catholics 'must place their fidelity to essential Christian principles and the needs of the common good before their personal opinions and individual interests.' It was only in 1968 that John xxiii's new orientation of the Holy See, with its tendency to stress the Church's universal religious vocation, placing it outside political competitions and marking its detachment from Italy's domestic political struggles, had filtered through to the Italian Episcopacy, so that the conference's time-honoured appeal to Catholics to vote together was replaced by the suggestion that Catholics should 'vote according to their individual consciences'. This suggestion was, of course, interpreted by individual bishops in different ways, so that it was still possible to find the traditional appeals in many pastoral letters, particularly in southern dioceses. In 1972, there was a return to old ways with the traditional appeal of the CEI.

C*

The Vatican's political activity was not limited to electoral propaganda. At various times the Church has attempted to dictate policy to Christian Democrat Party leaders; and to do so, the Pope has not hesitated to take sides in internal party disputes. Under Pope Pius XII, there were a whole series of incidents which marked the Pope's determination to direct Italian affairs; they were, moreover, not always successful, and sometimes they were unfortunate. Thus Pius XII attempted, unsuccessfully, to persuade De Gasperi, when Prime Minister, to institute a clerical regime on the morrow of the Christian Democrat triumph at the polls on 18 April 1948. He endeavoured to take advantage of the cold war not only to destroy the Communist Party but also to persuade all Italians to return to the Church's bosom. To this end, Pius XII proclaimed 1950 a Holy Year to promote the return of those of little faith; and to ensure its success, the Holy Office issued on 14 July 1949 the celebrated decree prescribing excommunication on all 'the faithful who profess communist, materialist and anti-Christian doctrines and all those who defend or propagate them ...' The years that followed are studded with examples of the Vatican's intervention in Italian policy: for example the Christian Democrat Party needed the Vatican's support before it would enter into 'opening to the left' alliance with the Socialist Party in the early sixties; it was the Vatican which had to apply pressure on Fanfani, one of the prominent Christian Democrat Party leaders, before he would withdraw from the contest, so that Parliament was able to elect the President of the Republic on the twenty-first ballot in December 1964. Although the list is long and continuous, one can say that since the papacy of John XXIII, the Church's intervention in Italian politics have been much less marked.

Another area where the Vatican has been active is in the administration. The Italian administration can help the Church in a variety of ways, from issuing regulations to authorizing grants. The Vatican has an interest, therefore, in people sympathetic to the Church occupying the important posts in the civil service. Joseph LaPalombara, in his study *Interest Groups in Italian Politics*, presents plenty of evidence of the intervention of the clergy in the administration; and of the *quid pro quo* the kinds of recommendations that civil servants seek from bishops to secure promotion. While it is impossible to assess how widespread such practices are, they cannot be unimportant, given that political intervention in the administration has a long tradition in Italy. The effect of Pope John's papacy seems to have been, as far as an outsider can judge, towards less interference in the administration as it has been towards greater abstention from party politics.

This chapter has not attempted to answer the question of whether the Vatican (or the Catholic Church) is, as some observers claim, stronger than the Italian government; this would have required a long and thorough analysis of the relations between the Vatican and the Italian government and their position on a wide range of contentious issues, and it will be decades before the material for such an analysis is available. It has, however, investigated briefly the elements on which an assessment of the Church's power is based. These are: (1) its privileged position in Italian life; (2) its enjoyment of a parallel state-structure (Curia and ecclesiastical institutions), and hence of a considerable, if declining capacity of mass mobilization; and (3) the will to exercise its privileges to the full and defend its prerogatives, the extent of which will become clearer when, and if, a new Concordat is signed. One thing is therefore certain: whatever the Catholic Church's true power, it is one which Italian governments of all political persuasions can expect to have to take account of, and ignore only at their peril. The cautious, some would say servile, attitude of the Communist Party towards the Church is proof, of a sort, of the veracity of this proposition.

4 Political Parties: The Politics of Patronage

Parties and the Party System

Italy has been widely considered, particularly since the passing of the French Fourth Republic, to provide the classic case of the multi-party system in contemporary Europe. There are nine parties operating nationally: Communist, two Socialist,* Social Democrat, Republican, Catholic (Christian Democrat), Liberal, Monarchist* and Neo-Fascist. In addition, a number of local parties, such as the Sardinian Action Party, the *Union Valdôtaine* and the *Südtiroler Volkspartei* (SVP), have been able to elect one or two Members of Parliament as spoksmen for their regions. None of the national parties, however, has succeeded in winning a majority of the popular vote in any postwar General Election. Government has been based, therefore, on coalition of the centre parties, now right-oriented as in the fifties, now left-oriented as in the sixties; and it has been marked by cabinet instability, since Italy has had thirty-five governments in the thirty years since the fall of Fascism.

This classical view of the Italian party system engenders more confusion than understanding of postwar Italian party politics. First, the party system has been dominated by a permanent government party – Christian Democracy, which has consistently polled two-fifths of the vote in all postwar General Elections (see Table 4.i) and has been the hub of all governmental coalitions since 1946. Indeed one of the key factors of postwar Italian politics has been the impossibility of forming a government which is not acceptable to the Christian Democrats. Secondly, the principal opposition party, the Communist Party, which has

* In July 1972, the left-wing Socialist Party (PSIUP) merged with the Communist Party and the Monarchists merged with the Neo-Fascists.

increased its share of the poll from one-fifth in 1946 to over 27 per cent in 1972, is, by origin and definition, an anti-system party, and so has been kept in permanent opposition since 1947. Although the party has never explicitly denied its Marxist goals, it has followed a reformist line, proposing structural reforms for the construction of Socialism. Its opponents have preferred to argue that should the Communist Party come to power, it would destroy the Parliamentary system; and the electorate have so far followed them. Hence the nub of the Italian party system has been the exclusion of the Communist Pary from government. Thirdly, the minor right-wing (Liberals, Monarchists and Neo-Fascists) and minor left-wing (Socialists, Social-Democrats and Republicans) parties have rarely, if ever, totalled more than a third of the electorate all told, and so no one party or group has been able to provide a credible alternative to Christian Democracy. Their highest aspiration, in fact, both individually and collectively, could only be the conditioning of the Christian Democrats towards either conservative or reformist policies.

Cabinet instability has been a major component of the functioning of the party system, but so too have electoral stability and its corollary political immobility. Cabinets may fall and ministers may change office, but the same persons remain ministers in consecutive cabinets. In one sense, therefore, the Italian party system has worked in Parliament in a manner remarkably like that which Sir Lewis Namier described in his account of eighteenth-century England. There has been a permanent government or 'Court' party (Christian Democracy (DC); the court being the Vatican since the fall of the monarchy); a permanent opposition or 'out' party (Communist Party (PCI); a group of government supporting parties (the minor coalition partners); and finally, a group of alternative government supporting parties (the minor parties opposing this coalition, but hoping to enter the next one). The stability of the party system was founded on the ability of the government parties, with the assistance of the Church and American influence, to persuade a majority of electors that the Communist Party was pledged to the overthrow of democracy. This has been achieved, thanks to the cold war, by identifying the Communist Party with the Soviet Union, the destruction of Western civilization and the Anti-Christ.

The Namier party model is a useful tool in helping us to

Italy – Republic without government?

Table 4 i : Election results of National Parties 1946-72
[votes, percentages and seats (votes in millions)]

Chamber of Deputies	1946 Votes	%	Seats	1948 Votes	%	Seats	1953 Votes	%	Seats
PCI	4.4	18.9	104⌐	8.1	31.0	183⌐	6.1	22.6	143
PSIUP	4.8	20.7	115⌐						
PSI							3.5	12.8	75
PSDI				1.9	7.1	33	1.2	4.5	19
PRI	1.0	4.4	23	0.7	2.5	9	0.4	1.6	5
DC	8.1	35.2	207	12.7	48.5	305	10.9	40.1	263
PLI	1.6	6.8	41	1.0	3.8	19	0.8	3.0	13
Mon	0.6	2.8	16	0.7	2.8	14	1.9	6.9	40
MSI	1.2	5.3	30	0.5	2.0	6	1.6	5.8	29
Others*	1.4	5.6	20	0.6	2.4	6	0.7	2.7	3
Total	23.0	100.0	556	26.2	100.0	574	27.0	100.0	590
Turnout	24.9	89.1		26.8	92.2		28.4	93.8	
Electorate	28.0			29.1			30.3		

Senate	1948 Votes	%	Seats	1953 Votes	%	Seats
PCI	7.0	30.8	72⌐	4.9	20.2	51
PSIUP						
PSI				2.9	11.9	26
PSDI	0.9	4.2	8	1.0	4.3	4
PSDI/PRI	0.6	2.7	4			
PRI	0.6	2.6	4			
DC/PRI				0.2	0.8	3
DC	10.9	48.1	131	9.7	39.9	113
PLI	1.2	5.4	7	0.7	2.9	3
Mon.	0.4	1.7	3	1.6	6.5	14
MSI				1.5	6.1	9
Others*	0.9	4.1	6	1.8	7.4	14
Total	22.7	100.0	237	24.3	100.0	237
Turnout	23.8	92.1		25.5	93.8	
Electorate	25.9			27.1		

*Including the regional parties SVP (*Südtiroler Volkspartei*) PSA (*Partito sardo d'Azion*
and U.V. (*Union Valdôtaine*) which have all elected members in their regions.
In 1946 MSI represents UQ; PLI represents UDN; and Monarchists represent BNL.
In 1948 PCI and PSI presented joint lists as FDP; PSDI represents US; PLI
   represents BN
In 1953 Monarchists represent PNM
In 1958 Monarchists represent PNM and PMP
In 1963 Monarchists represent PDIUM
In 1968 PCI and PSIUP presented joint lists in Senate; and PSI and PSDI presented
   joint lists for both Chamber and Senate as PSU
In 1972 PCI and PSIUP presented joint lists for Senate; MSI and Monarchists presented
   Joint lists for Chamber and Senate; and PSDI represents PSU born as result
   of split with PSI in 1969.

Source: *Italy: Documents and Notes*, 6 of 1971, pp. 419–34; and 3 of 1972, pp. 198-

Votes	1958 %	Seats	Votes	1963 %	Seats	Votes	1968 %	Seats	Votes	1972 %	Seats
6.7	22.7	140	7.8	25.3	166	8.6	26.9	177	9.1	27.2	179
						1.4	4.5	23	0.6	1.9	—
4.2	14.2	84	4.2	13.8	87	4.6	14.5	91	3.2	9.6	61
1.3	4.5	22	1.8	6.1	33				1.7	5.1	29
0.4	1.4	6	0.4	1.4	6	0.6	2.0	9	1.0	2.9	14
12.5	42.4	273	11.8	38.3	260	12.4	39.1	266	12.9	38.8	267
1.0	3.5	17	2.1	7.0	39	1.9	5.8	31	1.3	3.9	21
1.4	4.8	25	0.5	1.7	8	0.4	1.3	6	2.9	8.7	56
1.4	4.8	24	1.5	5.1	27	1.4	4.4	24			
0.5	1.7	5	0.4	1.3	4	0.5	1.5	3	0.8	1.5	3
29.6	100.0	596	30.8	100.0	630	31.8	100.0	630	33.4	100.0	630
30.4	93.8		31.8	92.9		33.0	92.8		34.5	93.1	
32.4			34.2			35.6			37.0		

Votes	1958 %	Seats	Votes	1963 %	Seats	Votes	1968 %	Seats	Seats	1972 %	Seats
5.7	21.8	59	6.9	25.2	84	8.6	30.0	101	8.3	27.6	91
									0.3	0.8	3
3.7	14.1	35	3.8	14.0	44	4.4	15.2	46	3.2	10.7	33
1.2	4.4	5	1.7	6.4	14				1.6	5.4	11
						0.6	2.1	2	0.9	3.0	5
			0.2	0.7	4						
10.8	41.2	123	10.0	36.5	129	11.0	38.3	135	11.4	38.1	135
1.0	3.9	4	2.0	7.4	18	1.9	6.8	16	1.3	4.4	8
1.3	4.9	7	0.4	1.6	2	0.3	1.1	2	2.8	9.2	26
1.2	4.4	8	1.5	5.3	14	1.3	4.6	11			
1.4	5.3	3	0.8	2.9	6	0.5	1.9	2	0.2	0.8	3
26.2	100.0	246	27.5	100.0	315	28.6	100.0	315	30.1	100.0	315
27.4	93.9		28.8	93.0		30.3	93.0		33.7		
29.2			31.0			32.5					

† PCI/PSIUP/PSI/PSA

understand the mechanisms underlying party representation. By focusing attention on Parliament as the key component in defining party activity, it spotlights one of the major characteristics of postwar Italian politics, i.e., the distance (and independence) of party representation from its electoral base. In eighteenth-century England, the link between Parliament and the country was cemented, where it was necessary under a restricted suffrage, by 'old corruption'. In postwar Italy, the links are necessarily different, if only because its regime is one of universal suffrage. Nonetheless, they all contribute to promoting electoral stability, which is one of the pillars of the system.

Four factors promote electoral stability, the first is the ideological tradition of the two leading parties. Both the Christian Democrats and the Communists are heirs to particular Italian subcultures, the Catholic and the Marxist, which became deeply entrenched in the nineteenth century, and ensure, through their associational networks (Church and Catholic organizations for the one, Labour organizations and Co-operatives for the other) the electoral strength of these parties in those regions (e.g. 'White' provinces of the North East, and 'Red Belt' of the Centre) where they organize specific populations. The second is the 'Southern system', which means that all parties are organized in the South and Islands on the basis of extensive personal *clientele* (the politicians are local bosses using their parties as their own exclusive electoral machines). The third is the cold war, with its tendency to divide the world into two blocks, which has acted as an element of polarization within the country. Inside Italy, the line of demarcation between the two groups passed right through the Socialist Party, which explains much of its unhappy postwar history of splits and reunifications. The fourth is the use of Proportional Representation, which is the most static of all electoral systems.

The consequences of this situation in which Parliament is independent of its electoral base in the country has been a party system dominated by parliamentary intrigue and factionalism, and interminable debates, discussions and *palabres* over the government 'formula' (i.e. the group of parties participating in the government majority). The Christian Democrat Party, because it cannot be replaced as the major governing party in the foreseeable future, has had virtually no interest in promoting dynamic policies that might attenuate the distance of Parliament from the country. On the contrary, it has had powerful incentives to resist them because, having a confessional base, any action provoking social mobility can only undermine the strength which is, at present, recruited from all social classes. Hence it has acted as the dominant bourgeois party and its leaders' constant preoccupations – outside the advancement of themselves and their friends to the top posts in Italian society and satisfying the patronage requirements of individual Catholic organizations – has been the disqualification of their greatest rivals, the Communist leaders, from office by the mechanism of limiting the so-called 'democratic area' (i.e. the area from which the government formula is selected), and the preservation of the party's internal unity, since a split is the one sure way in which it could lose power. Such a power structure places a premium on immobility, because dynamic action promotes disunity.

The preoccupations of the Communist Party are apparently diametrically opposed to those of the Christian Democrats, and hence complementary. Aware that it is too weak to form an alternative government at present, it has striven to prevent the formation of stable Christian Democrat cabinets out of fear that they might isolate it. This dialectic relationship between the Communists and the Christian Democrats has been responsible paradoxically for the immobility as well as such dynamism as the parliamentary system has shown in the postwar period. The Communist Party, from its place of imposed opposition, has been forced to become the prime mover in promoting liberal democratic reforms, and its votes have assisted the passage of important government legislation through Parliament. The 'apparatus' party leaders appear satisfied with the present situation because, as a result of a unique feature of Italian Parliamentary procedure, i.e. the power of standing committees to legislate, the party enjoys the best of both worlds for an opposition party : a cut of patronage from collaboration in committee behind closed doors; and the stance of unsullied opposition or prospective government responsibility in public debate on the floor of the House. This has enabled the party to make modest, if significant, gains in each postwar General Election.

Finally, the minor parties, whether of the left or the right, because of the contradiction between their aspirations for power and their inability to control the government by replacing the Christian Democrats, are continually forced to renounce their political *raison d'être* for fear of worse. If, by chance, they push their support of principle to the point of resignation, they can either be replaced by one of the alternative government support- ing coalition parties, as the Liberal Party was by the Nenni Socialist Party in the early sixties and vice-versa in 1972, or brought into line by the threat of a military *coup* as the Nenni Socialist Party was in July 1964.

This functioning of the party system was just about adequate for the 1950s, when economic reconstruction and development was the imperative demand of the population. Organization of political hegemony was relatively simple; it was based on a division of labour: the economic operators ran the economy and the political leaders managed party representation. All was well because the economy operated very successfully; and not too much Galbraithian squalor and spoliation was visible. In the sixties, however, this political hegemony encountered serious difficulties. The southern countryside was being left abandoned by the massive rural exodus and the northern cities were becom- ing choked and their amenities submerged under the weight of economic development. Talk of social reform dominated politi- cal discussion: the need for controlled urban development, the reorganization and reform of the legal system, the health service, the educational system and so on. The Student Movement, the 'hot autumn' of 1969, and the riots in Pescara, L'Aquila and Reggio di Calabria of summer 1970 were only a few of the more important consequences of the decline in the political hegemony of the politicians. In these circumstances, it is no surprise that there was much talk of a grave crisis in Italian Parliamentary democracy.

Party Organization

All the national parties copied, sooner or later and with more or less success, the Communist Party model of a mass party and gave themselves a branch-like structure. They are organized at three levels: at the local level in the commune, the party section (or the cell in the workplace in the case of the Communist Party) was part of the provincial federation, the intermediate unit, which was part, in turn, of the national unit, the National Executive or Central Committee. The Executive Committees at all levels (i.e. sections, federations and National Executive) are elected at periodically held congresses of delegates representing the paid-up membership at that level, which debates policy and elects delegates to the congresses at the superior level. The supreme party body is the National Congress which elects the National Executive or Central Committee and Secretariat that controls the party in the periods between Congresses. Congresses also ratify party policy; they are held at irregular intervals, but usually every other year for most parties.

At the same time, all parties promote collateral para-political organizations, such as labour unions, cooperatives, women's and youth movements, and even professional associations and sports' clubs. Thus the three mass parties, Communist, Socialist and Christian Democrat, were initially flanked by the General Confederation of Italian Labour (CGIL) as a result of the Pact of Rome of June 1944 on united union policy. After the union split of July 1948, the Catholics set up the Italian Confederation of Free Trade Unions (CISL), and the Social Democrats and Republicans, the Union of Italian Labour (UIL); they were joined in 1948 by the CISNAL, a Neo-Fascist union. In the commercial field the Communist Party promoted the League of Cooperatives; and in the agricultural field the Christian Democrats organized the National Federation of Small Farmers (*Coldiretti*), and the Communist Party first the *Federterra* (for agricultural labourers) and later the Peasants' Alliance. In addition, most parties publish their own daily papers: *L'Unità* (Communist), *Avanti!* (Socialist), *Il Popolo* (Christian Democrat), *La Voce Repubblicana* (Republican), *Il Secolo d'Italia* (Neo-Fascist), etc. Some parties have even founded their own publishing houses: *Editori Riuniti* (Communist), *Cinque Lune* (Christian Democrat), *Edizioni dell'Avanti!* (Socialist); and where possible patronize cultural associations and clubs oriented ideologically in their direction. The object of this many-sided activity has been to ensure the party a permanent political presence in civil society.

Most party organizations are stronger in the North than in the South and Islands. Thus the Communist Party sections and cells were more numerous in the industrial centres of the North and the Centre than elsewhere. The Nenni Socialist Party is best organized in Lombardy, Liguria, Emilia, Tuscany and Sicily, and worst organized in Piedmont, the Venetias and the mainland South. On the other hand, Christian Democrat Party data suggest that it is as strong in the South as in the North and Centre, but Congress discussion reveals that many southern sections exist on paper only. In the South the party depends as much on the parish as on the formal sectional organization for the continued penetration that ensures the Chistian Democrat vote in rural areas in successive elections. The Monarchist and Neo-Fascist Parties are also stronger in the South than in the North, but the former's formal organization is virtually non-existent, and the latter's has been pretty weak.

Italian parties are parties of direct membership. Membership is an individual act and there are no arrangements for associate membership like those which exist in the case of the trade unions and the Labour Party in Britain. Most parties fix the minimum age of membership at 18 years, although it is 21 years for the Republican and Social Democrat Parties, and 14 years only in the case of the Neo-Fascists. Moreover most parties require that members accept, and even profess, their goals and ideals. In addition, the Christian Democrat statute requires that its members have 'an irreproachable moral and political behaviour', while the Communist Party statute contains special provisions for dealing with those members who have held important posts in other parties, or are seeking readmission to the party after having been expelled.

Membership is high, particularly in comparison with other countries with direct membership parties, such as France and Germany. Three parties claim to be mass parties with over half a million members: the Communist and Christian Democrat Parties, with around one and a half million each, and the Socialist Party with about 500,000. Approximate figures for other parties are Social Democrats (PSU), 100,000; Republican, 40,000; and some 250,000 spread among the three right wing parties (Liberals, Monarchists and Neo-Fascists) and which have a tendency to move from one to the other according to the political climate (at present, the situation is in favour of the Neo-Fascists). Distribution of party membership follows the localization of party sections fairly closely. Thus over a third of the Communist Party members are found in two regions of Central Italy, Emilia and

Tuscany, and the remainder are unevenly distributed over the country. In general, there are still twice as many members in the North as in the South: northern members are concentrated in large and medium-sized towns and southern members are dispersed in the countryside and agro-towns. The geographical distribution of the Socialist Party is more uneven than that of the Communist Party: strong and weak federations nestle side by side in different parts of the country. In general, Socialist Party membership strength in the North and Centre is tied to Socialist traditions; in the South it is linked to the political positions of national and local leaders (cf Mancini in Calabria, etc.). This contrast has become more marked since the Socialists entered the government coalition in 1964; and some leaders fear that a return to opposition will have serious consequences on membership.

The territorial distribution of Christian Democrat membership does not follow any expected pattern. Southern membership levels now exceed those of the 'White' provinces of the northeast. This Christian Democrat penetration of the South reverses the immediate postwar situation, and is due to the important positions that local leaders have been able to build up thanks to twenty years of continuous office. All the southern regions have their bosses: Moro in Apulia, Colombo in Basilicata, Gava in Naples, etc. Indeed the high annual turnover of southern Christian Democrat membership confirms the artifical nature of many of the southern 'congressional' membership figures. Membership of minor parties conforms to a similar pattern: either they have a stronger northern membership, like the Republicans and Liberals, or they have a higher southern membership which is largely bogus, as often in the case of Monarchists and Neo-Fascists.

The social composition of party membership reflects the different groups to which the parties appeal. The Communist Party is a proletarian party: about three-quarters of its members are recruited from the proletarian classes. However, if in the early postwar years the backbone of the party was formed by the industrial working class, it has subsequently changed to one of working-class families. This is because many industrial workers have quit, but the family members of those who have remained have joined where they did not previously. Regional differences are strong: in the North and Centre the industrial working-class family is strong, but in the South it is the peasantry who form the bulwark of the party. The various Socialist Parties are not basically working-class in composition. Before reunification between the Nenni Socialists and the Saragat Social Democrats in 1966, only about a third were workers and another third peasants (mainly small farmers). Since 1966 this proportion of workers and peasants has diminished, while the middle-class members have increased in all Socialist Parties, although the extent is difficult to evaluate because of lack of data. The principal reason for party membership of many socialists appears to be family tradition, of son following father; and the chief motive for going along to the party section is recreation, i.e. to play cards or watch television rather than to talk politics.

The Christian Democrat Party is, as it so vociferously claims, an all-class party, i.e. it recruits members from all classes in Italian society. The percentage of proletarians is only half that of the Communist Party, but still accounts for almost a third of party members. Bourgeois groups also number a third of party members and comprise the urban and rural middle classes in a proportion of about two to one. The proportion of this group has increased in the postwar period, which shows that the Christian Democrats now recruit the professional intelligentsia who formed the personnel of the pre-Fascist Liberal Party. This is a consequence of the Christian Democrats' dominant position in contemporary Italian politics. But it must not be forgotten that the greater part of this group is made up of professional people from the Catholic organizations. Over a third of party members are women, which is the largest percentage of any Italian party. The middle and upper classes furnish the majority of members of the other parties: professional men in the Republican Party; professional and businessmen in the Liberal Party, etc. The Monarchist Party at the moment of its greatest success in the mid-fifties was a mixed bag of nostalgic aristocrats, petty bourgeois on the make, and urban poor of the big southern cities.

Party personnel fall into four grades: at the lowest level are found the party activists who are ready to be mobilized for party proselytism and propaganda; at the next level come the party officials who man, generally without pay, the local sections; at the third level are the provincial federation officials, many of whom are permanently employed by the party, and all of whom are prospective recruits to the Italian political class; finally, at the top are the national party leaders and parliamentarians who control the party. Of course the pyramid is much steeper at the top level because there may be a greater distance, in terms of political power and influence, between a top party leader and an ordinary Member of Parliament, than between the latter and a federation official. It is difficult to give precise figures of each grade of party personnel. Party activists of both the Communists and Christian Democrats are a veritable army of some 100,000 strong each (i.e. between 5–10 per cent of the membership); a figure of 15,000 was advanced for the Socialist Party some years ago. The other parties certainly cannot match the Communists and Christian Democrats in their number of activists. Local party officials of both the Communist and Christian Democrat Parties number about 50,000 each; and a proportionally smaller number for the other parties. The provincial officials provide a hard core of between 1000 to 5000 people, dedicated to politics according to party; and finally a figure of between 100 and 500 depending on the size of the party represents the national party leadership and parliamentarians. Top leadership in any party, at any one given moment, rarely exceeds some twenty to thirty carefully selected individuals. Moreover, influence in party leadership is not static : a man who is important in today's conjuncture may very well not be tomorrow.

The important point about party personnel is that there is a qualitative jump between the local and the provincial level : in all parties the activists and the local officials mirror the party membership in their social composition, but that of provincial and national officials does not, being predominantly middle-class in all parties. For example, over half of the Communist Party local officials are workers and peasants, but less than two fifths of the party's provincial and national officials have a proletarian background. Similarly, over four-fifths of the Christian Democrat provincial and national officials come from the middle and upper classes and not one is a worker or a peasant, whereas some 15 per cent of its local officials are workers. Thus if the Communist Party is, as has been claimed, a vehicle of social promotion at the local level because of the wide access to positions of public responsibility that it offers to persons of humble origins, the avenue it opens is much narrower at the higher echelons.

Nonetheless, the avenue is still sufficiently wide to provide a model for aspiring party workers and local officials. In the Christian Democrat Party, power is open to the professions. Indeed the two professions which predominate are teachers (in the North) and lawyers (in the South), and both are extensively recruited from Catholic organizations. Over two-thirds of party officials began their political careers in this way. A similar pattern, without the emphasis on Catholic organizations, prevails in the other parties.

Elections and the Electorate

On the fall of Fascism, Italy reverted to the electoral system in force before its rise: proportional representation. Italy was ruled in the nineteenth century under a relatively narrow franchise, and by a system of simple majority, single-ballot voting in one-member constituencies, like that used in the United Kingdom and the United States today. This was replaced in 1919 by universal male suffrage and a system of PR by the method of the highest averages. The new system lasted only two elections (1919 and 1921): after taking power in 1922, Mussolini passed through Parliament, in a period of political confusion, legislation known as the Acerbo Law which provided that in future elections the party obtaining a simple (but not necessarily an absolute) majority should get two-thirds of the seats. Armed with this majority after the 1924 elections, Mussolini held no more elections and ignored the Chamber of Deputies which he eventually abolished.

The CLN governments not only restored PR but extended the suffrage to women. Thus Article 48 of the Republican Constitution asserts the principle of universal suffrage for all citizens over twenty-one years of age, declaring that the 'vote is personal and equal, free and secret'. In addition, it describes its exercise as a 'civic duty'. Finally, it excludes all limitations on the right to vote 'except for civil incapacity or by reason of irrevocable penal sentence or in cases of moral unworthiness indicated by law'. Article 56 provides that elections to the Chamber of Deputies shall be based on 'universal and direct suffrage, in the proportion of one member for 80,000 inhabitants or fractions greater than 40,000'. Articles 57 and 58 provide that elections to the Senate of the Republic shall be organized on a regional basis, with one senator for every 200,000 inhabitants, and restrict the electorate to electors over twenty-five years of age. In 1963, the number of members of the Chamber of Deputies was fixed at 630, and that of the Senate at 315 elected members with an additional number of life appointments (former Presidents of the Republic and presidential appointments).

The list system of PR was adopted for both houses, but while the pure form prevailed for the lower house, a modified form was adopted for the upper house. For the Chamber the country is divided into thirty-two constituencies which are formed from groups of two and three adjoining provinces. Each party presents a list of candidates (not greater than the number of seats allocated to the constituency on a population basis) separately in each constituency, or it may combine with one or more parties to present a joint list. The Communist and Socialist Parties presented a joint list (Democratic Popular Front FDP) in 1948; and the Monarchists and Neo-Fascists (National List) did the same in 1972. The number of candidates of each list elected is proportional to the number of votes which it receives in each constituency – in fact, the method of distribution used is the corrected quotient $N + 2$ for all constituencies. Fractional remainders are gathered in a national pool and divided on a proportional basis depending on the national vote. No party participates in the distribution of fractional remainders if it has not elected at least one candidate in one of the constituencies. This explains why the left-wing Socialist Party (PSIUP) was allocated no seats in the 1972 elections, despite polling more than 450,000 votes nationally, which was more than the Republican Party won in three successive elections and the Monarchist Party in 1968.

The full force of proportionality of the list system is to some extent modified by the system of preference voting within each list. The voter not only selects a list but has the opportunity of indicating (either by name or list number) his preference among candidates. The number of preference votes that can be given varies according to the size of the constituency, but is usually either three or four. In addition, the voter has the right to strike out the names of any candidates on the list to which he is opposed. The candidates elected on each list are those who receive the highest number of preference votes (after subtracting the

75

strikings out) in proportion to the number of seats allocated to that list in the constituency. This means that there are two contests going on at each election: (1) for the party list vote; and (2) for the preference vote. The importance of the latter is that it can reverse the tendency of the list system, which gives precedence to the party programme over the personality of the candidates.

For the Senate, each region is divided into a number of single-member constituencies equal to the number of seats allotted to the region on the basis of the population. Each party presents a candidate in all or some of the constituencies. Since the seats are assigned on a regional basis (i.e. there are no fractional remainders gathered together in a national pool, joint lists are more frequent than for the Chamber. Thus, the Communists and left-wing Socialists (PSIUP) presented joint lists in 1968 and 1972; the Monarchists and Neo-Fascists in 1953, 1968 and 1972, and the Republicans joined with the Christian Democrats in certain Central Italian constituencies in 1958. A candidate who receives more than 65 per cent of the poll is automatically declared elected; the remainder of the seats are distributed on a proportional basis within the region. The successful candidates in each list are those in the constituencies in which the party polls its highest vote according to the number of seats allocated to it. Thus one constituency can elect two senators (for example, if the vote is evenly distributed between two parties and the other national parties poll only a negligible number of votes); and another can elect no senator (for example, if the vote is evenly divided between all the lists competing, so that the vote in that constituency is not among the highest proportionally for any one list [see Table 4.ii]).

In 1953, an attempt was made to throw out the proportional principle for the Chamber of Deputies, but it was frustrated by the electorate. The governing coalition of Christian Democrats, Social Democrats, Republicans and Liberals, fearing heavy losses in the forthcoming elections, bulldozed legislation through Parliament whereby the coalition of parties which received fifty per cent plus one of the votes cast would obtain two-thirds of the seats in the Chamber. The *legge truffa* (swindle law), as it was dubbed, was so obviously intended to manufacture a comfortable parliamentary majority for the government parties where

Table 4. ii

Senatorial Elections: Senators Elected with a Quorum of 65 Per Cent and
Number of Senators Per Constituency, 1948–63

Quorum of 65%

Elections	Senators to be elected	Senators with 65%	Parties DC	SVP	Lomb.	Regions of election Ven.	T-AA	Abr.	Sic.
1948	237	15	14	1	3	6	4	1	1
1953	237	6	5	1	1	2	3	—	—
1958	246	5	4	1	—	2	3	—	—
1963	315	3	2	1	—	2	1	—	—

T-AA = Trento Alto Adige
Abr. = Abruzzi
Sic. = Sicily

Number of senators elected per constituency

Elections	No senator	1 senator	2 senators	3 senators
1948	34	153	34	—
1953	47	137	45	—
1958	39	146	44	2
1963	27	122	74	15

Source: A. Spreafico, 'Il Senato della Repubblica: composizione politica e
stratificazione sociale' in M. Dogan and O. M. Petrarca, Partiti politici e
strutture sociali in Italia (Milan, 1968), pp. 615–6

they did not have one in the country, and was so reminiscent of
the Acerbo Law by which Mussolini had performed the same
operation in 1924, that it was fought tooth and nail by the opposition parties. In the election the government coalition fell short of
the necessary majority by a few thousand votes so that its operation remained a dead letter. In fact, the government was so
shaken by the savage attack of the opposition that it agreed to
the law's repeal the following year.

Proportional representation is the most stable of all electoral
systems. The reason is that since voting landslides occur very
rarely, it is the electoral legislation translating votes into seats
that has the final word in determining the parliamentary consequences. PR systems accentuate electoral stability by adding
stability of representation to it because they accurately relate
seats to votes won and lost. This contrasts with the simple-
majority, single-ballot system which accentuates mobility in
representation because it turns small changes in votes into larger
turnovers in seats, Similarly, the former encourages minor party
representation which is discouraged by the latter. These simple

propositions can be verified by comparing British and Italian electoral results in the postwar period. Since 1945, the so-called 'cube rule' (whereby the change in the number of seats is the cube of the swing in votes between the major parties) has operated in British elections, so that swings of around 2 per cent in the vote for the parties have provoked changes in seats in the House of Commons of around 8 per cent. In Italy, much larger swings have given smaller changes in seats; in the 1968 elections the swing was 3.1 per cent and less than twenty seats (i.e. 3 per cent) changed party affiliation. Indeed as a result of the growth in electoral stability in Italy, more seats change party affiliation in the course of a parliament than at a general election. This was certainly the case in the sixties; for instance, in the fourth Republican Parliament (1963–8) between twenty-five and thirty members of the Chamber changed political affiliation. Moreover, the twenty-three Socialist deputies who split away from the PSI to found the left-wing PSIUP were returned at the 1968 elections. It would have been true for the next parliament too, if the technical rule that a party list must elect at least one candidate in a constituency had not deprived the PSIUP of representation in the Chamber (i.e. circa ten seats).

If, therefore, the electoral system accentuates stability of representation, it has been powerfully abetted by the remarkable growth in the partisan stability of the electorate in the postwar period. Vote movement between parties (i.e. swing) in elections for the Chamber has declined from 21.4 per cent between 1946–8 to 3.5 per cent between 1953–8 and 3.1 per cent between 1963–8; and a similar phenomenon has occurred in Senate elections. In fact this is a general, and not a specifically Italian, phenomenon. All electorates are basically stable, as the example of most Western countries testifies, except when a traumatic political event causes a fundamental electoral re-alignment. The cold war and the manner of its presentation to the Italian electorate in 1948 – the stark choice between civilization and barbarism, Christ and Anti-Christ, God and the Devil, Good and Evil, etc – was a traumatic political event which was responsible for the fundamental alignment in Italy that has survived throughout the postwar period.

A number of indices illustrate the nature of this stability. First, electoral turnout is, and has remained, high. In contrast to the pre-Fascist period, when turnout rarely reached 60 per cent of the restricted electorate, it has never dropped below 92 per cent since 1948. Moreover the regions where it was highest, like the 'Red' provinces of the Centre, have remained the regions where it is still highest. Second, the degree of voting stability can be measured by examining the electoral returns at the communal level on a countryside basis. The Cattaneo Institute of Bologna did this for 7144 of the 8000 Italian communes for the elections of 1946 and 1963. Communes were classified as 'absolutely' stable where the party's share of the vote did not fluctuate more than 10 per cent and 'relatively' stable where it did not exceed 30 per cent. The results for the three major parties are set out in Table 4.iii. Galli and Prandi commented on these results: 'the figures confirm the general conclusion that Italian party voting is relatively stable. Although there was considerable fluctuation within some communes between elections, the fluctuations within a zone were fairly modest.' Both Communist and Christian Democratic votes are more stable in those regions – 'red' and 'white' – where their vote is backed by an institutionalized subculture; and less stable in those regions – mainland South and Islands – which are dominated by the southern system of *clientele*.

Table 4. iii

Percent of Communes in which there was Absolute and Relative Stability in the Vote for Major Parties in Elections to Chamber of Deputies in 1963 Compared with 1946

| | Christian Democracy | | Socialist Party | | Communist Party | |
	Absolute	Relative	Absolute	Relative	Absolute	Relative
Industrial triangle	38·5	82·2	14·1	57·1	58·2	96·1
White provinces	37·3	86·5	18·5	68·6	74·3	99·4
Red provinces	41·1	87·7	23·3	72·2	44·2	90·1
Mainland South	22·0	54·6	52·8	84·3	28·6	66·8
Sicily	18·6	62·3	47·6	80·8	26·5	59·7
Sardinia	29·1	62·5	56·3	75·1	23·2	68·9

Source: G. Galli, and A. Prandi, *Patterns of Political Participation in Italy* (New Haven, 1970), p. 54

The third index is the fierceness of the fight for the preference vote. Although we lack systematic data, it is clear from all the evidence that the preference vote fight and the factional struggle (of which it is an intimate part) have increased with the stability of voting by lists. Indeed one can say that there is an inverse relationship between the intensity of the battle for the list vote and that for the preference vote. The importance of the preference vote fight lies in its effect on the internal balance within a party; it raises or lowers the strength of the various factional leaders within the party machine, and thereby influences the kind of alliances and orientations the party will engage in. One of the paradoxes of Italian politics is that preference voting increases with illiteracy, i.e. is greater in the backward South than in the more developed North. Hence it indicates that the greater part of the electorate is uninterested in this aspect of Italian elections. The reason for the higher preference vote in the South is the 'Southern system' : the fact that patronage is the fundamental link between the *clientele* and the politician. For example, Aldo Moro and Giulio Andreotti won the highest number of preference votes, 290,000 and 350,000 respectively, the former in the elections of 1968 and the latter in those of 1972 when each was Prime Minister. In 1972 Moro's personal tally dropped by over 100,000 votes : he was only Foreign Minister. Similarly, Giuseppe Mancini, the PSI Secretary, won a very high preference vote in Calabria in 1968 when Minister of Public Works; in 1972 he was out of office and his preference vote dropped so alarmingly that it was feared at first that he would not be re-elected!

Fourth, the parties' electorates follow those of the parties' organizational strength (see Table 4.iv). This led Galli and Prandi to conclude that the 'Catholic world since 1946 has had a form and structure capable of influencing moderate and conservative as well as Catholic opinion at a time when Italy had no tradition or activating force on which to build an influential secular party to represent moderate and conservative points of view'; and that a 'combination of organization and ideology [had] enabled the Communist Party rather than the divided and much more poorly organized socialist parties to mold left-wing opinion and to translate into votes for the party a variety of tendencies and tensions.'

The socio-demographic composition of the parties' voters is set out in Table 4.iv. The Communist Party is strong in the 'red' provinces and weak in the 'White' provinces; its electorate is predominantly lower class, male, under forty years of age, and

Table 4. iv
Socio-Demographic Characteristics of Party Voters

	PCI %	PSIUP %	PSI %	PSU %	PRI %	DC %	PLI %	MSI/Mon. %
1 SEX (1970)								
Men	59	63	58	56	51	37	42	62
Women	41	37	42	44	49	63	58	38
2 AGE (1970)								
21/40	52	66	51	47	59	47	46	43
41/60	33	33	39	39	32	36	37	34
Over 60	15	1	10	14	9	17	17	22
3 CLASS (1970)								
Upper/middle bourgeoisie (business/ professional/ managers)	1	2	3	4	3	2	6	3
New middle class (white-collar)	5	10	10	14	18	9	10	10
Old middle class (shopkeeper/ artisan/peasant)	12	9	17	19	24	20	21	18
Working class (industrial/ agricultural)	38	25	31	24	9	13	10	24
Housewives	27	23	25	27	33	40	37	24
Other occupations	17	31	14	12	13	16	16	21

Source: *Demoskopea* (May-June 1971), pp. 8–11

4 CHURCH-GOING (1962)								
Went to church	14	*	38	51	(No)	67	51	49
Did not go	86	*	62	49	(data)	33	49	51

* Party founded in 1964 from PSI split

Source: *Bolletino della DOXA* (26 February, 1963), p. 53

5 VOTE BY REGIONS (1963)								
Industrial triangle	23	*	17	8	1	36	10	3
White provinces	13	*	16	7	½	54	5	3
Red provinces	38	*	15	6	2	30	5	4
Mainland south	25	*	11	5	1	40	6	8
Islands	23	*	11	4	4	40	7	7

* Party founded in 1964

Source: G. Galli and A. Prandi, *op. cit.*, pp. 332–5

non-church-going. Sidney Tarrow has shown that it attracts workers in the North and peasants in the South, to which must be added the share-croppers and middle-class groups in the 'Red' provinces. The vote of the Socialist Parties, on the other hand, is greater in the North where more of the membership is found than in the South, although its greatest gains in the postwar period have been in the South. The movement of the parties' centres of gravity towards the South is confirmed by the social composition of the voters, who are more middle-class and less working-class than in the immediate postwar period. They have remained, moreover, predominantly male, although more church-going than of yore.

Galli and Prandi have indicated that the Christian Democrat electorate has a double nature. It is strong in the 'White' provinces, and to a lesser extent in the South; but relatively weaker in the 'Red' provinces and the industrial triangle. Thus it taps two sources of support : (1) organized Catholicism; and (2) un-organized conservatives looking to the State. Its social composition is composite, as the party proudly claims, but with a bias to women and the rural population. Church-going, the rural and female electorate, all emphasize the importance of the role of the Church in its electoral success, since numerous surveys have indicated that these are the groups who heed the appeal of the clergy to 'make their choice with a watchful Christian conscience, etc.'. Indeed one of the party's deputies is reported to have remarked that 'one needs fifty million lire and fifty Priests to elect a Christian Democrat deputy'. It must not be thought, however, that the Church is alone; the strength of the small farmers' organization, the *Coldiretti*, which controls all aspects of the farmers' lives through its dominance of the *Federconsorzi* must not be overlooked. Finally, the Liberal Party vote is located in the fashionable residential districts of the big cities; and its support comes from the well-to-do urban bourgeoisie and middle classes. On the other hand, the Monarchist Party, in its heyday in the mid-fifties, won the support of the petty bourgeoisie and urban poor of the big southern cities, like Naples. Many of these voters have turned to the Neo-Fascist Party, particularly after Reggio di Calabria, and have been joined by small and medium entrepreneurs in the North since the 'hot autumn' of 1969.

Party Finance and Power Structure

Italian parties keep their financial affairs secret, so any analysis is largely conjectural. Nonetheless, all observers are agreed that they spend large sums on their multiple activities. Professor Passigli, author of one of the few serious studies, estimated that the Communist Party's annual expenses in 1963 were of the order of 12 billion lire (about £6 million); that of the Christian Democrats a little less, say 10 billion lire; and that of the Socialist Party around 5 billion lire (£2½ million). On top of this have to be added campaign expenses which have been conservatively estimated at about half a billion lire for the larger parties. Thus it represents less than 10 per cent of the expenditure of the major parties, but for the smaller parties it can represent as much as half their normal annual expenditure.

As regards party income, one thing is clear: membership dues and other fees do not cover expenditure. For example, direct contributions from party members (membership dues, special contributions, Members of Parliament's salaries, fund-raising drives, like the *Festa dell'Unità*) raise, at most, 3 of the 12 billion that the Communist Party spent in 1963. The flow of direct contributions is less favourable in the other parties. Hence several other sources are used to meet the difference. First, control of local government can be used in two ways: members can either be put on the payroll of local organizations etc. within local government patronage; and more important, commissions can be received on contracts where public money is spent. Share-outs of communal and provincial departments depend on the type of coalition envisaged and the power relations between the constituent parties. Where the Christian Democrats and Communist parties are dominant, they do not surrender key financial departments like those of Public Works or Welfare. A second and prime source for the government parties is central government patronage; and the importance of the patronage at stake is clear from the struggles that go on among the coalition partners to secure the appointment of their *protégés* which have often paralysed government action. For example, in the words of one observer: 'RAI (the state-owned radio and television service) is one of the eldorados of the patronage system, employing thousands of unnecessary people, including over 20,000 'special contributors'.

A recent article in *La Stampa* described the head of RAI, Signor Barnabei, as an eastern potentate, surrounded whenever he goes to the Houses of Parliament by a horde of supplicant MPs asking him to employ their protégés.' The chief source would appear to be the various public corporations and state-owned enterprises, most notably ENI and IRI. Passigli noted that

> in spite of being accountable to Parliament for their operations, public corporations enjoy a considerable degree of autonomy. More-over, most state-owned industries are formally private corporations where the State, through having a controlling interest, acts as a private share-holder. Their real budgets are largely disguised and offer, under various miscellaneous headings, possibilities for direct financial contributions. The fact that the actual recipients of these contributions tend to be various organizations and individuals does not substantially change the role of public money, though it has far-reaching consequences since it allows a careful discrimination among the various groups in the Catholic Party; the recipient of support tends to be the individual faction rather than the party.

A third source of direct contributions to the government and right-wing parties is made up of the various interest groups and private companies. *Confindustria* (Confederation of Italian Industry) is reputed to finance the Liberal Party, but has also certainly helped the Christian Democrats financially in the past. Industrial groups like Fiat, Pirelli, Olivetti and others, which supported the 'opening to the left', can be taken as having been likely to contribute to party funds of the Christian Democrats, Social Democrats and Republicans, while others, like Edison and *Assolombarda* (Association of Lombard Industrialists), which opposed it vigorously, almost certainly contributed to right-wing opposition parties' funds, like those of the Liberal and Monarchist Parties, and even perhaps the Neo-Fascist Party. The cement group, *Italcementi* is reputed to have financed the Neo-Fascists. The main channel of these funds is in the form of direct contributions from individual companies and interest groups, but often it takes a round-about route via auxiliary organizations rather than direct to the party.

The Communist Party as a permanent opposition party has not been able to benefit from government patronage. The gap here between expenditure and direct contributions has been covered through the promotion of a number of commercial activities. It is known that the party operates a number of industrial and commercial enterprises, including a large garment concern which maintains retail stores in most Italian towns. It has also attempted to operate a chain of department stores. However it is fairly certain that the major flow of income to the party has come from transactions with the Soviet Union by Communist-controlled enterprises which turned over most of the profits to the party. It is claimed that the party's financial problems in the late sixties, particularly those which have beset the party press, have been caused by the liberalization of trade with Eastern Europe which has reduced a major source of revenue. Galli claims that it has been reduced to a third of the party's needs. Similarly, the United States has provided funds for the Social Democrat Party : (through American Labour Unions) and the Christian Democrats (through the CIA).

All Italian parties are leadership parties. We have already noted that they split themselves into two levels : (1) at the grass-roots, where a co-operative and associative life is organized which is oriented, within a particular sub-system of values, towards recreational activities rather than political discussions; and (2) at the federal and national levels, where political discussion is the centre of activity. Pavolini's description of the Socialist Party in 1958 is more or less valid for all parties. He writes that

The rank and file ... participate very little in political discussions in the true sense, contenting itself with affirmations about socialism and deprecating factional struggles considered unpropitious for unity and harmony among socialists. The leaders, whether party officials or elected office-holders, are the only ones to concern themselves with politics in the true sense, which thereby becomes an encounter and clash at the summit, leaving the rank and file more or less indifferent. ... At a higher level, on the key issues of general policy only a few groups take part : Members of Parliament (not all), a few communal and provincial councillors, officials of the provincial federations, and a small nucleus of young intellectuals. ...

The local sections comprise, therefore, homogeneous social and cultural groups in which educated people seem out of place. Those interested in a political career are forced to join at the federal level; a university education normally permits an individual direct entry. Galli and Prandi have succinctly described the career of a budding politician and its effect on the party :

A political career often begins at the provincial level, with entrance into the office of the provincial directorate, where clerks are mostly engaged in paper work. Yet what might be called 'the living party', that of the ordinary people of varied social backgrounds and interests, of political and cultural debate, finds expression in the party section, with which those launched on political careers in the provincial offices have little contact. The provincial executive offers political support, alliances, and opportunities to become known to the electorate.

As the party official advances in the party hierarchy an increasing amount of his time is divided between the provincial and central offices of the party or of parliament. He seldom sees the rank and file party members; he seldom engages in conversation with them; he arrives in a rush at the section to deliver a speech, and then as quickly departs for the provincial or national capital. As he becomes increasingly committed to the party apparatus, he loses contact with the party as an expression of social needs.

In this way the political leader's competence in terms of input – his capacity to sense, understand, and interpret the needs of the rank and file – tends to disappear. At the same time his competence in terms of output, that is his ability to translate social needs into action, is progressively reduced by the commitment of his time and energy. He is besieged by the things he must do to keep or improve his position.

Since the party politician increasingly represents the party machine rather than its rank and file, he is continually in the company of party and front-organization functionaries or representatives of specific sectional or local interests. He needs them; they need him; and this reciprocal dependence is transformed into tasks and responsibilities that the leader assumes to in order to maintain this relationship.

He is beset with some overlapping of responsibilities that characterizes many activists at local level. And like the activist who is committed to too many tasks, the party official never refuses any task that offers him more and better control over the machine. In this manner he prevents others from having access to positions of leadership; and since he can devote too little energy to each of his multiple commitments, the party as a whole loses its capacity for political initiative and for reacting to social needs.

The pre-eminence of the leadership within the Communist Party is not in doubt because of its Leninist structure and the emphasis placed on party discipline. The leadership is elected, but in fact it has been able to control election and dismissal. A system of co-option has in reality been in operation. The crux of this control is the method of 'democratic centralism' which in practical terms means bureaucratic centralism. It is based on the career patterns of party officials. The Communist Party is the only Italian party which acts as a vehicle of social promotion for the proletarian classes. A political career for a person of modest origin means becoming a full-time official. Entry into the national leadership is possible only for those who reach office-holding positions at the provincial level; and three-quarters of provincial officials, regardless of social origin, are full-time paid career men. Since the party apparatus is in the hands of people whose livelihood depends on their party career, it is easy to see how the party leadership controls the party apparatus.

The Communist Party is an apparatus rather than a parliamentary party. While its top leaders have simultaneously been Members of Parliament, their power has always been based on their position in the party hierarchy. Moreover strict party discipline ensures that the party retains full control over who is elected to parliament. It follows that parliamentarians have little freedom of action in opposition to the central committee.

All this points to the monolithic party structure western writers often associate with Communist Parties, but it would not be an accurate picture of the Italian Communist Party today. The Italian leaders, unlike their French colleagues, have permitted a revisionist discussion and critique at the risk of a breakdown of the party's unity and discipline. But they were frightened at some of the consequences and kept it within much narrower grounds than originally intended. Galli has indicated that the party's three strong points are: (1) the inheritance of the power positions and traditions of the key organizations of the labour movement; (2) the control of local government and a whole network of collateral organizations in the 'Red belt'; and (3) the amount of time its parliamentarians, without governmental responsibilities, can devote to following and defending the sectional interests of various groups of the population. The limits of the party leadership in imposing a particular line emerge when the contradictions between the reality of the line and the reality of the interests of these groups become too painfully apparent. The party cannot demand for too long what the social area which it claims to represent does not want. If it does, it will suffer a similar crisis to the one the French party suffered in the late fifties and early sixties : a greatly reduced membership and a much narrower sphere of influence.

Control of the Socialist parties by the leadership is much less secure than that of the Communist Party. In general, Nenni and Saragat maintained control of their respective parties by a combination of caution in policy and personal appeal. It has been claimed that it was Nenni's charismatic personality which enabled him to prevail over a hostile apparatus in the factional struggle over Socialist autonomy and reunification. It was insufficient to prevent party splits. Nonetheless it would seem that the relatively weak apparatus which the Socialist parties now have are generally able to keep control of the parties, if they take account of the power positions built up by the factions on the basis of their local 'notables' personal *clientele*. This dependence on parliamentary personnel indicates a shift in the nature of the Socialist parties from the apparatus party, which was founded at the time of the Liberation, to the parliamentary parties that now exist. Nonetheless since parliamentarians dominate the Central Executives, the apparatus is in their hands and, therefore, such a distinction is not crucial as it was in the old German Social Democrat Party.

The power structure of the Christian Democrat Party is complex. In essence, it is a confessional party whose vocation is government, but continued dominance can only be won at the cost of attracting the support of groups critical of, if not hostile to, its confessional ideology. This need to reconcile contradictions dominates its power structure, which is difficult to characterize with any certainty. In the De Gasperi period, the party was a parliamentary party; that De Gasperi so considered it is clear from his last speech to the party congress in 1954. In his postwar political activity he attempted to take more account of the electorate's reaction than of the party's; and also more account of certain economic groups than of either, because he believed that continued electoral support depended on successful economic reconstruction. His position in the party was reinforced by his prestige as the pre-Fascist leader of the party, as well as by his position as Prime Minister in the politically dramatic period of the cold war. Thus although De Gasperi's position as party leader was rarely in doubt, it did not free him from difficult battles with different party groups at various times. In fact, he too succumbed increasingly after April 1948 to the temptations of a leadership founded on brokerage and in consequence on immobilism in place of one of initiative and decision.

De Gasperi's death and Fanfani's attempt to strengthen the party organization complicated rather than simplified the internal party power structure, because it increased the contesting elements at the very moment that the lynch-pin of party unity disappeared. This was because the Christian Democrat Party does not control, much less lead, its electorate. The electorate is controlled by the Catholic organizations and individual party bosses through the preference vote. In such a situation, the fact that politicians of very divergent social views militate in the party creates an incipient basis for factionalism. It is encouraged, even exacerbated, by a complex of factors. First, the stability of partisan representation, which assigns a dominant position to the Christian Democrats, means that there is no electoral alternative to Christian Democrat dominated government coalitions in the foreseeable future. In consequence, the various combinations of party alliances are parliament-created as opposed to electorally imposed. Second, the dominant position of the Christian Democrats in the party system is recognized by all. Thus interest groups feed factionalism with the 'polycentric' flow of funds to factions and leaders rather than to the central party fund. Third, factions are prevented from perpetrating splits by the individual leaders' realization that the only result would be the loss of the party's dominant position and their own share of power. Moreover since the party is the political expression of the Catholic movement, a party leader disobeying Vatican wishes would be disowned by the Church and very likely lose his next election.

In these circumstances, the object of Christian Democrat politicians is simple : to create their own faction (Table 4.v indicates their success). The means : conquest of a large provincial federation or the office of Under-Secretary (or, better still, both combined). Thus Giulio Andreotti (Prime Minister in 1972) built his career on control of the Roman federation and as Under-Secretary to the Prime Minister's Office in the first Parliament;

Italy – Republic without government?

Emilio Colombo (Prime Minister 1970–2) used control of the Potenza federation and the Under-Secretaryships of Agriculture and Public Works in the same Parliament (both were leaders of *Impegno democratico* in 1972); Mariano Rumor (Prime Minister 1968–70) founded his career on control of the Verona federation and as Under-Secretary of Agriculture in the first Parliament (he was leader of *Iniziativa popolare* in 1972), etc. The importance of the office of Under-Secretary is that, as a result of an informal division of ministerial labour, he is left free to distribute the patronage of the ministry in his constituency in his own name, and not in that of the minister. The strategy: to join a faction and use its support to gain office; to exploit the office to build up his own position independent of the faction. When his position is sufficiently strong, the politician can quit the faction that gave him his initial opportunity and form his own faction.

Table 4. v
Christian Democrat Factions in 1971

Factions	Leaders	Congress Votes	Members in Nat. Exec.	Ministers	Under-Secretary	Press
Iniziativa popolare	Piccoli Rumor	20·4%	6	3	6	*Notizie Parlamentari*
Impegno democratico	Colombo Andreotti	15·1%	3	3	6	*Concretezza Impegno democ.*
Nuove cronache	Fanfani Forlani	17·4%	6	2	5	—
Taviani	Taviani	10·5%	4	2	5	—
Amici di Moro	Moro	13·4%	4	1	4	*Progetto*
Base	De Mita Misasi	11·0%	4	2	2	*Radar Politica*
Forze nuove	Donat-Cattin	7·0%	5	2	3	*Forze nuove Sette giorni*
Forze libere	Scalfari	3·5%	2	1	1	*Forze libere*
Nuova sinistra	Sullo	1·7%	1	—	1	*Nuova Sinistra*

Source: G. Sartori, 'Proporzionalismo, frazionismo e crisi dei partiti' in *Rivista Italiana di Scienza Politica* (December 1971), p. 650

The classic example of this strategy is furnished by Paolo Emilio Taviani of Genoa. After election to Parliament in the early postwar years, party office and Under-Secretaryships, he was appointed Minister of Defence for five years and then Minister of the Interior as a representative of the *Doroteo* faction, and was able to use the formidable apparatus of both these ministries to control 10 per cent of the party membership. In 1967 he quit the *Doroteo* faction, and constituted his own faction, despite the fact that politically his position was indistinguishable from that of the *Dorotei*. When Rumor formed his first cabinet in November 1968, Taviani demanded the portfolio of the South for his support. His position was strong enough to ensure that he triumphed despite tough competition. Thus his faction was able to extend its clientele in the South and gain national dimensions. Earlier, the late Ferdinando Tambroni had used the resources of the Ministry of the Interior, to which he had been appointed as a representative of the *Fanfaniani*, to become a faction leader in his own right at the Party National Congress of 1959 and Prime Minister in the ill-fated summer of 1960. Fiorentino Sullo, starting from a leading place in the left-wing *Base* faction and a period in the *Doroteo* faction, attempted the same manoeuvre with less success : his personal faction, *Nuova Sinistra*, controlled less than 2 per cent of the Congress vote in 1971, but it earned him a ministry without portfolio in the two Andreotti governments of 1972.

It is therefore clear that the top party leadership sits in Parliament. Membership of Parliament is an essential requirement for ministerial office. However this does not make the party a parliamentary party in the British sense, since party decisions can be, and are, taken independently of a Christian Democrat Prime Minister. Of course it plays a more important role in party decisions than it does in the Communist Party, for the reasons outlined above (i.e. it is the *sine qua non* of a leadership position). All in all the Christian Democrat party resembles the Socialist parties in this respect; it exhibits the power structure of most Italian parties.

The various aspects of the Italian parties we have outlined attest to their striking similarity. They all claim to represent an exclusive ideological point of view; they all have a similar articulated branch-type structure; and they all sponsor permanent satellite organizations and a party press. Two of them have been more successful than the rest : the Communists and the Christian Democrats. Despite local differences, control of all parties lies with party leaders through paid party officials who control local section meetings and provincial congresses which elect delegates to national congresses. Factionalism exists in all parties although it is more severe in the Socialist and Christian Democrat parties than in the Communist and some minor parties. Thus while policy is decided and debated at the top of all parties, the consequences of factionalism are everywhere the same : the leaders so absorbed in the tactics of survival that they have little time and energy left for the strategy of achievement.

The lack of an electoral alternative has led to all parties seeing their role as the occupation of as many posts as possible in the state institutions, not to transform society but for patronage : the occupation of posts is *per se* a symbol of political strength. This operation has almost reduced them to the role of defenders of sectional interests. They can achieve more than most interest groups not because they embody general interests but because control of the state apparatus at national and local level gives them the right to patronage. It was because the operation of the party system so reduced the sphere of action of the government parties that a group of politicians under Moro's leadership promoted the 'opening to the left' and socialist reunification. It was hoped to introduce a certain mobility into the system as well as to effect a number of urgent reforms which would tip the balance of power in favour of the reformers. It failed because the Socialist parties were too weak to provide a credible alternative to the Christian Democrats and the conservatives proved too strong for the reformers. Hence the Socialists were quickly assimilated to vassal status in respect of Christian Democracy. The Socialist split of 1969 was the recognition of the failure of this strategy. In fact, of course, the operation of the party system in the postwar period has been the illustration of a simple fact: the two major parties have been strong enough to dominate partisan representation in its static form but not strong enough to dominate it dynamically and work the party system according to a two-party logic. Hence the Namierite form of the party system and its consequences : immobility, factionalism and parliamentary manoeuvre. At the present time, the gravest danger to the parliamentary system comes from within the party system : a danger resulting from its own political inefficiency. So far it has been judged with indulgence – the consequence of twenty years of Fascism – but unless it does sufficient to prevent the antithesis between the lethargy of the institutions and the aspirations of the people from becoming too great, it could be undermined.

5 Interest Groups: The Politics of Clientela and Parentela

Interest groups apply pressure in the political system wherever they think it likely to be worthwhile. It is possible to reduce the complex activity of interest groups to a number of general propositions. Thus, for example, we can say that they are generally active in two different spheres: (1) in the decision-making centres of the state system of institutions; and (2) in the policy-forming centres of civil society. Both these spheres of activity imply different methods of pressure. Thus pressure on the decision-making centres of the state system of institutions can either be directed at the legislature, or at the executive and administration; pressure on the policy-forming centres of civil society can either take the form of trying to influence public opinion directly (for which there exist a whole range of weapons from deeds – strikes and public demonstrations – to words – control of the mass-media : press, radio, television, cinema, etc.), or of attempting to control party life (by financing parties or soliciting party office).

Interest-group activity varies from group to group and country to country. The activity of a particular group will depend on its perception of the decision-making process in the political system in which it is operating and the channels of access open to it. For example, it may well be that a particular group perceives that effective decisions are taken by the administration but lack access to it. On the other hand, it may well be represented in the legislature and hence be forced, *faute de mieux*, to concentrate its efforts there. Nonetheless, despite these problems of individual groups, it is true to say that the predominant activity of the major groups will reflect, more or less accurately, the reality of the decision-making process in that country. Finally, it is generally believed that groups that are active in attempting to influence public opinion directly, do so because they lack access to the decision-making centres. This may well be the cause for individual groups, but, in fact, no group, however well it is served with access to and influence over decision-making centres, will neglect opportunities of creating a favourable ideological climate for itself and its claims.

The Groups and their Characteristics

It is impossible to know how many interest groups exist and are active in Italy, because all voluntary associations as well as all organizations are, in their relations with the political system, interest groups. It is likely that their number is of a similar order to that in other Western European countries, if for no other reason than that they are similar in other respects. For example, they are highly differentiated both organizationally and territorially. In the only full-scale study of Italian interest groups Professor LaPalombara estimated that there were some 3000 different voluntary associations with headquarters in Rome which might intervene in the political process. These comprised : Catholic Confraternities (61); Administrations of Foreign Buildings (6); Associations, Centres and Entities for International Relations (29); diverse cults, Knightly Orders and Foreign Institutes (35); Artistic Associations (212); Fine Arts and Archaeological (27); Musical (18); Mass-Media (38); Tourist (20); Commercial and Industrial (65); Employers' Syndical Associations (285); Trade Unions (176); Independent Syndical Associations (269); Veterans' Organizations (56); Political Parties and Movements (62); Sports Clubs and Associations (over 500); Philanthropic and Humanitarian Groups (161); Mutual Aid Societies (41). Two things impressed Professor LaPalombara : first, that 'every conceivable interest group, and many that seemed inconceivable, were organized into secondary associations'; and second, that most interest groups operate within the subcultures (Communist, Catholic, Socialist, etc.) of the political system, resulting in an enormous proliferation of pressure groups, because each professional/occupational category is organized in a number of parallel ideological groups. We have already noted the energy the parties expended in promoting collateral organizations to extend their political influence throughout society; this is the other side of the coin. Close links between parties and interest groups have been one of the characteristics of postwar Italian politics.

The most important interest groups are the so-called economic groups; those which were founded specifically to promote and defend the interests of different economic groupings, like businessmen and industrialists, shopkeepers and farmers, artisans and workers. The best known of these are those which are organized in national confederations: the employers' organizations, such as *Confindustria* (General Confederation of Italian Industry), *Confragicoltura* (General Confederation of Agriculture), and *Intersind* (State-Holding company employers), etc., on the one hand, and the unions, CGIL (General Confederation of Italian Labour), CISL (Italian Confederation of Free Trade Unions), UIL (Italian Labour Union), *Coldiretti* (National Confederation of Small Farmers), etc. on the other. A second series of groups are the private corporations and holdings, like Fiat, Pirelli, Montedison, Olivetti etc., alongside which must be placed the public corporations, IRI (Industrial Reconstruction Institute) and ENI (State Hydrocarbons Corporation), as well as the insurance agencies INAM (National Institute for Workers' Compensation), INPS (National Institute for Social Security) and INAIL (National Health Insurance Institute). Finally, there are a considerable number of associations promoting and defending moral and ideological causes. The majority of these play only a secondary role in the political process since the parties are, generally, better equipped for the job, and usually colonize any such associations that spring up in their ideological area. One such group which has played an important part in recent Italian politics is the Divorce League.

Confindustria is the central organization which claims to represent all Italian businessmen; it speaks for both trade associations and local business organizations. However LaPalombara has indicated that it accounts for only some 80,000 of Italy's estimated 680,000 firms. A further 15,000 small firms are grouped in *Confapi* (National Confederation of Small Industries), a would-be rival. If firms employing more than twenty workers are considered alone, then it is generally agreed that *Confindustria* represents the overwhelming number of potential members. In this connection, it is worth recalling that the Italian business com-

95

munity is extremely concentrated : a relatively small number of firms (less than 200) possess most of the capital and dominate the market. In addition, *Confindustria* grouped all the major para-state holdings and state enterprises until the government forced them to withdraw from it in 1957, when they formed their own association *Intersind*. Thus the confederation's orientation towards big business is natural. In fact, it has been such that many small businessmen have complained that the big firms use the confederation to keep the small ones in line. Certainly the problem of presenting a united businessmen's front has been one of the Confederation's perennial problems; in this, it has been aided by the fact that businessmen are not split, like other interests, into different ideological formations. However the real power of Italian industry lies in the big corporations and holdings, and their leaders know it. Agnelli and Pirelli, like Falck and Valletta before them, do not delegate authority to subordinates or even to *Confindustria* spokesmen. They do not hesitate to intervene directly in the decision-making process when their immediate interests are at stake.

The Italian Labour Movement has traditionally been weak and divided. There are three major confederations, two lesser confederations, and numerous small independent trade unions; but they organize only a minority of Italian workers. They claim a total membership of about 9 million out of a working population of about 19 million, but it is generally agreed that this figure is notional as all confederations greatly exaggerate their membership; a figure of 6–7 million would be more accurate. In the early sixties the Communist-oriented General Confederation of Italian Labour claimed 3½ million members (probably 3 million); the Catholic-inspired Italian Confederation of Free Trade Unions about 2½ million (probably 2 million); the Social Democrat Union of Italian Labour 1½ million (probably 800,000) and the Neo-Fascist CISNAL a million (probably 500,000). In general, membership reached a high peak in the early fifties and has been gradually declining. However the period 1968–9 saw an abrupt reversal of this tendency and membership has taken a sharp jump upwards.

Division has traditionally had two causes. First, the unions were political in inspiration and have remained largely so. They were founded by working-class and peasant parties; and although a united movement was created on the fall of Fascism it failed to survive the cold war. However the political reasons for their divisions have been diminishing and the movement towards trade-union unity has been one of the major political developments of recent years, although it looks like falling short of full unification. Second, chronic financial weakness has kept the confederations unduly dependent on parties. Unions were forced to charge low dues, and even these were paid infrequently and irregularly. Hence they could not be a major source of union funds; these came from party sources which strengthened party influence over the unions. To this extent the parties saw them less as workers' organizations in their own right and more as instruments of the parties' own social penetration. They also used the unions as a recruiting and stamping ground for party leaders.

This situation has been reversed by a number of developments : (1) the growth of full employment and the consequential strengthening of the bargaining position of the unions; (2) the decline of the cold war and with it the realization that inter-union hostility greatly weakened union bargaining power; and (3) the creeping paralysis of the party system, and the inefficacy of government action. There was some sense in the unions supporting parties when they were economically weak and the parties politically strong, but there was less when the unions' bargaining power was growing and the parties and government were becoming increasingly impotent. Hence the growth of union emancipation from party ties has gone hand in hand with the movement towards union unity. The unions decided, therefore, to play a direct role as interlocutors of government. They found that they could force the government to do things in a way that no other interest group could, as, for example, in 1969 when they forced the Rumor government through a strike to take some hasty action on the Pensions Bill. This was followed by a series of national strikes for housing reform, reform of the Health Service, etc. in 1970–1. By 1972, they had reached a cross-roads because the original momentum for unification had been sapped by the UIL, which dragged its feet alleging that the new-style union would be an instrument of the Communist Party.

The *Coldiretti* (National Confederation of Small Farmers) is the most powerful organization in the agricultural field. In the

97

early sixties, it claimed 14,360 local sections, 1,773,618 families and 3,561,711 members, representing over 8 million persons. Its influence is based on two institutions. First there are the *Federconsorzii* (Federation of Agricultural Syndicates) which exist in every locality to aid the farmer by bulk buying and selling of crops and equipment. They are private in conception but have been endowed with a number of quasi-public functions so that they act as field agencies for the government, and particularly the Ministry of Agriculture. At the same time they have extended their range of services of immediate economic concern to the farmer – they provide gasoline, equipment and fertilizers at cut prices (through arrangements with big business firms); can store crops to raise prices; arrange credit facilities (by arrangements with financial houses). Galli and Prandi concluded their survey of them in these words: 'In the course of 15 years the federation has become a powerful financial holding, controlled by Bonomi and a narrow circle of collaborators. It constitutes one of the pillars of Catholic hegemony (mediated by the *Coldiretti*) in rural Italy.' The second basis of the Coldiretti's influence is the *Casse Mutue* or Small Farmers' Health Insurance Agency, which was created in response to the *Coldiretti's* legislative pressure in 1955. It provides free sickness and accident benefits similar to those enjoyed by workers. The agencies administer mutual funds made available by the government and peasants' contributions on a local basis. They are managed by boards of directors elected locally for a three-year term over which the *Coldiretti*, through its massive and ruthless organization, has gained overwhelming control.

The power of the *Coldiretti* comes from its ability to mobilize a massive rural vote for the Christian Democrat Party; in consequence, it has been able to count on a following of at least a sixth of the party's parliamentarians in each postwar parliament. However, the economic miracle has done much to undermine its privileged position in party and government by promoting a massive rural exodus. Instead of being a dominant element in the Christian Democrat Party, it has become just another element in the factional struggle.

In the other fields, the groups are divided along ideological lines. Thus there are Communist, Catholic, Social Democrat, Monarchist and Neo-Fascist Veterans' Associations. Similar divisions exist in Women's movements and Family Associations, Youth and Students' movements, etc. In addition, there are groups of intellectuals, not directly attached to parties, which set themselves up as Study Centres to carry out research and provide material on subjects of their interest, since it is well-known that information is half the battle in promoting a project or interest.

Patterns of Interest Group Activity

The influence of interest groups is difficult to assess. Many act in a discreet, not to say semi-clandestine way. Without hard documentation, one is often forced to make very sweeping and superficial statements or none at all. Interest groups are powerful. At least the majority of politicians and commentators are convinced that they are; and the configuration of the party system confirms that conviction. But how powerful are they? That is the question. All we intend to do is to outline the most important of the specifically Italian patterns of their activity.

(a) INFLUENCING PUBLIC OPINION : THE PRESS

Professors Lazarsfeld and Merton once outlined the true role of the mass-media in Western industrial society when they admitted :

increasingly the chief power groups, among which organized business occupies the most spectacular place, have come to adopt techniques for manipulating mass publics through propaganda in place of more direct means of control . . . Economic power seems to have . . . turned to a subtler type of psychological exploitation, through the mass-media of communication . . . These media have taken on the job of rendering mass publics conformative to the social and economic status quo.

The Italian radio and television service is, as noted in the last chapter, a state-controlled monopoly owned by IRI, so not surprisingly it has been predominantly an instrument of Christian Democrat and the minor government parties' propaganda. Since 1960 the parliamentary parties have been given time to outline their programmes during electoral campaigns. Commercial publicity is allowed on a regulated basis; and many companies have not been slow to avail themselves of the possibility of proposing their products to a larger audience.

99

Italy – Republic without government?

The press, however, still remains an important means of influencing public opinion. The basic features of its structure are set out in Table 5.i which shows the dominant position of the papers owned by the big industrial groups. In fact one has only to think of *La Stampa* (Fiat), *Il Giorno* (ENI), *La Notte* and *Il*

Table 5. i

Ownership and Circulation of Daily Newspapers in 1961 (in thousands)

Party Press	Large n.	copies	Medium n.	copies	Small n.	copies	Total n.	%	copies	%
Left	2	430·0	1	70·0	2	80·0	5	5·6	580·0	12·0
Centre	—	—	—	—	6	81·0	6	6·7	81·0	1·6
Right	—	—	2	140·0	1	15·0	3	3·4	155·0	3·2
	2	430·0	3	210·0	9	176·0	14	15·7	816·0	16·8
State-holding cpn.	2	330·0	1	75·0	1	30·0	4	4·4	435·0	9·0
Catholic groups	1	140·0	1	70·0	15	240·0	17	19·2	450·0	9·3
Business groups	10	2160·0	2	120·0	7	144·0	19	21·4	2424·0	50·2
Confindustria	—	—	1	50·0	15	162·5	16	17·9	212·5	4·7
Independent	—	—	5	280·0	14	205·0	19	21·4	485·0	10·0
	15	3060·0	13	805·0	61	957·5	89	100·0	4822·5	100·0
Sporting	2	315·0	2	140·0	—	—	4		455·0	
Total	17	3375·0	15	945·0	61	957·5	93		5277·5	

Source: I. Weiss, *op. cit.*, p. 154

Giornale d'Italia (Pesenti and Italcementi), *Il Roma* (Lauro), etc. It is no surprise to observe that they account for more than half the circulation of Italian newspapers. In 1956, a representative of *Confintesa* (a private businessmen's front) claimed that it was able to control 90 per cent of the Italian press. Subtracting the circulation of the left-wing party papers, gives us a figure very close to 90 per cent. As regards the daily press, there is no doubt about the dominant position of the business groups. If, on the other hand, periodicals are taken into account, the influence of Catholic opinion reveals itself. On the basis of a careful analysis Weiss calculated that the various associations and agencies into which the Catholic world is articulated controlled some 1800 publications which had an overall circulation of 16 million copies. These figures represent a third of all publications and a half of the circulation of all periodical literature in Italy. Much of this literature reaches people and groups untouched by the rest of the press – it is distributed by hand and so represents the only form of reading of many people in the small rural centres. Pope John XXIII understood its significance when he declared 'the Catholic press is one of the most serious means that the word of God can use to arrive in the home and be understood and loved . . . Hence, all Catholics have a vital duty to support and defend it.'

The predominance of business and Catholic interests in the press ensures that the overwhelming bias of the media is all of a piece. The existence of a reduced dissenting sector (the rise of the leftist and underground press, culminating in the appearance of two dailies, *Il Manifesto* and *Lotta Continua*, has been one of the novelties of the sixties) does much to obscure the true situation, by suggesting the importance of a plurality of opinions which is, in fact, much more theoretical than real. One must call attention to the limitations of the Italian press as a means of influencing public opinion. We have already noted the lack of development of civil society in certain regions of Italy. In 1960, Italy took only eighteenth place out of the twenty-five European countries with regard to the development of the means of communication : Italy had an index of 24.0 compared with 100.0 for Great Britain; and found itself behind Iceland (66.3) and Ireland (43.1). At that time, the radical political journalist Enzo Forcella wrote, 'We must not forget that we live in a country of 30 million electors of whom barely one in six reads a newspaper. Even if we agree that the five million readers can find trustworthy reports in the newspapers, which is far from being an established fact, it still leaves 25 million people without any source of information at all, or any opinion at all.' The situation has almost certainly changed to Italy's advantage in the last decade, if only because of the rapid rise in the number of television sets throughout the country. Nonetheless the relative inefficacy of the press as a means of influencing public opinion probably goes a long way towards explaining why Italian interest groups believe it so important to be represented in the decision-making centres of state institutions. Certainly lack of readership accounts for the peculiarly esoteric style of much of Italian political journalism.

(b) DIRECT REPRESENTATION IN PARLIAMENT AND LOBBYING

Professor LaPalombara concluded his study of interest-group activity in Parliament in the fifties with the statement. 'Groups seem to be omnipresent at Montecitorio and Palazzo Madama'. We have already noted that all Italian parties are vehicles for making direct group representation not only a possibility but also a reality. Certainly there are advantages to be gained for interest groups from direct representation in Parliament. Where a group cannot achieve this it seeks contacts; and for this reason it is claimed that a fair number of parliamentarians, particularly among lawyers, are on retainers from interest groups to look after their interests. The first advantage comes from the fact that Italian Parliamentary Standing Committees have the unique power of legislating without reference back to a plenary session. While it is true that the great issues of public policy are not decided in committee, the so-called less important and technical bills are; and under the cover of technicalities, decisions of wide import, such as, for example, export and import regulations and tariff procedures, can be taken to the advantage of influential interests.

A second advantage can be gained from the appointment of a sympathetic parliamentarian as committee reporter on a bill which concerns an interest group. The reporter has the task of gathering the technical information about the proposal and is free to choose the groups from which to solicit information as well as the type of information selected. In the conduct of his investigation he is in a position to hurry or delay the discussion of the bill. Furthermore, he makes the major speech on the bill and this and the material he furnishes can affect the reaction of the House to it. It is claimed that the action of the reporter can, at the least, delay the legislation; at the most, permanently defeat it.

A third advantage to interest groups of permanent representation and lobbying can be gained from the provision of information. Parliament almost totally lacks adequate secretarial and research assistance; the study, office and reference services of both houses are primitive. Parliamentarians turn naturally to organized groups which are in a position to supply the relevant information. Hence groups which are able to maintain research units are in a strong position to influence legislation or, at the very least, the frame of reference in which a standing committee or the House debates the problem.

Which, then, are the groups with direct representation in

Parliament? Broadly speaking the most important are Catholic Action, *Coldiretti,* some of the auxiliary or collateral party organizations (women's movements and professional associations) and, until 1968, the principal trade-union confederations. It is difficult to know exactly how many Catholic Action leaders are in Parliament because of the overlapping with specialized Catholic organizations. Professor LaPalombara states that the number is considerable, and that Catholic Action is responsible for their election. As regards the auxiliary organizations, each party usually selects a number of leaders who are given candidatures and elected as much to reassure the membership of the party's concern for their interests as to pursue specific legislation, although here again there is often no conflict between the two elements. As mentioned, the *Coldiretti* could count on about a sixth of the Christian Democrat parliamentarians to promote and defend its interests.

No specific mention has been made of *Confindustria* representatives in Parliament. This is because after the failure of its attempt in 1956 to promote a businessmen's front in Parliament (*Confintesa*) it has preferred an outside approach through lobbying and discreetly financing sympathizers. Thus, during the fifties, Giulio Andreotti, the Christian Democrat minister, was used to put the *Confindustria* viewpoint. Similarly, CIDA (Italian Confederation of Plant Managers) used its leader, Giuseppe Togni, a leading Christian Democrat parliamentarian and minister, who was also identified with the Montecatini chemical group.

It has been suggested that interest groups sought direct representation in Parliament because it gave them greater leverage over rule-making than was otherwise available to them. This leverage was believed to be greater for Catholic groups (Catholic Action, *Coldiretti,* Catholic unions) whose parliamentarians were always members of the majority government party. However, if this was so, we must ask why certain groups, and specifically the trade unions, which had an important representation, abandoned it. It was not that they had a greater access to the agencies of public administration; indeed, it was their lack of this access which had led them to develop their own direct representation in Parliament. But it became an increasingly inefficient way of exerting pressure for the unions; they found in the later 1960s that they could intervene more effectively in the political process as interlocutors of the government by means of direct action. The reason would seem to have been the consequences of the primary focus of interest groups on Parliament; the desire of all groups to be represented at the party and parliamentary levels has exaggerated the phenomenon of factionalism in both the party and parliamentary systems. The interest groups did not create factionalism; its origin is to be sought in the fragmentary nature of Italian society; and, hence, the fragmentary nature of partisan representation. But, given the immobility of the parliamentary system, factionalism is a natural corollary. Interest groups have merely added to it by making considerable sums available to individual or groups of politicians, rather than directly to national party headquarters. To appreciate why interest groups have behaved in this way, we must consider the other pole of Italian interest group activity with state institutions, its relations with the bureaucracy.

(c) BUREAUCRATIC INTERVENTION : CLIENTELA AND PARENTELA

It is a commonplace in the postwar period to say that state intervention in a so-called mixed economy–welfare state has brought interest groups and the administration much closer together. The growth in government subsidies and in the regulation of social and economic activities has made the goodwill of civil servants important to the success of many groups' policies. Similarly, civil servants need information and co-operation from interest groups if they are to intervene successfully in economic and social affairs. Hence interest groups have much to gain from access to and intervention in the administrative process. For example, the administration has been accorded *de facto* rule-making power in many fields; in addition, the growth of delegated legislation and the creation of specialized agencies and advisory bodies to control certain activities and advise the government have similarly led to an increase in the administration's powers. Interest groups have not been slow to invade these bodies and agencies: in 1960, Felice Ippolito, Secretary General of the National Committee of Atomic Energy (CNEN) complained of the activity of the Edison Electrical Company in placing its men :

It is a daily struggle; even for the naming of the lowest expert to a meeting of Euratom, the electrical companies insist on the right to choose a man in their complete confidence, and continually make unjust, indiscriminate, defamatory attacks on whoever upholds a thesis not consonant with their interests. I, also, have been accused by their newspapers of being a public servant who is an enemy of Italy only because I do not identify the interests of Italy with the interests of the Edison group.

Professor LaPalombara has outlined two structures which he believes determine the pattern of interest-group intervention in the administration. In the first place, what he calls the *clientela* group, i.e. the group which dominates the activity of the sector within the department's competence; and, in the second place, what he calls the *parentela* group, i.e. the group which has won a special relationship with a department based on control of appointment or patronage, in brief, which has colonized a department.

The client relationship between a ministerial department and the groups working in its field of action is the most common type of group-administration relationship. The administration requires information and co-operation to organize activity in the field; and these commodities can only be supplied by groups. However not all interest groups are equal in the eyes of civil servants. As Professor LaPalombara himself notes: 'Few groups in a highly fragmented society can lay claim to the characteristics of representativeness, respectability, authoritativeness and proximity.' He goes on to observe that the trade unions are split; that the Veterans' Associations cover the whole spectrum of political ideology from extreme left to extreme right; that the professional people affiliate on the basis of different partisan interests rather than common economic or professional ones, etc. Even the *Coldiretti* which dominates the agricultural sector is not cohesive in terms of concrete policy objectives. Hence he comes to the conclusion that *Confindustria* is the most perfect example of a client group in its relations with the Ministry of Industry and Commerce. In consequence, it might be expected to wield an overwhelming influence with that Ministry. If this is the case, which Professor LaPalombara is not prepared to deny, we must not forget the importance of a specific factor, the technical capacity of the civil service, a fact which we shall have to examine further. Interest groups do not supply information in a non-structured way, but rather in the way which supports the conclusions that they wish to be drawn from it. Because the Italian civil service is woefully weak in technicians, the ministerial departments are often incapable of assessing it critically, and accept the information and the conclusions and/or proposals drawn from it. A civil servant admitted to Professor LaPalombara in 1958 that 'an association like *Confindustria* is rich in technicians who present the bureaucrats with massive studies to support their own ideas regarding the action which the ministry should take. The bureaucrat then is in a very weak position if he seeks to oppose *Confindustria,* particularly, when the latter says "you must do the following regarding this industrial sector or you will cause bankruptcy, and unemployment".' The fact is that there was not a single ministry that had at its disposal the number of technicians and research facilities that *Confindustria* had organized at that time.

Professor LaPalombara claims that the view that *Confindustria* is all powerful is exaggerated because of the *parentela* relationships between interest groups and ministerial departments which exist parallel to the *clientela* relations; and that *Confindustria* is not so favoured in this relationship as other groups. The basis of the *parentela* relationship is the hegemonic quality of the governing Christian Democrat Party. It is a permanent government party which has been in power uninterruptedly for over twenty-five years, and is unlikely to be removed from office by election in the foreseeable future. Moreover, although it has to form coalitions to have a majority in Parliament, its power outweighs those of its partners; 'they', as Professor LaPalombara has felicitously said, 'are essentially *guests in power.*' This fact is fully appreciated by civil servants. Two further factors are required to make the *parentela* relationship effective. First, the willingness of the Christian Democrats to intervene in the administrative process. As already noted the government parties have seen their role as the occupation of as many of the key posts in the State as a symbol of their political strength. Hence the bitter struggles within the Christian Democrat Party between the various factions and the coalition partners over appointments and promotions.

The second factor is the capacity of the interest groups to condition the party. It goes without saying that given the dependence of the Christian Democrat Party on the Church and the Catholic organizations to mobilize the Catholic vote, Catholic organizations, Catholic Action *en tête* are in a strong position to impose their men on the party, and in the administration. Three points, however, must be made to qualify the implications of this statement : (1) the very fierceness of the factional struggle in the Christian Democrat Party denotes that no Catholic organization is overwhelmingly dominant; (2) the fact that electoral support is now more important in terms of the preference vote than in terms of policy; and (3) the fact that Catholic organizations' interests are often more passive (i.e. the defence of Catholic privilege) than progressive in policy terms, which means that they are more interested in patronage for patronage's sake.

Finally, we can ask with Professor LaPalombara whether *clientela* or *parentela* is the more significant as a strategy for intervening in the administration. He adopts the proposition that the most productive strategy is one of position : the ability to create and maintain fixed channels of access is more important than the ability to exercise pressure through an agency outside the administrative system (i.e. the party). In these terms a client relationship is more productive than a *parentela* one. In the former, the interest group renders itself indispensable to the administration almost without the administration being aware of the group's pressure activities. On the other hand, the *parentela* relationship has to be renewed with each new issue. It is interesting that in the case of the two most important and active groups, *Confindustria* and Catholic Action, both are very aware of their weaknesses. Catholic Action is busy establishing *clientela* relations where it can; and *Confindustria* is forever looking for the possibility to renew the *parentela* relationship it enjoyed under Fascism and in the immediate postwar years. The new trade-union strategy is an attempt to avoid the pitfalls of the one and the other by acting as a direct interlocutor of the government, representing as it were the direct confrontation between society and the State. It is certain that one of the consequences of the *clientela* and *parentela* activities of interest groups in a political system as immobile as Italy's is to exacerbate factionalism, and hence reinforce the vicious circle that has been established.

Part III
The Italian State

'The executive of the Modern State is but a Committee
for managing the common affairs of the whole bourgeoisie.'

Communist Manifesto

'One can do worse than think of the government as a
hierarchy of committees.'

After Galbraith

Part III
The Italian State

6 Executive and Legislature: A Classic Parliamentary Government?

The Republican Constitution of 1948 instituted a parliamentary system of government in Italy. In so doing it merely gave *de jure* form to a *de facto* situation, because all the anti-Fascist parties were committed to restoring parliamentary government on the fall of Fascism. Although there was some disagreement as to the form this should take the Constitutent Assembly adopted, in fact, what has been called the classic form of parliamentary government; the executive is politically responsible to Parliament, but retains the right of dissolution. The functioning of a parliamentary government, however, depends on the party system which works it. For example, a parliamentary government operated by a two-party system functions very differently from one run by a multi-party system or one controlled by a single dominant party. Italy has a multi-party system powerfully conditioned by a dominant government party. This situation has, naturally, strongly moulded the contours of the classic form of parliamentary government adopted by the Constituent Assembly.

The Role of the President of the Republic

The problem facing the Constituent Assembly in respect of the office of Head of State was twofold: on the one hand, the electorate had rejected the monarchy; and, on the other hand, the Assembly was pledged to introduce a parliamentary and not a presidential republican regime. Hence neither the English monarchy nor the American Presidency could serve as models. It was natural, therefore, that it should look to the French President of the Republic as a prototype. Nonetheless there are significant differences between the powers of the Italian President and the Presidents of the French Third and Fourth Republics, which need to be borne in mind. Observers and commentators agree that the President is something more than a figurehead, but as Professor Kogan has pertinently observed, 'nobody, including the President, is quite sure of "how much more" . . .'

(a) THE FUNCTIONS OF THE OFFICE

The President is elected for a period of seven yeai. by a joint session of both Houses of Parliament, with the participation of three delegates from each region in order to guarantee the incumbent a somewhat broader electoral basis. Eligibility is restricted to candidates who are fifty years and over. Unlike the French Constitutions of 1946 and 1958, which explicitly permit the retiring President to be re-elected, the Italian Constitution is silent on this point. Although no retiring President has been re-elected, Presidents Gronchi and Saragat were both in the running for a further term of office. According to Article 83 of the Constitution, the election of the President 'takes place by secret ballot and requires a two-thirds majority of the Assembly. After the third ballot, an absolute majority is sufficient.' Since the election of Enrico De Nicola as Provisional President of the Republic by the Constituent Assembly by an overwhelming majority on the first ballot in June 1946, there have been five presidential elections. Each time the number of ballots has increased alarmingly : four in May 1948 for Luigi Einaudi; four in May 1955 for Giovanni Gronchi; nine in April 1962 for Antonio Segni; twenty-one in December 1964 for Giuseppe Saragat; and twenty-three in December 1971 for Giovanni Leone. The length and asperity of these elections – the last two went on for a fortnight – are a clear indication of the importance that the parties and their leaders attach to the office of President and the lengths they will go to secure the election of candidates they believe to be favourable; or to block those of persons believed to be hostile to them.

The Constitution invests the President with a wide range of functions : he is Head of State and representative of national unity. As such he has power of appointment in specified cases (principally the nomination of five life senators during his term;

and five Constitutional Court Judges); can veto legislation; authorize the submission of government bills to Parliament; call special sessions of Parliament, dissolve Parliament (on the advice of the Presidents of the two Houses); dissolve Regional assemblies; call elections and referenda; ratify treaties on their approval by Parliament; declare war after a decision of Parliament; promulgate laws and issue regulations; grant amnesties, pardons and reprieves; and bestow honours. In addition, he is Commander-in-Chief of the Armed Forces; Chairman of the Supreme Defence Council and Chairman of the Higher Council of the Judiciary. Nonetheless Article 89 states: 'No act of the President of the Republic is valid unless countersigned by the Ministers proposing it, who assume responsibility for it. Acts which have the force of legislation and other acts indicated by law are countersigned also by the President of the Council of Ministers.' In a similar vein, Article 90 declares that the President 'is not responsible for acts performed while exercising his functions', except for treason or other impeachable offences.

The question, therefore, is which are the presidential acts that are covered by Article 89? Some acts are clearly outside its scope because the Constitution says so. Three are important: (1) the suspensive veto of legislation; (2) the dissolution of both Houses of Parliament; (3) the appointment of the President of the Council of Ministers. For other acts, the position is ambiguous. Thus for example, the cabinet claimed the right in 1955 to select the five Constitutional Court Judges to be nominated by the President, but first Einaudi, and then Gronchi, stood firm with the backing of Parliament and legal opinion. The argument which carried the day was that if the Constitution had wished the government to exercise this power it would have granted it to the cabinet. Other acts, like delivering speeches, paying official visits, holding conversations, writing letters and sending telegrams are, of their nature, informal and can be made the subject of countersignature only with difficulty. The question becomes more one of whether the President must reflect faithfully the views of the cabinet or not. Each successive president has clearly thought not, and, indeed, all have felt free to say and do what they believed was in the national interest. The differences have been that some have acted more discreetly, like De Nicola and Einaudi, and others have acted more openly, like Gronchi, Segni and Saragat. In-

113

deed, Gronchi's clashes with the official cabinet position were notorious: his sending of Giorgio La Pira, the unconventional Christian Democrat Mayor of Florence, to Mahommed V's coronation in Morocco as his personal representative to discuss oil concessions for ENI, the national hydrocarbons corporation; and his famous visit to Moscow in early 1960, which was only approved by the cabinet under his veiled threat of going without government consent, were only two of the more clamorous. But in 1954, Einaudi insisted that the Prime Minister Scelba nominate a Foreign Minister who would accept and sign the Trieste agreements; and the request was met. Earlier, in August 1953, after the failure of De Gasperi's last government, he had been instrumental in the appointment of Pella as Prime Minister, and he endeavoured to force the government coalition to keep Pella in office when his cabinet fell apart in spring 1954. Again, nothing formally prevented Segni inviting the Commander-in-Chief of the Carabinieri, General De Lorenzo, to the Quirinale Palace in July 1964, and asking him to ensure public order but one can ask why Segni did not consult the Prime Minister, whose personal responsibility it was. Similarly, the telegrams of condolence which Saragat sent the relatives of the policeman, Antonio Annarumma, and the victims of the Milan Bomb incident during the 'hot autumn' of 1969, alleging precise criminal responsibilities while the matter was *sub-judice,* are all examples of presidents' personal intervention into political life.

(b) THE POLITICAL INFLUENCE OF THE PRESIDENT

Although he is not considered a formal part of the legislative process, the President has been endowed with a number of powers for influencing the legislative process on his own responsibility. We have already noted that he can only 'promulgate', and not 'sanction', laws. Nonetheless he may 'by means of a motivated message, requested a new decision of the Houses' (Article 74). In normal circumstances, he has thirty days to exercise this suspensive veto; and no special majority is required to override it. This action has been used sparingly. For example, President Einaudi returned only four of the 3000 laws he promulgated in his seven-year term. In none of these cases was the law reconsidered; and it appears that his successors and Parliament have accepted to some extent the distinction he drew between political policy (which is the exclusive concern and responsibility of the cabinet) and public policy. Einaudi claimed that the President could and should (as he himself did) intervene not only in regard to the constitutionality of legislation but also in relation to its compatibility with public policy as this could be inferred from the principles of the Constitution. That the President should not intervene in questions of political policy was argued from the fact that, unlike the presidents of the French Third and Fourth Republics, he was not accorded the right of participating in cabinet meetings. Gronchi preferred, however, to use his political influence in the legislative process before the bills were approved by means of public statements, personal contact and suggestion, rather than when they came to him for signature. And Segni by contrast used his veto power seven times in his two years of office, although never on a major issue.

The Constituent Assembly expected that it would be in the appointment of the President of the Council of Ministers (or Prime Minister and, upon the latter's recommendation, of the Ministers) that the President would exercise his most important executive power. This expectation has not been disappointed, but its realization has come less from the constitutional power itself than from the parliamentary situation with which successive presidents have had to deal. The power of appointment of a prime minister is one that is always formally in the hands of Heads of State in liberal democracies. In states with strong two-party systems, the Head of State has virtually no effective choice because the leader of the majority party in Parliament effectively controls it. But in multi-party states, like Italy, where no party has an over-all majority and factional conflict in the major party is strong, the Head of State's choice is more open and must be exercised more frequently. Hence the opportunity for manoeuvre is real. In Italy, the limits have been, since 1948, that the Prime Minister must be a member of the dominant Christian Democrat Party. At every ministerial crisis, the President goes through a routine series of consultations with former presidents, former prime ministers, party secretaries, and the Presidents of both Houses. If the majority party leaders are agreed, they will give him a name; and he will invite that person to form a government. This is what happened between 1947 and 1953, during the period of De

Gasperi's ascendancy. On the other hand, if the parties, and above all the Christian Democrats, are not agreed, the President will receive a list of names and it will be up to him to decide whom to invite. Normally he will do this on his assessment of whom he thinks is most likely to form a working majority.

There are numerous examples of the President of the Republic using his judgement in this way. Leone's appointment as Prime Minister in July 1963, after Aldo Moro had failed to form the first 'organic' centre-left coalition (i.e. with the active participation of the Socialist Party) was Segni's personal choice, and he personally supervised the composition of the all Christian Democrat cabinet. But perhaps the most notorious example of presidential discretion in the appointment of a Prime Minister was Gronchi's choice of Tambroni in the spring of 1960. It appears that Tambroni was not one of the names suggested to Gronchi in the course of consultations during the ministerial crisis by the governmental party leaders after the failure of first Segni and then Fanfani to form a government. Moreover when he presented his cabinet to Parliament for the formal vote of confidence and got a majority only thanks to the support of the Neo-Fascist Party, the Christian Democrat Party Executive invited him to resign which he did. Gronchi, however, refused to accept his resignation after a second failure by Fanfani; and he did everything in his power to save the government despite popular protest in the country. A couple of months later the massive popular demonstrations of protest, which included loss of life, forced Gronchi to change his mind and accept Tambroni's resignation.

The presidents developed two further techniques which gave them an increased control over the choice of prime minister. The first was that of laying down the type of government that should be formed, and even the contents of the proposed government's programme. Saragat in July 1969 and February 1970 charged Rumor with 'forming a new organic four-party centre-left government' which considerably reduced Rumor's room for manoeuvre; and Nenni claimed in 1965 that Segni had presented the Socialist Party with an ultimatum with regard to its participation in the second Moro government in July 1964, in the form of a veto on a whole series of reforms which were part of the party's programme of government. The second was the consultation in ministerial crises of a whole series of people extraneous to this delicate phase of the political process. Thus Segni made a habit of consulting the Governor of the Bank of Italy, the Commander-in-Chief of the Carabinieri and the Chief of Police. It is true that his successor, Saragat, did not continue this practice.

We may conclude with the proposition that the President's power is in inverse proportion to that of the cabinet. A strong, united, long-lived cabinet would reduce the President to something of a figurehead. Weak, divided, and short-lived cabinets give the President power and influence. His term of office is fixed and relatively long, and, moreover, is not subject to votes of confidence. This greater security of tenure of office means that he can act as an instrument of initiative and imperative coordination when it is lacking elsewhere. The constitutional lawyer Alberto Predieri has argued that as Chairman of the Supreme Defence Council and Commander-in-Chief of the Armed Forces, the President could actually assume the direction of national affairs himself in a crisis situation threatening the survival of the State. However that is to argue that extreme situations provoke extreme remedies. In the normal course of events, it is very unlikely that even a Christian Democrat President would find a party united behind an experiment with personal presidential politics.

The Position of the Cabinet

The function of the executive, Weber said, is the imperative coordination of government activity. The Italian Constitution attempts to achieve this in two ways. On the one hand, it recognizes the commanding position of the head of the cabinet (President of the Council of Ministers or Prime Minister); and on the other, it seeks to give the cabinet strength as an institution of collective decision-making. Thus Article 95 first proceeds to state that 'The President of the Council of Ministers directs the general policy of the government and is responsible for it. He maintains the unity of political and administrative action, and promotes and coordinates the activity of the Ministers.' In a second paragraph, it goes on to say that 'the Ministers are collectively responsible for the acts of the Council of Ministers, and individually for the acts of their various departments.' Furthermore, it endeavours to bolster the concept of collective responsibility in the provisions that institute the principle of cabinet responsibility to Parliament. It is the cabinet, and not the Prime Minister, which must present itself before both Houses of Parliament to seek a vote of confidence within ten days of its formation. Similarly, it is the whole cabinet which must resign on the passing of a vote of no-confidence. Incidentally, on the model of the French Fourth Republic there are restrictions on the use of votes of no-confidence to prevent the cabinet being overthrown by surprise attack : motions of no-confidence require the signature of at least one tenth of the members of that House; and three days must elapse between the presentation of the motion and its being called.

Table 6. i
Duration of Italian Governments and Cabinet Crises 1948–73

Prime Minister	Crisis Days	In office Mths.	Days	Formation Date	Parties Represented
De Gasperi V	16	19	19	23 May 1948	DC, PSLI, PRI and PLI
De Gasperi VI	10	17	19	27 Jan. 1950	DC, PSLI and PRI
De Gasperi VII	17	22	3	26 July 1951	DC and PRI
De Gasperi VIII	20	—	12	16 July 1953	DC
Pella	13	4	19	17 Aug. 1953	DC and 'technicians'
Fanfani I	11	—	12	17 Jan. 1954	DC
Scelba	14	16	12	10 Feb. 1954	DC, PSDI and PLI
Segni I	9	22	4	7 July 1955	DC, PSDI and PLI
Zoli	12	13	0	16 May 1957	DC
Fanfani II	20	6	25	1 July 1958	DC and PSDI
Segni II	24	12	9	19 Feb. 1959	DC
Tambroni	30	3	24	26 Mar. 1960	DC
Fanfani III	7	18	7	26 July 1960	DC
Fanfani IV	19	14	25	21 Feb. 1962	DC, PSDI and PRI
Leone I	36	4	15	22 June 1963	DC
Moro I	29	6	22	4 Dec. 1963	DC, PSI, PSDI and PRI
Moro II	26	17	30	22 July 1964	DC, PSDI, PSI and PRI
Moro III	33	27	13	23 Feb. 1966	DC, PSI, PSDI and PRI
Leone II	19	4	26	24 June 1968	DC
Rumor I	24	6	23	13 Dec. 1968	DC, PSU (i.e. PSI and PSDI) and PRI
Rumor II	31	6	2	5 Aug. 1969	DC, PSI
Rumor III	50	3	7	29 Mar. 1970	DC, PSU (i.e. PSDI) and PRI
Colombo	31	17	12	6 Aug. 1970	DC, PSI, PSU and PRI
Andreotti I	33	—	11	17 Feb. 1972	DC
Andreotti II	121	11	17	26 June 1972	DC, PSU, and PLI
Rumor IV	25	—	—	7 July 1973	DC, PSI, PSU and PRI

Source: *Keesings Contemporary Archives*

(a) CABINET INSTABILITY BUT MINISTERIAL STABILITY

The Italian Constitution has not been very successful in its objective of formal imperative coordination because one of the characteristics of postwar Italian politics that we have already noted is cabinet instability. Italy has had thirty-five cabinets since the fall of Fascism in 1943. The average duration of a cabinet is, therefore, approximately ten months (see table 6.i). The first point to make is that cabinet instability in Italy is not what it seems on the surface, because behind the façade of continuous cabinet crises, there is a significant continuity of party, persons and posts. In fact the form that cabinet instability has taken in Italy is the 'musical chairs' of continuous coalition between the same partners : frequent changes of cabinet, less frequent changes of office and rarer changes of personnel. Indeed as a result of the frequency of cabinet reshuffles in Britain, more men have held cabinet office in postwar Britain than in Italy. The United Kingdom is widely believed to be an exemplar of cabinet stability, but the figures for the average length of time in the same office are not very different for the two countries as Table 6.ii indicates. Moreover, the average minister has a much longer active career in Italy than in Britain. Thus, for example, men like Fanfani and Moro, Andreotti and Colombo, Rumor and Taviani, have been in office almost continuously for over twenty years (over fifteen years as ministers). In consequence, Italy's ministers have many more years of cabinet experience than their British colleagues, for whom ten years is rare and fifteen exceptional. This is a fact of some importance when assessing the relations between executive and administration. It gives the lie to the simple proposition that in countries where cabinet instability is rife, the government is run and policy is made by higher civil servants ensconced in office because of their security of tenure.

A second point which we would make is that there appear to be two kinds of ministerial department (what we shall call the 'command' and the 'patronage') and two types of ministerial personnel (what we shall call the 'top' and the 'middle' level politicians). Thus on the one hand there are ministries with a much more stable ministerial personnel (Interior, Defence and the Economy) which have only had eight or nine heads in twenty-two years; and others which have had a succession of them (Mer-

Table 6. ii

Average Period in Same Office for Selected Ministers: Great Britain and Italy, 1955-70

Office (Great Britain)	months	Office (Italy)	months
Foreign Secretary	22·5	Minister of Foreign Affairs	16·4
Chancellor of Exchequer	25·7	Minister of Treasury	25·7
Home Secretary	30·0	Minister of Interior	22·5
Minister of Defence	25·7	Minister of Defence	25·7
President of the Board of Trade	22·5	Minister of Industry	18·0
Minister of Education	18·0	Minister of Education	20·0
Secretary for Scotland	45·0	Minister for South	45·0
Minister of Agriculture	36·0	Minister of Agriculture	18·0
Postmaster General	30·0	Minister for Posts and Telecommunications	15·0
Minister of Public Works	20·0	Minister of Public Works	18·0
Average minister	26·1	Average minister (20 ministers)	20·0
Average administration	30·0	Average cabinet	12·0
Average prime minister	45·0	Average prime minister	18·0

Sources: R. Rose, 'The Making of Cabinet Ministers', *British Journal of Political Science* (October 1971), p. 408; and *Annuario Politico Italiano 1965* and *Keesings Contemporary Archives*

cantile Marine, Foreign Trade, Posts and Telecommunications, and Education have had double that number in the same period). Similarly, there are a number of key politicians (Scelba, Pella, Vanoni, Fanfani, Moro, Taviani, Andreotti and Colombo etc) who over the years have alternated between the 'command' posts, often spending a prolonged period in one department (Scelba, Tambroni, Taviani and Restivi in the Interior; Pacciardi, Taviani, Andreotti and Gui in Defence; Pella and Colombo at the Treasury; Colombo and Andreotti in Industry, and so on). On the other hand, there are Christian Democrat ministers who remain in successive cabinets but change departments : Jervolino,

Mattarella, Bosco, Mazza and Natali are typical examples, but there are many others, mainly southerners. Ministers from the coalition partners usually fall into the latter category, even when they receive important posts, not only because their parties are 'guests in power' (a favourite trick is to make the leader of the leading opposition party Deputy Prime Minister, an office with prestige but no power, because without a department; this happened to Saragat, Nenni and De Martino), but because it is easier for them to reach office because of the needs of coalition arithmetic, but correspondingly more difficult to hold it for any length of time. This analysis of different types of department indicates an hierarchy of office and person which constitutes an informal mechanism for continuity and co-ordination in executive government that cabinet instability belies.

A third point to be noted is that, despite the heterogeneity of party and faction, there is a great similarity in the social background of ministers. In fact, over 80 per cent of Italian ministers between 1945 and 1970 came from the upper middle class, and over 90 per cent had a University degree (two-thirds of them in law!). It suggests that behind the façade of ideology, there is more common ground than is often supposed.

(b) CABINET INSTABILITY AND ITS EFFECTS ON POLICY-MAKING

In spite of ministerial stability, Italy still suffers from cabinet instability and this has consequences for the quality of the country's executive government. A prime minister who is assured of a permanent parliamentary majority is able to control not only Parliament but also the cabinet. Moreover, the cabinet can be enabled to exercise the specific powers of Parliament. This happy situation has been refused to the majority of postwar Italian premiers. Indeed, De Gasperi alone, for a part of his premiership, enjoyed this position; and then only in exceptional circumstances. Not only was he the undisputed leader of the Christian Democrat Party, but in a first period he was also the leader of the governments of national unity; and in a second period he was the leader of a pro-Western government in the throes of the cold war. In addition, the Christian Democrats had an absolute majority in both Houses between 1948 and 1953. Yet in eight years of continuous office, he formed no fewer than eight cabinets. His successors have lacked his ascendancy over their colleagues. Such prestige and authority as they have gained has come from the control over the party which they were able to win at any particular time. In default of uncontested power in the party they could only count on being the presiding officer of the Council of Ministers and the person with whom the government's programme was politically identified. On the other hand, they had to construct their cabinets from a mosaic of parties and factions with the added disadvantages of knowing full well that : (a) ministers were first and foremost delegates of their respective parties and factions, which hence had first call on their loyalties; and (b) each prime minister's endeavour was seen, at best, as a temporary arrangement. Either the Prime Minister had rivals in his cabinet, to whom he had to give office because of their party standing; or he had them outside the cabinet in Parliament or the Party Executive because they had refused to accept a post. Sometimes, a Prime Minister was able to retain his position for almost a whole Parliament, like Moro who, thanks to his infinite patience and immense capacity for brokerage was able to keep the various heterogeneous elements of the centre-left coalition together, or when it split to persuade the vital elements back. More often, the Prime Minister lasts a year or two and then gives way to a colleague, like Rumor and Colombo recently.

The two most important consequences of the cabinet's instability appear to be its ineffectiveness as a collective decision-making body, and the quality of co-ordination of executive government. This must not be exaggerated, but it forms part of the chain of political immobilism, even if it is not the cause. First of all, cabinet deliberations are secret, but while only the highest level issues are brought up for discussion and decision, it appears that much of the discussion involves, in fact, no more than the reporting by various ministers to their colleagues of their activity so as to keep them in the picture. However despite Kogan's belief that an Italian tradition of minding one's own business accounts for lack of discussion, discussion there is, and disagreement. Factional rivalries are fanned by the fact that most departmental Under-Secretaries are of a different political affiliation from the Minister, and can brief a party representative in the cabinet, even if he is responsible for a different department, and so they can enter the discussion to oppose or try to change a project under discussion.

Similarly, the long ministerial experience of many ministers means that they are well briefed in the problems of many departments. Finally, the hierarchy of ministerial personnel obviously plays a role. A top-level politician will carry more weight than a middle-level one, even if the matter concerns a 'patronage' department and not a 'command' one. While it is impossible to assess the weight of different factors in cabinet discussion, given the secrecy, it is clear that disagreement can play an important role, if only because more cabinets have fallen as a result of internal discord than have been forced to resign due to an adverse vote in Parliament.

In consequence, it is not surprising that Italian ministers should prefer informal means of consultation and co-ordination. They add the advantages of cutting down paperwork and unnecessary discussion to that of not providing rivals and adversaries with valuable information. This practice has led to what one student of Italian politics has called a 'dramatic lack of co-ordination'. When it became clear that these methods were insufficient – the multiplicity of ministries made the need for co-ordination of effort overwhelming – resort was had to the creation of interministerial committees. There are any number of these : Interministerial Committee for the South; Interministerial Committee on Prices; Interministerial Committee on the European Communities etc.; and the more recent Interministerial Committee on Economic Planning which is destined to replace the previous Interministerial Committee on Reconstruction. However their utility has been much affected by cabinet instability; it is a truism to say that if the cabinet is divided, the interministerial committee is unlikely to provide harmony. But the effect of cabinet instability has gone further. First, many ministers leave an interministerial committee's deliberations with no serious intention of implementing its decisions in their own sphere of responsibility. Second, changes in the political situation have required corresponding changes in governmental coordination structure. For example, during the four-party centrist coalition under De Gasperi, the interministerial committee was used as the principal institution of co-ordination because of the need for all parties to be represented. In the later fifties, when minority Christian Democrat cabinets were more often the rule, the co-ordinating function shifted from the interministerial committees to a particular ministry. The formation of the 'centre-left' coalition saw a return to the use of interministerial committees for co-ordination. The creation of the Interministerial Committee for Economic Planning is a clear indication of this renewed tendency. It is a question not only of all parties being adequately represented so as to have a say in policy, but also of the allocation of posts to suit all parties which has led inevitably to an increase in the number of posts to satisfy all ambitions. It is this latter factor, which is itself a reflection of cabinet instability, that is responsible for the fact that the machinery of administration, although perfectly adequate for executive co-ordination, has not operated with the efficiency that was expected. This problem, like so many others, is fundamentally a political one.

The Power of Parliament

Alfred Grosser has observed that 'the nature of the national legislature is a function of the structure of the State, centralized or federal.' Italy is apparently no exception. The Constitution adopted a bicameral system with an absolute equality of powers between the chambers. If in federal states, like the United States or the Federal Republic of Germany, bicameral arrangements are justified on the ground of representing popular sovereignty through two channels – one the citizens the other the territorial collectivities – no such justification can be alleged in Italy's case. Indeed the only explanation of the adoption of a bicameral system with a parity of powers between each House is the centralized tradition of the state. Certainly the conservative forces in the Constituent Assembly defended such a position when they argued that a bicameral system was necessary to give balance to the legislative process, greater maturity to the legislative debate and greater stability to Parliament. Not surprisingly, it has fulfilled none of these hopes. One original intention was to give the upper House some specific form of regional representation which would have justified the concept of the parity of powers, but when the Christian Democrats also raised the idea of interest representation in the upper House, it sounded to the anti-Fascist majority in the Constituent Assembly so much like an effort to resurrect Fascist tainted corporativism that the latter made sure that all thought of special representation was banished from the final text of the

Constitution. In consequence the Italian Parliament is composed of two Houses, the Chamber of Deputies and the Senate of the Republic, with similar membership and identical powers.

Some constitutionalists have argued that Italy now has a system of 'imperfect bicameralism' characterized by the superiority of the Chamber. They claim that party leaders and the most representative party members tend to prefer the Chamber to the Senate; that there is a tendency to select the Prime Minister and important ministers from the Chamber rather than the Senate; and for governments to take votes of no confidence in the Chamber more seriously than those in the Senate. There is some truth in the arguments, but two Prime Ministers (Zoli in 1958 and Leone in 1968) were senators and many important ministers have also been senators. Moreover, in March 1972 President Leone dissolved Parliament after Andreotti's first cabinet had been defeated in the Senate without waiting for the vote in the Chamber. Finally, the President of the Senate takes constitutional precedence over the President of the Chamber as the second personage in the State and replaces the President of the Republic, in the case of the latter becoming unable to carry out his functions, until a new election can be held, as Carlo Merzagora did President Segni in 1964. Hence not too much weight need be attributed to the 'imperfect bicameralism' thesis.

The Chamber of Deputies is a typical European lower House. Its 630 members are elected for a five-year term by universal suffrage on the basis of one representative per 80,000 inhabitants; any citizen over twenty-five years of age on the date of election is eligible for membership and all citizens who have reached the age of twenty-one are eligible to vote for the election of deputies. The Senate is elected for a term of five years on a regional basis of one Senator per approximately 200,000 inhabitants, but with the proviso that no region is to have less than six senators with the exception of Friuli-Venezia-Giulia (3) and Molise (2) and the Val d'Aosta (1) for a total of 315 elected members. Any citizen of forty years of age is eligible for election, and all citizens who have reached the age of twenty-five are eligible to vote in senatorial elections. A certain number of persons can become life senators as of right : all former Presidents of the Republic on the completion of their term of office; and the five senators appointed by the President of the Republic for meritorious services to the nation.

Both Houses have similar electoral systems: a pure list system of PR for the Chamber of Deputies; and a modified list system for the Senate. Hence it is no surprise that their memberships in terms of party representation are very similar. The larger parties are slightly stronger in the Senate, but the differences are politically insignificant. In fact, similarity of representation has been increased by the fact that general elections to both Houses are held on the same day. Originally, the Senate was given a six-year term, but after having been dissolved thrice on the same day as the Chamber, its term was amended to five years in 1965. In consequence, political conflict between the two Houses – for the resolution of which the Constitution made no provision – has not emerged.

(a) ITALIAN PARLIAMENTARIANS : THE DOMINANCE OF THE MIDDLE
     CLASS

It has been claimed that Italian legislators resemble American legislators more than other European ones because they are made up in good part of lawyers. It could be argued, however, that they are not only typical of European parliamentarians in the sense that lawyers are the most important profession in most parliaments, but above all because they are overwhelmingly middle class. Indeed according to Professor Sartori's detailed study of Italian deputies between 1946 and 1963, 81.9 per cent came from middle and upper-class families. Thus in Italy, as elsewhere in Western Europe, there has been an increasing trend for parliamentarians to be recruited from families in professional and commercial occupations rather than from the older agricultural, and often aristocratic, groups; and to have professional occupations themselves (see Table 6.iii). Another typical feature of the Italian Parliament is the under-representation of women; women have never accounted for even 10 per cent of the membership of either House in any Parliament; and in the Fourth Parliament (1963–8), there were only 31 women out of a total of 945 parliamentarians. One can advance a general proposition of European dimensions, but also relevant to Italy, i.e. that membership confirms the transition from ascribed to achieved status. Since the majority of Italian deputies and senators have a higher class status than that which their fathers had, it is clear that a large proportion reached Parliament through their own achievements. Moreover, since over 70 per cent have a university degree, education would seem to have been the key to their success. In fact so indispensable has education become in Italy, that Rolf Dahrendorf's statement with reference to Europe that 'Nowadays the road to the top leads almost invariably through a successful university career' is true there too. Important as achieved status has become, ascribed status continues to matter. Dahrendorf noted its continuing significance too, but claimed that it often took the masked form of self-recruitment. In Italy election to parliament takes the form of co-option, i.e. the selection of a future MP by an established member who uses his influence to secure the requisite number of preference votes for his protégé.

Table 6. iii
Professional Activity of Deputies and Senators, 1948–63

	First parliament (1948–53) Senate	Ch. of D.	Second parliament (1953–58) Senate	Ch. of D.	Third parliament (1958–63) Senate	Ch. of D.
Landowners & businessmen	5·3	5·2	6·6	4·4	5·9	2·7
Liberal professions ⎧ lawyers	33·3	24·8	28·4	22·9	31·6	15·9
doctors	7·0	2·6	7·4	2·0	6·3	2·1
architects & engineers	2·3	1·2	2·5	1·1	2·0	1·7
⎩ others	3·3	2·0	4·9	0·9	4·8	2·6
Judges	1·8	0·9	2·5	1·6	1·6	0·9
University lecturers	9·6	11·4	6·6	10·9	6·7	8·9
Primary and secondary teachers	4·4	10·1	4·5	7·9	5·1	10·8
Journalists	4·7	4·9	4·5	5·4	3·6	7·5
Political leaders and organizations	12·0	21·7	13·6	21·6	14·6	23·4
Union leaders and organizations	5·3	5·2	6·1	8·0	5·1	10·0
Executives	5·2	2·0	5·8	2·6	4·8	4·1
Clerks	0·3	4·1	0·8	4·8	1·6	4·4
Manual workers	1·2	1·6	2·1	2·3	0·8	2·7
Other occupations	3·3	1·8	1·6	1·8	4·3	1·3
No occupation	0·5	0·5	2·1	1·8	1·2	1·1
Total	100·0	100·0	100·0	100·0	100·0	100·0
N.	(312)	(574)	(243)	(596)	(253)	(596)

Source: A. Spreafico, 'Il Senato della Repubblica: Composizione politica e stratificazione sociale' in M. Dogan and O. M. Petrarca, *Partiti politici e strutture sociali in Italia*, p. 631

Four specific traits of Italian parliamentarians are noteworthy. First, there is the importance of the place of the liberal professions, which is greater in the Senate (circa 40 per cent) than the

Chamber (20–30 per cent) where it has suffered a gradual decline, principally owing to the fall in the number of lawyers. Second, there is the prominence of 'professional politicians', almost twice as great in the Chamber (20 per cent) as in the Senate (10 per cent). Along with Union officials, they represent the entry of the lower classes into Parliament : a worker's only chance of election is as a result of a career as a Communist Party or Union official. Professor Somogyi noted in his statistical analysis of the composition of the Chamber of Deputies that 'the lower stratum has a significant weight only in the Communist Party, where it accounts for a little over a quarter of the cases, 25.9 per cent. For the other parties, representatives of this stratum are very few or are not found at all.' Third, there is the importance of the various teaching professions which account for almost 20 per cent of deputies. Finally, we may note the very poor representation of the productive sector (i.e. landowners and farmers, businessmen, managers, clerks and workers) which does not exceed 15 per cent of membership of either House. It indicates two things : (1) that there is a distinction between political and economic leaders and the representation of their interests; and (2) that the recruiting ground for political leaders is the tertiary or services sector. In fact the full-time professional politician is increasingly replacing the traditional 'notable' (21 per cent elected in 1946, 45 per cent elected in 1972). This has important consequences for Italian politics; and insofar as it is true of other Western European countries it goes a long way to explaining similarities between them.

(b) PARLIAMENTARY ORGANIZATION AND PROCEDURE

Both Houses meet by right at least twice a year, at the beginning of February and the beginning of October. In addition each may be called into special session by the President of each House, the President of the Republic, or on the initiative of one third of its members. The reason for the variety of methods of recall of Parliament is that at certain moments of Italian history the government has made crucial decisions while Parliament was in recess, and has then presented it with a *fait accompli*. The Constituent Assembly was determined to prevent a recurrence of this procedure, and, since the opposition has always won more than 30 per cent of the seats, it would seem that it has been successful.

Certainly there have been no occasions in the postwar period
when the opposition has claimed that it was prevented from discussing a matter because Parliament was in recess. Indeed the
principal criticism (although not specific to the opposition) has
been the length of sessions. To complete its business Parliament
is almost continually in session with the exception of the summer
recess and two short breaks at Christmas and Easter.

Each House is master of its own procedure; and elects its own
officers, President and presidential bureaux etc. Each House is
organized into a number of standing committees. There are fourteen in the Chamber and eleven in the Senate; they are arranged
to correspond to the various fields covered by the different
ministerial departments. There are twenty ministerial departments
and only half that number of committees; so some fields are
combined. The standing committees in the Chamber are grouped
as follows : constitutional matters, Foreign Affairs, Budget and
State-controlled Enterprises, Internal and Religious Affairs,
Justice, Finance, Defence, Education, Public Works, Communications, Agriculture, Commerce, Labour, and Public Health. The
Senate has no Constitutional Matters Committee, no Budget and
State-controlled Enterprises Committee, and combines Public
Works and Communications. Membership of standing committees
is proportional to the size of the parliamentary groups. The first
three Standing Committees in the Chamber have a membership of
30 to 35; and the remainder between 45 and 50. The Senate
Standing Committees have a membership of between 20 and 25.
Normally a senator or deputy is a member of one standing committee, but when a parliamentarian becomes a Minister he automatically resigns his standing committee membership and is
replaced by another parliamentarian from his party group. In
this way some parliamentarians can become members of more
than one standing committee.

The membership of standing committees follows the experience
and presumed competence of parliamentarians, but the bulk of
individual parliamentarians do not appear to attach importance
to sitting on a particular standing committee. On the other hand,
the Christian Democrats have tried to keep the control of standing committees in their own hands as far as possible in the same
way as they have tried to keep a tight rein on the organization
of both Houses. Until 1968 the Presidents of both Houses were

either Christian Democrats or independents allied to the Christian Democrats, but in that year the Christian Democrats permitted the election of a Socialist, Pertini, as President of the Chamber. Moreover, for many years the Christian Democrats chaired all the standing committees of both Houses; and hence managed their agenda, organized their consultations with other groups, their publication of documents, and statements of policy, etc. Since 1963, a number of minor 'centre-left' party parliamentarians have been elected presidents of standing committees. For example, Ugo La Malfa, the Republican Party leader and former Budget Minister, became President of the powerful Budget Committee. The importance of control of committees lies in their virtual autonomy (the chairman having control of business) and so in their usefulness in burying controversial legislation.

(c) PARLIAMENT AND THE LEGISLATIVE PROCESS

'The legislature makes the laws; the executive carries out the laws', so runs the well-known parliamentary adage. Article 70 of the Constitution states that 'the legislative function is exercised collectively by the two Chambers', but Article 71 goes on to say that 'the initiative in legislation appertains to the government, to each member of the Chamber, and to organs and bodies on which it may be conferred by constitutional enactment.' The latter include, so far, the Regional Assemblies and the National Council of Economy and Labour. In addition, this initiative can be taken by private citizens, if 50,000 will sign a draft petition, but up to 1971 they had never done so. Passage of legislation is by a simple majority of the votes cast in both houses in turn, and an absolute majority of each House must be present to constitute a quorum. All bills are passed on introduction to the appropriate standing committee which may decide on one of three types of procedure:
(1) to act as an advisory body; (2) to act as a legislative body; and (3) to act as a drafting body.

The first procedure is the normal one adopted in all continental European parliaments; the committee studies the bill and reports back to the whole House. It may propose amendments or consult other standing committees, or just sit on it and so effectively kill it. Moreover, the committee appoints one of its members as a reporter to present its view to the whole House; and if there is a minority view, a specific member can present a minority report. The second procedure has already been mentioned as a device unique to the Italian Parliament. The standing committees can take a final decision on any bill and pass it as legislation. In this case any member of the government can appear before the committee, and any member can come and speak, but only committee members vote. Excluded from this procedure, however, are a number of important subjects: basic constitutional, electoral and budgetary matters and treaties. Furthermore, the Constitution provides a safeguard against abuse of this procedure in the form of the possibility of referring any bill back to the full House on the request of one tenth of the members of the full House or one fifth of the committee's members. The third procedure is resorted to only in exceptional circumstances. In this case the committee's draft of the bill is voted on by the whole House without debate.

Voting on single articles and amendments is by show of hands, or by roll-call if a number of members demand it. However the rules of both Houses require that the final approval of all legislation by the whole House, like motions of investiture, be by secret vote. The secret vote was introduced to give parliamentarians a certain independence of party instructions. It has not had this effect because it is fairly easy to discover the views of different groups in debate. In January 1959, various right-wing members of the Christian Democrat Party continually voted against the governmental legislation of the left-centre Fanfani cabinet because they disliked its political orientation. However when the government made an issue a vote of confidence, the dissident Christian Democrats supported the government to prevent its overthrow. This parliamentary harassment was symptomatic of growing factional tension within the party which led directly to Fanfani's resignation. Fanfani resigned not because of his parliamentary defeats, but because factional conflict within the party made his political position untenable. Nonetheless, the principal adverse consequence of the secret vote is that it prevents the elector from knowing how his representatives have voted on certain issues in Parliament.

All bills which are passed in identical form in both Houses are sent on to the President of the Republic for signature and become law on publication in the *Gazzetta Ufficiale*. A bill which is defeated in one House cannot become law. If the bill is amended in the other House, it must return to the first one for reconsideration. Since there is no provision for a Conference Committee, this kind of shuttle between the Houses can continue for years and lead to a bill being 'killed' by a dissolution, which has the effect of annulling all uncompleted legislation. Thus, for example, the legislation setting up the Constitutional Court was shuttled between both Houses for eighteen months until they agreed on the same text. There is, however, an abbreviated procedure for bills of declared urgency.

Table 6. iv
Summary of Italian Legislative Activity, 1948–68

	I Parlt. 1948–53	II Parlt. 1953–8	III Parlt. 1958–63	IV Parlt. 1963–8
Number of sittings of whole House				
Chamber	1,114	738	789	844
Senate	984	653	697	804
Number of sittings of Chamber Committees				
In advisory capacity	1,860	1,186	1,757	2,130
In legislative capacity	1,405	1,270	1,485	1,476
Total	3,265	2,456	3,242	3,606
Number of sittings of Senate Committees (Total)	1,733	1,488	1,502	2,136
Government Bills				
Presented in Chamber	2,149	1,574	1,484	1,437
Approved by Chamber: by whole House	500	433	421	398
by committees	1,496	1,006	919	861
Presented in Senate	2,382	1,577	1,462	1,417
Approved by Senate: by whole House	564	431	429	400
by committees	1,550	1,036	929	868
Private Members' Bills				
Presented in Chamber	1,155	2,132	3,152	3,573
Approved by Chamber: by whole House	87	63	63	47
by committees	344	592	639	724
Presented in Senate	650	985	1,144	1,481
Approved by Senate: by whole House	61	45	48	51
by committees	239	489	486	548
Total laws passed, both Houses	2,317	1,897	1,797	1,767

Source: *L'informatore CIPS, Elezioni politiche 1968*, No. 1, p. 12

In common with other Western European countries, legislative initiative is largely in the hands of the executive, but private members play a more important role than elsewhere (see Table 6.iv). At the same time, what is also clear is the immense legislative output of the Italian Parliament. If one compares Italian legislative activity with that of West Germany, the differences are startling. In the first West German Parliament (4-year term, 1949–53) 545 bills were passed as against 2317 in the first Italian Parliament (5-year term, 1948–53); and 497 and 424 compared with 1897 and 1797 in their respective second and third Parliaments. In the fourth Italian Parliament, the number was still high – 1767. It is not surprising, therefore, that much Italian legislation is confused, fragmentary and conflicting. In any event, this productive capacity would be impossible without the recourse to legislation by committee (see Table 6.iv) because both Houses spend less than a fifth of their time in plenary session on legislating. The greater part of it is dedicated to ideological motions, interpellations and the draft budgets. Further, since not only is 75 per cent of all legislation passed in committee, but 90 per cent of it unanimously, it is clear that the area of agreement between all parliamentarians regardless of party is very great, however violent the ideological clashes on the floor of both Houses.

During the first four Parliaments (1948–68), public and press were excluded from committee meetings despite their fundamental importance in the activity of the Italian Parliament. Moreover, a summary of proceedings was published only at a later date and not widely circulated. Hence their legislative activity was non-public and unpublicized legislation by small groups often representing special and vested interests. In 1968 both Houses undertook a detailed revision of their procedures. As a result, detailed reports of committee meetings are now available as well as closed-circuit television of proceedings for the benefit of journalists and interested members of the public.

One consequence of this situation is the rise in the proportion of Private Members' bills approved in the life of a Parliament from 12 per cent in the first to over 30 per cent in the fourth. Italy is one of the few countries which places no limit on the initiative of back-benchers. They have shown little restraint : in the first Parliament they presented 1155 bills in the Chamber and 650 in the Senate; in the fourth the numbers had risen to 3537 and 1481 respectively. Most of the legislation is of a minor nature. In fact the system clearly encourages the presentation of Private Members' bills in favour of either a restricted number of individuals, or of occupational categories, interest groups and localities. In addition, some Private Members' bills are inspired and drafted by sectional interests in the administration (i.e. administrative regulations and executive decrees). According to an analysis by Professor Predieri, 28 out of 29 Private Members' bills approved in the first semester of 1960 were bills in favour of sectional interests. Rare, and getting rarer, are Private Members' bills discussed outside the Standing Committees (less than 20 per cent in the first Parliament; down to circa 5 per cent in the fourth).

Thus while the Italian parliamentarians can boast that they do actually participate in the 'legislative power' more than most of their European colleagues, their activity is, nonetheless, similar as far as government bills are concerned: they sometimes amend, rarely reject, and usually sanction them. The success of government legislation depends as much on the humour of the Christian Democrat Party as on that of the coalition partners. In view of the Christian Democrats' dominance of the government coalition, and its strong position in Parliament, it is master of the legislative programme. No legislation can be passed without its approval; in this perspective the success of the Divorce Bill in 1970 was the exception that proves the rule. If the Christian Democrat factions are divided over an issue, as they have been over much of the centre-left's programme of social reform, then the legislation stagnates or is withdrawn. Jacques Nobécourt, the *Le Monde* correspondent in Rome, believes that the Italian Parliament has no reason to be envious of either the *Bundestag,* the House of Commons or the Assemblée Nationale as far as the debating and passing of basic legislation is concerned; and adds, 'the obvious complaints are simply a result of the regulations'.

One further legislative device established by the Constitution must be mentioned, because the implementing legislation has at last been approved. This is the possibility of repealing, a law totally or partially, by popular referendum; specifically excluded from these provisions are tax, budgetry and amnesty legislation, and treaties. On the demand of one fifth of either House, five Regional Assemblies, or 500,000 electors, a referendum must be held. It is supervised by the Constitutional Court, which is responsible for seeing that the correct procedure is adopted (right number of signatures etc.) All those eligible to vote for the Chamber of Deputies are entitled to vote in a referendum; and a simple majority of valid votes cast is all that it is required for the offending text to be repealed. To prevent the referendum being used to disrupt normal parliamentary legislation, four restrictions have been introduced : (1) the same bill may only be the object of one referendum during the life of a Parliament; (2) no referendum may be held in the first and last years of the life of a normal Parliament; (3) referenda can only be held on Sundays between 15 April and 15 June in each year; and (4) fifty days must elapse between the decree organizing the referendum and the vote.

No referendum has as yet been held under these provisions. However, as mentioned above, the opponents of the 1970 Divorce Law have collected the 500,000 signatures required for the holding of a referendum to repeal it. It was originally fixed for June 1972, but it was automatically suspended when the Chamber was dissolved in March 1972. It now appears that the first date when it can be held is April 1974. Nonetheless it is always open to Parliament to amend the Divorce Law and so obviate the holding of the referendum. Referenda have been rare in Italian history. Plebiscites were held in favour of unification in the territories annexed by the former Kingdom of Piedmont in 1860; and a constitutional referendum was held on the government's initiative in June 1946 to decide the institutional form of the new regime. Whereas the vote in favour of unification was overwhelming in 1860, in 1946 the Republicans defeated the Monarchists by a small majority of 2 million out of 23 million votes cast.

(d) PARLIAMENT AND THE CONTROL OF THE GOVERNMENT

The Constitution has furnished Parliament with a whole armoury for controlling the government. First and foremost the cabinet must have the confidence of the two Houses of Parliament. However the use of the vote of confidence depends on the organization of the parties in Parliament. While the cabinet commands an obedient parliamentary majority, it has little to fear from Parliament. One of the paradoxes of the Italian situation is that, although all governments are coalitions, and hence by definition lack a homogeneous majority, more cabinets fall as a result of internal discord than from an adverse vote in Parliament. This is because the parties are able to impose tight parliamentary discipline on their members. Moreover, in the Italian party situation the defeat of the government in Parliament is an inefficient

135

way of controlling the cabinet; a new coalition on virtually the same lines as its predecessor will be formed to go on from where the latter left off. Members of the government parties who are dissatisfied with government policy or legislation will endeavour to intervene in the party machinery before the Parliamentary vote. In fact, dissatisfaction with cabinet policy may well be the origin of the internal discord that causes a cabinet crisis.

A second method of control is through power of the purse. Here the same factors apply, i.e. the power of party discipline in all parliamentary votes. The situation is worsened by a number of general factors. In the first place, national budgets are very complex; few members can understand even the simplified versions prepared to help them. In addition, the budgets do not include the expenditures of many state and parastate agencies, even though they are formally accountable to Parliament. 'Their real budgets', as one observer has noted, 'are disguised.' In such a situation, it is not surprising that Parliament makes no real effort to examine them critically. In the second place, the limitation of budgeting for one year is not compatible with rational policy-making or efficient administration. Long-range planning demands that sums be committed for several years in advance; this is what, in fact, happens, but it is disguised. Moreover, Parliament only examines in any detail the provisional budgets and not the real expenditure. Hence it accepts the *fait accompli* and abdicates any real attempt to control expenditure critically. Nobécourt has remarked that 'the Chambers examine the budgets beforehand, but only study the balance sheets late and in haste.' In the third place, the clientele pressures put on back-benchers lead them to interesting themselves in and even contesting minor points of detail (a swimming pool or a school, or even a hospital, in their constituency and not in another locality) rather than the main lines of the budget. Interest groups of national dimensions intervene at an earlier stage with party leaders, or with the administration in the preparation of the budget. Hence the real struggle over the size and direction of the budget takes place before its presentation to Parliament, either at the planning stage, or in the Council of Ministers for the final arbitration.

A third possible method of control is through questions posed by individual parliamentarians, but it does not seem to have become a method of controlling the government in Italy. Both written and oral questions tend to get written replies; the government keeping oral replies to a minimum. Hence questions rarely lead to discussion or debate. For a debate, a motion must be presented, so there is nothing like the question time in the British House of Commons. Italian parliamentarians also prefer to write directly to Ministers or ministerial departments to hasten administrative decisions which interest them rather than ask questions. They do ask questions (over 20,000 per Parliament), but these are asked to obtain information and are not intended to control the government; they are used more as a means of demonstrating to their constituents their solicitude for local interests than as an effective weapon for bringing pressure on the government.

Executive-Legislative Relations

The Italian Constitution follows classic liberal doctrine in defining the Republican regime in terms of the relations between the executive and legislature. Republican Italy has a parliamentary government because the executive is politically responsible to the legislature. But we may ask if this statement has much political meaning. We have observed that, although cabinet instability is a characteristic of the Italian political system, it is not adverse votes in Parliament which have been responsible. Cabinets have resigned either as a result of disagreement between coalition partners or, more often, as a result of internal struggles in the Christian Democrat Party. Until recently, the dissolution of Parliament – the weapon with which the executive is provided in classic liberal doctrine to discipline Parliament – had not been contemplated. Moreover its use by President Leone in March 1972 was not to discipline Parliament but as a means of avoiding the feared consequences of a deteriorating economic and political situation and in particular the referendum on the Divorce Law.

A dissolution is unlikely to resolve a political crisis in Italy because party representation under proportional representation is not likely to be changed sufficiently to make the operation worthwhile. It would require very exceptional political circumstances, such as the dramatic situation of 1948, to destroy the underlying stability of the Italian electorate. And, given the static nature of the PR electoral system, it would require massive electoral swings towards one party to change parliamentary representation significantly. The truths of these assertions was amply borne out by the results of the elections of 7 May 1972. Moreover the formation of a new 'Centrist' coalition (DC, PSDI, PLI and PRI) by Andreotti in July 1972 for the first time in ten years which was their political consequence was already possible in the dissolved Parliament.

Assuming that a dissolution could resolve a political crisis by throwing up a coherent majority, it is always likely to be an exceptional occurrence. Elections are financially costly and parties are, therefore, anxious to avoid unnecessary expenditure. The system of preference voting for the Chamber of Deputies is expensive for individual candidates too; it also gives rise to a considerable amount of uncertainty in the sense that the turnover of successful candidates is high. Moreover, the pressures to become and remain a parliamentarian are high both in prestige and perquisites. No deputy would like to lose a life pension or other entitlements owing to an early dissolution and the loss of his seat. In consequence, the pressure on the executive from its back-bench parliamentarians against premature dissolutions will always be intense.

It is clear from what has been said that, despite cabinet instability, the executive dominates the legislature; and that both have been dominated by party rule, or *partitocrazia*, as many Italian political commentators despairingly call it. They claim that it has deformed the functioning of parliamentary institutions in Italy because the life of cabinets is decided by party executives and not parliamentary votes. They overlook the fact that parties are a fundamental feature of the life of all parliaments; and that the party leaders who are responsible for the party decisions are almost all parliamentarians. What they are bemoaning, in fact, is not so much party rule in itself but the inability of the ruling class to control party representation in Parliament.

7 Public Administration and the Military: Bureaucracy, Enterprise and Repression

Liberal constitutional doctrine is clear and unambiguous about the position of the public administration and the military; they are the instruments of democratic rule. They are subordinate to the executive and legislative powers. The government lays down the policy with the assistance of Parliament, and the administration and the military execute and administer it, each in their respective spheres. This doctrine underlies the arrangements adopted in the Italian Constitution. Thus the Prime Minister is not only responsible for directing the general policy of the government, but also for maintaining the unity of political and administrative direction, and co-ordination. In addition, Article 97 states that 'the public offices are organized according to legal dispositions in such a fashion as to ensure the effectiveness and impartiality of administration'; and Article 98 that 'public employees are exclusively at the service of the nation'. Finally, limitations on the right of affiliation with political parties for certain categories of public officials (judges, policemen and diplomats) and serving soldiers (officers) are also sanctioned.

In practice no one believes any more in the existence of a clear distinction between policy and execution, yet the theoretical presumption of such a distinction is the cause of much ambiguity. It forces observers to think in terms of 'policy' and 'execution' when all decisions are an amalgam of both. It also leads political scientists to discuss the relative influence on decisions of politicians and civil servants instead of examining where the ideas which determine the final decisions come from, and how they are brought into play. In saying what is really very obvious we must not overlook the specific functions of the administration and the military which give them their power and influence. The public administration and the military were created as instruments of government with specific functions which give them certain political weapons : the principal are a virtual monopoly of information in the case of the administration; and a virtual monopoly of arms in the case of the military. This means that they have the means for putting their viewpoint as a group in any political conflict. The fact that they control these weapons does not mean that they will push the logic of their situation to its logical conclusion, but any serious political analysis cannot afford to overlook this possibility.

We need to bear in mind that no part of the state system exists in a vacuum : the relations of the public administration and the military with the other institutions of the state system depend on their own social cohesion (i.e. recruitment and training) and on their links with civil society. In fact discussion of the public administration involves such questions as its organization, the character of its personnel, the subjects over which it has control, and the extent of the effective jurisdiction of its authority; and that of the military concerns questions such as the scope of its involvement in society, the character of its personnel, and its technical capacity.

The Italian Administrative System

The Italian administrative system consists of a complex of ministries, autonomous agencies, separate administrations, public and quasi-public corporations with varying legal relations with Ministers, the other state institutions and among themselves. The system is so complex that La Malfa, when, as Minister without Portfolio, he was entrusted with an inquiry into government holdings and agencies in 1951, described the whole sector as 'an uncharted jungle'; and a decade later Fanfani, as Prime Minister, declared that 'the public administration is really a clandestine organization, no one knows anything at all about it'. La Malfa claimed in his report to have found over a thousand different state undertakings and agencies, not counting provincial and communal ramifications which would have pushed the number into several thousands. As Professor Chapman has noted 'their status, their structure, the forms of control to which they were subject, and their place in the machinery of government was utterly incoherent. Some were public bodies, some were private firms, some technically autonomous state institutions. The legal status of some of these enterprises was so obscure that the courts were continually giving widely divergent judgments as to their position.'

The reason for this situation was succinctly summarized by the old Socialist leader, Pietro Nenni, when he told a journalist in 1967 that 'the Italian State was created in little bits, by sectors, a little royalist bit, a little Fascist bit, a little corporative bit, a little socialist bit. It is also true that many institutions appear to become worn out after twenty years . . .' But he forgot to add that instead of being lopped off, the dead wood is left to survive as best it can. Thus despite a measure of reform introduced into the system by the creation of the Ministry of State Holdings in 1956 to act as a holding agency for all branches of industrial and commercial activity and to assume responsibility for their supervision instead of the different ministerial departments, the Italian administrative system still remains a complicated network of institutions and agencies, long overdue for reform. For example, even after the reorganization of the Ministry of the Budget in 1965–7 to permit it to undertake economic planning, economic affairs remained split up between three ministries: Treasury (State Funds and Public Debt) and Finance (Collecting Revenue) as well as Budget (Economic Policy). The easiest way to approach its organization is to separate the traditional form of administration by ministerial department from the other state agencies which have escaped from the ministerial departments. This is what we have done. Nonetheless, we must mention that the Italian administration is expected to be legally as well as politically accountable. Two independent agencies, the Council of State (*Consiglio di Stato*) and the Court of Exchequer (*Corte dei Conti*) exist to exercise legal and financial controls, but since their major functions are judicial, they are treated later on.

(a) GOVERNMENT BY MINISTRY

Ministerial departments are still the core of the central administration in Italy as they are in every other Western European country. Initially, because the majority of pre-unification Italian states had

Table 7. i

Organization of Ministerial Departments 1970

Presidenza del Consiglio dei Ministri
(*Cabinet Office*)
Press Office
Central Statistical Office (ISTAT)
National Centre for Research (CNR)
Interministerial Committees
  (CIP, CIPE, etc.)

Ministry of Foreign Affairs
Staff and Administration
Ceremonies
Political Affairs
Economic Affairs
Emigration and Social Affairs
Cultural Relations
Overseas Offices (Insp. Gen.)
Press and Information
Diplomatic Careers, Treaties and Leg.
Documentation and Archives

Ministry of the Interior
Staff and Administration
Public Security
Civil Administration
Public Welfare
Civil Protection and Fire Services
Religious Affairs
Religious Funds and Aid
State Archives

Ministry of Justice
Judicial Organization and
  Administration
Civil Affairs and Liberal Professions
Penal Affairs
Prisons and Penitentiaries

Ministry of Budget and Economic Planning
Staff and Administration
Planning
Execution of Plan

Ministry of Finance
Staff and Administration
Fees and Indirect Taxes on businesses
Claims
Customs Duties and Indirect Taxes
Comparative leg. studies and
  Int. Rels.
Direct Taxes
Real Property Taxes
State Property
Local Finance

Organization of Tax Services
Extraordinary Finance
Lotteries (Insp. Gen.)

Ministry of Treasury
Staff and Administration
General Accounting Office
Treasury
Public Debt
Deposits and Credit Funds
Welfare Agencies
War Pensions
War Damages
Special Services and Claims
General Purchasing Office

Ministry of Defence
General Staff of Defence
Legislation and Legal Matters
Budget and Financial Matters
Organizational Matters,
  Mechanization and Statistics
Military Preparations
Administrative Inspections

Army
Personnel – Officers
Civil Personnel and General Matters
NCOs, Other Ranks and National
  Servicemen
Artillery
Defence Supplies
Establishments and Administration
Military Health
Motor Transport (Insp. General)

Navy
Personnel and General Matters
Naval Construction
Naval Health
Naval Establishments

Air Force
Personnel and General Matters
Aircraft supplies
Aircraft Construction and Armaments
Provisioning and Airports
Airfield property
Airforce Establishment

Carabinieri
Commandant General
Military Chaplaincy

Ministry of State Holdings
State Holdings

Ministry of Education
Staff and Administration
Primary Education
Secondary Education (First grade)
Arts, Sciences and Teacher Training
Technical Training
Professional Training
University Education
Antiquities and Fine Arts
Academies and Libraries
Diffusion of Culture
Adult Education
Cultural Exchanges
Private Intermediate Schools
School Building and Supplies
Artistic Education (Ins. Gen.)
School Upkeep (Ins. Gen.)
Physical Education (Ins. Gen.)
Pensions (Ins. Gen.)

Ministry of Public Works
Staff and Administration
Roads and New Railway Construction
Water and Hydro-electric Works
Maritime Works
Public Housing
Health Works
Town and Country Planning
Disaster Relief

Ministry of Agriculture
Staff and Administration
Agricultural Production
Land Reclamation and Resettlement
Land Improvement
Economic Control of Agric. Products
Mountain Economy and Forests
Food

Ministry of Transport and Civil Aviation
State Railways
Civil Motorways and Transport
  Concessions
Civil Aviation
Coordination

Ministry of Posts and Telecommunications
Staff and Administration
Posts and Telecommunications

Ministry of Industry
Staff and Administration
Energy Supplies and Basic Industries
Industrial Production
Mines
Artisans and Small Industry
Internal Commerce and Industrial
  Consumption
Private Insurance and Collective
  Interest

Ministry of Labour and Social Welfare
Staff and Administration
Labour Relations
Professional Training of Workers
Employment of Labour
Welfare and Social Security
Cooperation

Ministry of Foreign Trade
Staff and Administration
Trade Agreements
Valuations
Development of Trade
Imports
Exports

Ministry of Mercantile Marine
Staff and Administration
Shipping
Navigation and Maritime Traffic
Maritime and Port Labour
Maritime and Port Property
Maritime Fishing

Ministry of Health
Staff and Administration
Public Health
Social Medicine
Veterinary Services
Pharmaceutical Services

Ministry of Tourism and Entertainment
Staff and Administration
Tourism
Entertainment

Source: Presidenza del Consiglio dei Ministri, *L'Ordinamento costituzionale e amministrativo dello stato* (Rome, 1971), pp. 35–48

adopted the Napoleonic administrative system, government was carried out by five principal departments: Foreign Affairs, Justice, Finance, Defence and War, and Internal Affairs. The first four ministries had reasonably clearly defined fields of administration, and the public services that they provided fitted into a coherent pattern. The fifth ministry held the residual powers of government which, as Professor Chapman has observed, Ministries of the Interior or Home Affairs still do everywhere in Western Europe today. Under the pressure of rising industrialization and social changes, the public services were extended by entrusting the government with new functions. Thus the number of ministries had doubled by the end of the century; and during the First World War they grew from eleven to sixteen. Today there are nineteen ministries (see Table 7.i), which is more than in most other modern liberal democratic states and which, it has been claimed leads, to additional waste and inefficiency.

Each ministry is formally headed by a minister who flanks himself with his own personal cabinet composed of political collaborators. His *chef de cabinet* can be either a civil servant of middle or upper rank (usually he is a prefect), or an outsider. In either case he is expected to be loyal to the Minister and to see to it so far as he can that his policies are implemented. The main branches of the ministry are directorates (*direzioni generali*) which carry out the major functions of the ministry (see Table 7.i). Each directorate is headed by a Director-General, who is the senior civil servant in charge of his department, although some minor directorates are directed by Inspector-Generals. The directorates are subdivided into divisions under a Head of Division; and divisions are, in turn, subdivided into sections under the responsibility of a Head of Section. For example, the five directorates of the Ministry of Foreign Affairs are divided into geographical or topical divisions. In addition, there are a number of services: ceremonial, press, etc.

It is claimed that nothing occurs within a directorate without the personal approval of the Director-General. Certainly the opposition of the Director General concerned is fatal to a project. Moreover, it is a frequent complaint among civil servants lower down in the chain of command that decisions are held in abeyance pending the signatures of Heads of Section or Division, Inspector-Generals or Director-Generals, and not infrequently of the Ministers themselves. It is generally agreed that there is very little if any delegation of authority. Paradoxically, one of the consequences of the great centralization of authority in the administration is that effective power is somewhat dispersed. As a result of overwork, those at the top are unable to review all the decisions coming from below for signature. Hence they often sign what appear to be uncontroversial decisions without being fully aware of the content or implication. Similarly, those below are often careless because they assume that all decisions will be reviewed at the top: the upshot is confusion and fragmentation.

There is no one civil servant in charge of the ministry comparable to the British Permanent Under-Secretary. Instead there is a Council of Administration composed of all the director-generals, the under-secretaries and the Minister. The Foreign Office is an exception to this pattern because, like the French *Quai d'Orsay*, it has a Secretary-General above the director-generals, as does the Ministry of Defence, so as to unite the previous three service ministries. In the other ministries, co-ordination is left to the political leadership, to the under-secretaries (unless there are problems of incompatibility arising out of factional or party differences) or the *chef de cabinet*, or, in the last resort, to the Minister himself. The lack of any effective co-ordinating agency in most ministries results in overlapping of functions and jurisdictional uncertainties. Moreover the situation is compounded by a number of specific factors. First, ministerial offices are dispersed round the capital. It has been calculated that the central administration occupies some fifty thousand different premises in Rome spread all round the city and not fitted into any coherent pattern, so that two offices of the same ministry that work in close liaison often find themselves several kilometres apart and have to communicate by a messenger on foot, or by motorcycle in cases of great urgency. Second, there is no coherent legislation governing the organization of the public administration; Professor Spreafico claimed a few years ago that a hypothetical estimate suggested that it was regulated by more than 100,000 laws and regulations. 'Laws are added to laws', he wrote, 'in inextricable confusion, often slovenly and hastily framed, their texts obscure and full of error. It so happens that it is almost always difficult to establish which are the dispositions in force in a specific field at a specific moment, resulting in loss of time and serious disorganization.' Third, many matters are often dealt with by several ministries : public health is administered by eleven different ministries and public agencies; vocational training by twelve, etc. The result of all this is obvious : interference and duplication, slow and disorganized activity which is both costly and inefficient. It is no wonder that the uncertainties about the actual position of the different components of a ministry lead each to look after its own affairs.

All ministries have special advisory bodies to help them with administrative action and legislative policy. These administrative advisory bodies, like the Supreme Defence Council of the Ministry of Defence, or the National Health Council of the Ministry of Health, or the Council of Agriculture of the Ministry of Agriculture, are extremely varied in scope and membership. All combine civil servants and outsiders; in some cases membership is by ministerial appointment (Supreme Defence Council); in others (Council of Agriculture) it is by election from client groups (i.e. interest groups). Similarly, in some cases consultation is obligatory; in others it is optional. As Professor LaPalombara has remarked : 'While advice is in no instance binding, it is nevertheless an important means whereby decisions can be conditioned and hedged in. It is natural, therefore, that these advisory bodies have become foci for interest-group action on the administration.'

One advisory body, the National Council of Economy and Labour, was given constitutional status as an auxiliary body. Established in 1957, it is authorized to give its opinion on legislation on requests from the government, Parliament or the regional assemblies. Thus, for example, in 1965 the government asked for its opinion on the important questions of economic planning (consultation made obligatory), the second agricultural plan, labour disputes, social medicine, export credit facilities and company reform. Its opinions aroused such a favourable response from public opinion that the government took increasing account of them. It can also propose legislation to Parliament on its own account, although it has made little use of this initiative. In fact it waited until 1966 before it proposed a bill (on hours of work). Finally, it is authorized to carry out studies and inquiries with a view to presenting concrete proposals for reforms, as it did on social security in 1963, and the social situation in 1966, etc. It is composed of seventy-nine members chosen on a corporative basis from names put forward by the various social and economic organizations and from experts nominated by the President of the Republic, who serve for a five-year term. Its activity was such in the sixties that the government proposed a reform that would give it an organic place in the legislative and administrative process, but so far this remains a proposal.

All ministries have their field services. In fact the same hierarchical pattern that can be found in the central administration is found in the provinces; each ministry has a chain of command that extends from the centre in Rome down to the local offices, but some only have regional offices (like the Ministry of Public Works), others provincial offices (the majority), and a few have offices in the larger communes (Ministry of Labour : Labour Exchanges, etc.). Until now the prefect has been the major representative of the government and chief field agent of the Ministry of the Interior in the provinces. He enjoys general powers of command and intervention only with regard to the services of his own ministry – over civil servants of the prefecture itself, over the *Questura* (Police Headquarters), over the provincial fire brigade, and over the Mayors (*qua* state officials – see Chapter 9). Unlike the French prefect, he has no statutory authority to direct or co-ordinate state services in the provinces, i.e. he has no power to intervene in the various chains of command running from the ministries in Rome to their specialized field offices. In this sense there was more integration and co-ordination at the provincial level under Fascism, when the prefect was made the co-ordinator and supervisor of all public authorities in the province, than in the postwar period. With the transfer of powers to the newly created Regional Governments, some of the prefects' powers have passed to the regions. A Government Commissioner resident in the regional capital now only exercises the central government's powers of supervision over the region; powers of control have passed to a control committee. The provincial prefect remains responsible for the maintenance of public order, the supervision of certain local organizations and of public works carried out locally, but financed by the central government, etc. Similarly, some ministerial functions have passed to the regions (see Chapter 9).

(b) GOVERNMENT BY SPECIAL AGENCY

Public intervention in economic and social life began early in Italy. The Terni steel works were founded in 1884 to supply raw materials for the navy, but the really substantial developments had to wait until the first decade of this century. The Liberal leader Giolitti nationalized the railways and telephones while local governments municipalized a wide variety of public utilities; and a little later social welfare became a state responsibility. As a result of these developments, we can divide government activity by special agency into four categories.

First are the *amministrazione* or *aziende autonome* (autonomous enterprises) which control and administer the railways and telephone services, the postal and telegraph services, the State monopolies (like salt and tobacco, motorways, bananas etc.). They are entirely state financed and possess a slightly higher degree of autonomy than ministerial departments because their general administration is under the control of a separate Chairman and Board of Directors. The Minister responsible merely lays down the general lines of policy, but does not interfere with day-to-day running. In addition, they have a separate and independent budget from the ministry to which they are attached and publish separate balance sheets. Although attached to different ministries, according to the object of their activity, they are regarded as a single group of agencies because they have a similar legal physiognomy. They are distinguished from the state controlled industrial holding companies because of their closer relationship (i.e. less administrative and financial autonomy) with the traditional machinery of government.

The second are the major institutions, National Institute for Social Security (INPS) National Institute for Workers' Compensation (INAIL) and National Health Insurance Institute (INAM) etc., which are responsible for social security. Italian social security consists of a conglomerate of protective systems, generally based on insurance principles, and not of a single integrated system. Moreover, its scope has been enlarged – particularly in the extension of coverage to broad categories of non-wage earners – not by means of integration but by juxtaposition. Hence it is extremely complicated, because social security legislation is applied through a large number of distinct schemes, each of which, in principle, enjoys administrative and financial autonomy under state supervision. The various schemes are largely financed through employer and employee contributions for each worker and his family, supplemented by state subsidies (which are considerable). Coverage is complete: medical visits, prescription charges and hospitalization are all either free or refunded. Most doctors take part in these schemes despite low fees. One reason why the government has preferred to create and extend a whole series of special institutions rather than institute a ministry to administer a single scheme is that there already existed a wide network of Church-controlled charity, health, and welfare institutions as well as local relief agencies and some private business schemes. However there is increasing pressure for the administration of the various social security schemes to be entrusted to a single institution through a gradual process of unification.

The various insurance institutions are public corporations subject to public administrative law, with a separate legal personality and independent management, but since the War under the supervision of the Ministry of Labour and Social Security. The Minister lays down the policy guide-lines but does not intervene in the general activity of the institutions, which have built up enormous financial resources from the subscriptions and subsidies that they have received. For example, in 1964 INPS was providing pension insurance for over 19 million workers and family allowances covering about 7 million insured persons and receiving payments equivalent to 8 per cent of the national income. The institutions' internal organization is constructed according to the familiar pyramidal pattern of public administrations. This fact probably helps to explain why they have remained administratively separate from state intervention in other spheres of economic and social life. For example, all three institutions make available funds for industrial development, but they, not the government, retain the control of the utilization of their funds.

The third group consists of the so-called *enti autonomi di gestione* or 'administrative bodies' of which the best known are IRI (*Instituto per la Ricostruzione Industriale*) and ENI (*Ente Nationale Idrocarburi*). IRI was a bi-product of the inter-war depression; it was created as a temporary body to disengage the leading banks, threatened with ruin, from involvement in industry. Its task was to reorganize the banks' industrial holdings and sell them back to private interests. For various reasons (the difficulty of disposing of certain assets, and then the needs of a war economy) this did not happen, and IRI was transformed into a permanent industrial holding institution in 1937. But, as Posner and Woolf have observed, 'the way in which IRI had obtained its assets determined the new method of exercising state control, and was to have important consequences in the postwar period. For while IRI was itself a public law corporation, wholly owned by the State, but with considerable legal and financial autonomy, the firms it acquired in 1933, and continued to acquire in certain sectors remained joint-stock companies operating under private law : IRI kept a controlling interest, but private investors also held shares ... Thus emerged a public industrial sector with the same legal structure and *modus operandi* as the private sector.' ENI was created out of the General Italian Petroleum Agency (AGIP) in 1953 mainly to develop domestic resources of natural gas and keep them under state control; and in 1962 the centre-left government nationalized the private electrical industry and created a new public corporation ENEL (*Ente Nazionale di Energia Elettrica*) on similar lines (but with a number of significant differences as regards financial operations and made responsible to Ministry of Industry); more recently, it created several other holdings, EFIM, GEPI, etc. to aid various industries with their liquidity problems. Nonetheless, whatever the reasons for the creation of these bodies, it has become clear that their chief function has become increasingly one of giving the government a wide influence in the national economy, and it is this aspect which has attracted the attention of foreign observers.

The pattern of state organization in the industrial sphere can best be described as a three-tiered structure. At the base are the individual firms which continue to be joint stock-companies subject to private company law; they are grouped under and responsible to various public corporations and stockholding companies, which are responsible, in turn, to IRI and ENI which are responsible to the Ministry of State Holdings which stands at the apex of the pyramid. The *enti di gestione* stand, as it were, as a buffer between the ministry and the individual companies. The Minister has a number of statutory powers of control including the right to approve IRI's and ENI's general investment programmes and their means of obtaining finance; the government is also represented on IRI's and ENI's Boards of Directors and has the power of appointment of the Chairmen and managers. In practice the relationship between IRI and ENI and the Ministry has never extended beyond consultation : the Minister lays down the general policy directives which coordinate the programmes of both corporations, and the latter are responsible for their execution by co-ordinating financially and technically the various holding or operating companies which retain executive responsibility for running their own concerns. 'The underlying theory', Posner and Woolf have remarked, 'was that this type of structure guaranteed what was frequently described as "the speed and secrecy" requisite for action in an open market, and so ensured freedom from bureaucratic interference, as well as the stimulus of private competition thought necessary for efficient management. Not only was direct material control curtailed, but parliamentary financial control was restricted to the *enti di gestione,* exempting the operative companies from submitting their balance sheets to the *Corte dei conti.*'

IRI now controls some 150 firms engaged in such diverse activities as iron and steel production, shipbuilding and merchant shipping, chemical production and civil engineering, banking and public utilities (telephones, radio and television, motorways and airlines), as well as the manufacture of a whole range of products from motor cars and electronic equipment to domestic appliances. ENI controls 160 companies mainly concerned with the exploitation, production and distribution of oil and natural gas, but has also developed interests in the transportation, refining and marketing of petroleum products. Thus it has spread into nuclear energy, chemicals, textiles, plant engineering and building construction. ENEL has so far restricted itself to the electrical energy field, where it had much to do to rationalize a notoriously inefficient industry. Finally, however similar IRI and ENI are in formal organization and structure, they have been worlds apart in men and methods. As the radical economic journalist, Eugenio Scalfari, has observed 'ENI under Mattei had all the characteristics of a fief as regards its complete independence of the government and the undisputed authority of its head. IRI on the contrary found itself in a very different situation : its direction was exercised by a collegiate leadership not an undisputed head, the internal structure of the group was not centralized but decentralized, and its relations with the government were not those of proud autonomy but of discreet and silent reciprocal influence.' Moreover Scalfari adds that Cefis's succession to Mattei's post changed nothing in ENI's internal power structure or its relations with the government. Reaction to these methods on the introduction of economic planning led to the central administration receiving greater and more explicit control of both ENI and IRI than hitherto. For example, new formal procedures for approving the investment programmes of the *enti di gestione* were introduced on the reorganization of the Ministry of the Budget in 1967. But, as Scalfari concludes, from the power point of view 'the centre-left and economic planning did not succeed in changing anything. The ENI fief on the threshold of the 1970's is stronger and more autonomous than ever.'

The fourth category consists of the special institutions created to promote economic development. The first of these was the *Cassa per il Mezzogiorno* (Southern Development Fund), the control of which was vested in a special interministerial committee, the *Comitato dei Ministri per il Mezzogiorno*, because it was intended to have an extraordinary character (i.e. it was intended to carry on additional activity and *not* to replace traditional government activity in the South). A similar procedure was adopted for economic planning in the sixties, with the creation of the National Committee for Economic Planning (CNPE) in 1962, which was transformed in 1969 into the Interministerial Committee on Economic Planning (CIPE). Because both were multisectoral (i.e. covering the activities of several ministries) and co-ordination was of the essence, it was believed that an interministerial committee was the best agency to direct their activity. Unfortunately these new institutional arrangements fell foul of the traditional forms of government machinery since they were dependent on the traditional machinery of government for the execution of their projects, and this was often inadequate. Hence it is hardly surprising that the Southern policy did not produce the results originally anticipated; and while it is too early to pass a final verdict on economic planning, the results so far are not encouraging. In November 1971, the government took a step towards simplifying procedures: it abolished the Interministerial Committee for the South and transferred its functions to CIPE. In addition, it changed the role of the *Cassa*, turning it into a planning and advisory body for regional and inter-regional special projects.

The whole problem of the relations between ministerial departments and special agencies has been succinctly summarized by Gabriele Pescatore, the former Chairman of the Southern Development Fund.

In attempting to summarize in a comprehensive manner the overall action carried out by the State in the postwar period, it seems possible to say that its intervention has followed two different lines of economic policy. In other words, while the extraordinary intervention was conceived and developed on the basis of an organic planning policy, the intervention of the ordinary administration does not appear to have evolved in response to an integrated [global] vision of economic policy. This has meant a great imbalance in the complex of state action in the South, as the activity of the Fund has ultimately remained isolated from an organic and wide context of traditional interventions, so much so that the special interventions have produced results inferior to those that should have been achieved.... The formula adopted by Parliament in creating the Fund was a compromise.... The complex integration of the Fund within the organic framework has been prevented by what we have called the lack of homogeneity between the type of intervention of this new institution and that of the ordinary administration. From this point of view, one cannot overlook the fact that the compromise adopted by Parliament has ended in the main in being more harmful than favourable to the special institutions.

The Civil Service: Structure and Recruitment

The Italian civil service, like that of most Western European countries, is divided into four classes: the administrative (*carriere direttive*), executive (*carriere di concetto*), clerical (*carriere esecutive*), and messengerial (*carriere del personale ausilario*). Briefly, the administrative class is responsible for the general supervision of the work of the entire ministry, for preparing and advising the Minister on major questions which require his decision, and for dealing with the whole field of government policy as it affects and is affected by the work of the ministry. The executive class comprises the staff responsible for the detailed management of routine business, for supervising the clerical class, for the day to day operation of the more complicated branches of administration, for taking decisions which do not involve questions of administrative principle or ministerial policy, and for assisting and preparing the work of the administrative class. The clerical class comprises the typists, secretaries, mechanical and counter staff. The messenger class is made up of porters, messengers, chauffeurs, and other odd-jobmen, like the numerous ushers (*bidelli*) one finds in Italian ministries. In addition, the Italian civil service recruits a number of specialists as well as general administrators: engineers, economists and scientists, but like most European countries it has found difficulty in recruiting an adequate number of technical experts, with the honourable exception of hydraulic, transport and civil engineers. Finally, it must be remembered that teachers and judges are also permanent state employees (see Table 7.ii).

Table 7. ii
State Employees by Category

	1 July 1948	1 July 1958	1 Jan. 1970
Ministries			
judges	4,684	6,282	14,112
civil servants	151,609	178,801	184,213
teachers	210,933	316,836	602,116
military	266,836	316,650	356,719
workers	99,598	60,135	} 165,746
non-specified	12,575	3,837	
Total	746,235	882,541	1,322,907
Aziende Autonome			
civil servants	297,013	267,624	188,682
teachers	—	—	2
workers	30,821	23,672	} 185,450
non-specified	346	47	
Total	328,180	291,343	374,113
Grand Total	1,074,415	1,173,884	1,697,020

Source: A. Spreafico, *L'amministrazione e il cittadino* (Milan, 1965), p. 71 and ISTAT, *Annuario Statistico, 1971*.

The four classes of civil servants number some 200,000 persons, of whom 30,000 make up the administrative class of higher civil servants. The higher civil servants are the key group in the public administration because it is they as a group who determine the nature of the administration as a corps (i.e. its attitudes and activity). They are unevenly distributed throughout the administrative machine. For example, the Ministries of Finance, Treasury, Interior and Agriculture have a large number of higher civil servants, while those of Mercantile Marine, Tourism, the Cabinet Office and State Holdings have very few. Indeed the latter was restricted to an overall staff of one hundred by Parliament when it was created in 1956, such was the official horror of bureaucracy! Professor Kogan reports that in 1961 the Foreign Office had a supernumerary staff in the messengerial class but was unable to fill all the 528 posts in the diplomatic-consular corps. In addition, numerous ministries and special agencies have depleted research sections or none at all because they are unable to staff them.

Entry into the Italian civil service is by written examination. Candidates for the administrative class must have either obtained a university degree or reached the rank of assistant secretary in the executive class. Similarly candidates for the executive class must possess the secondary school leaving certificate, or have reached the rank of archivist in the clerical class and possess the intermediate secondary school certificate. Unlike Great Britain, Italy has no Civil Service Commission; each ministry announces and holds its own examinations. An examination commission must formally be appointed for each examination, and the syllabuses announced. In the two higher classes there must be at least two written papers, and there are also oral examinations on related subjects. Attempts are being made to limit the very frequent reservation of a percentage of posts to certain categories of persons (orphans, children of war widows and veterans etc.).

Recruitment by written examination is intended as a means of selecting candidates on merit. To do so presupposes that the examinations are conducted impartially, and are appropriate. A study of middle and higher civil servants carried out by ISAP in 1965–6 indicates that the majority consider the entry examinations neither impartial nor appropriate. As one academic examiner for the Diplomatic Corps told Professor Kogan in 1958, 'I know the Diplomatic examination is supposed to be beyond influence. If it is, it is the only one in Italy, and I still don't believe it.' In other words the suggestion is that political recommendations and clientele connections play their role here as they do in the appointment to special and temporary posts (for their numbers, see non-

F*

specified in Table 7.ii above). In addition, the examinations have remained of a general type, being more of a test of a generalist than a specific culture, humanistic rather than technical; and hence unconsciously favour candidates cast in the social and intellectual mould of existing higher civil servants. Finally, specialized training in administration for higher civil servants is still in its infancy. The *Scuola Superiore della Pubblica Amministrazione* set up in the Royal Palace in Caserta in the early sixties has had, as yet, little impact on civil service methods and thinking; it offers only two-month training courses of uncoordinated lectures by an ever changing staff.

Entry into the higher civil service ensures the successful candidate of a life-time career. No one has ever failed to survive the eighteen-months probation period. Poor performance leads, at most, to being overlooked in promotion, but generally not even this, as promotion is largely by seniority. As long as he does not commit some irreparable howler, the civil servant will make a dignified career. Appointment to top posts (Director-General and Prefect) and specifically to the key top posts (the Auditor-General, Director General of the Treasury, Director-General of Civil Administration in the Ministry of the Interior, Secretary-General in both the Foreign Office and Defence Ministries, etc.) involves party politics. As we have already observed, appointment to a particular key post is a test of power between the coalition partners, or between the Christian Democrat factions, that may involve Ministers, the cabinet, the President of the Republic and party executives. The failure of a party or faction to get their man appointed is evidence of its weakness; success becomes a symbol of strength.

Hard data on the personnel selected by these methods are hard to come by. In Italy, as in the rest of Western Europe, there are few reliable statistics available on the social origins of civil servants. In general, we can accept Professor Chapman's description of the origins of the Western European civil services as being generally true of Italy. 'Excluding the industrial workers,' he writes, 'the public service epitomizes the various levels of the middle class. The clerical official representing the lower middle class, the executive official the middle middle-class, the administrative official the upper middle class. Even when their salary scales do not fully correspond to their position in society, the different grades of the public service adopt the social customs and outlook of their appropriate social grading'. An unofficial survey published in 1960 revealed the following data on the social origin of the civil service: (father's occupation) civil servant: 50.3 per cent; professional and businessmen: 18.7 per cent; worker or artisan: 17.4 per cent; landowner or farmer: 10.9 per cent. Other data suggest that a greater proportion come from the lower as opposed to the upper middle class than in other Western European countries. Regional origin is set out in Table 7.iii. From this it is clear that the two major characteristics of the civil service are that it is middle class and comes predominantly from the South.

Table 7. iii
Region of Birth of Groups of Higher Public Officials, 1963

	Population	Administrative class	Prefects	Directors General	Ordinary judges	Administrative judges (1968)
	%	%	%	%	%	%
North	44·6	13·7	6·0	11·5	7·0	8·9
Centre	18·6	21·3	18·1	26·0	16·0	25·9
South	24·7	40·7	54·1	46·9	{77·0}	46·3
Islands	12·1	24·3	21·8	15·6		18·9
N.		(31,717)	(133)	(96)	(5,703)	(624)

Sources: A. Spreafico, *L'amministrazione e il cittadino*, p. 151; and E. Colasanti, 'La magistratura amministrativa italiana: un profilo statistico', in *Politica del Diretto* (February 1971), pp. 113, 130.

The most obvious reason for the predominance of southerners is the comparatively poor pay of civil servants. It is often half or a third of the salaries that can be had for comparable positions in private industry. Given the lack of alternative employment in the South and the limited opportunities of private law practice in its provincial centres, the civil service seems a more attractive proposition to southern graduates than to their northern counterparts. It must be remembered that the universities of Rome and the South are responsible for two-thirds of the country's law graduates. Moreover, the civil servants receive important fringe benefits like pensions, paid leave for various reasons, good holidays, excellent severance pay based on seniority, free health care, indemnities for loss of health due to the job, and a thirteenth-month's salary in addition to security of tenure.

The consequences of this situation are striking. It leads to the phenomenon of the accumulation of jobs and posts. At the lower levels of the administrative hierarchy, civil servants often take a second job to make ends meet. They can do this because many ministries and agencies work a single session (*orario unico*) from 8 am to 2 pm. This leaves them free to devote their evenings to another job or form of employment. At the top of the hierarchy, it takes the form of the appointment of many higher civil servants to lucrative directorships as state nominees on the Boards of Directors of state corporations and monopolies, and companies. Certain officials in certain ministries, such as the Treasury, Finance and the Interior, regard such appointments almost as a vested right, and the additional salaries, expense accounts and so on, form an important part of their emoluments. For example, nine of the fourteen directors of IRI are top civil servants. In the spring of 1962 Premier Fanfani issued a circular forbidding this practice, but it does not seem to have met with much success.

Low salaries attract mediocre personnel and give no incentive to promote administrative efficiency. For example, many ministries are often unable to fill all the posts advertised for competitive examination, 'despite the fact that the jury used criteria of measured and reasonable benevolence in its own assessments', to quote one jury. Civil service morale is consequently low; featherbedding, loose and indisciplined working methods are rampant. The continuation of complicated and out-dated procedures within the administrative machine creates the conviction, which is widespread, that the administration is corrupt; and that efficient and understanding service can only be obtained by greasing the palms of public officials (i.e. the use of the famous *bustarella* [money-laden envelope]). The popular image is probably exaggerated. However, it is true that the complicated maze of administrative procedures places a premium on the person who knows his way around the administrative machine. In addition, the accumulation of posts (whether inside or outside the administration) at all levels of the hierarchy militates against officials being efficient in their primary post. Finally, the lack of adequate technical staff implies a dangerous dependence on certain pressure groups for information and its evaluation.

Finally, it accounts for the top civil servants' view of the State and its citizens. They see the State as a giant inspectorate, 'a sort of gigantic registry office that stamps, controls and collects.' Few top civil servants have a dynamic conception of the State as an agency which should give a lead in public life. Similarly, citizens are viewed as being passive and submissive; they are not seen as forming part of a dynamic political and social reality, but as being shut up in their own individualism. One Treasury inspector has commented that : 'if the upper and lower civil servants are criticized for having a distorted conception of the State, it is the fault of the politicians who have done nothing to change it, because they have everything to gain from a servile administration and everything to lose from an autonomous and entrepreneurial one. For its part, the civil service is well aware of the advantages that accrue to it from the present situation'. Top civil servants, he might have added, know that administrative confusion has an immediate political pay-off : it can be used to favour friends and harass opponents.

The inefficiency and the inability to attract first-rate technical personnel have resulted in the creation of specialized agencies every time there is a new task or policy to be carried out. This was the meaning of the creation of the Southern Development Fund, the Ministry of State Holdings, the National Committee for Economic Planning and the Interministerial Committee for Economic Planning, etc. However, the advent of the regions has suddenly made genuine reform possible for the first time, with some real shifts of power and a consequent shake-up of the civil service. The responsible Minister, Remo Gaspari, has stated that some 20,000 of the existing 60,000 upper civil servants in Rome would be eliminated in the next few years, and only 6000 will be given jobs and status commensurate with those of private and public industrial managers. Naturally enough, the civil servants are not resigned to their fate and have fought the transfer of powers to the regions all along the line. Other elements of the Gaspari Reform, expected to be in force by 1975 are : (1) recognition of the civil servants' own field of responsibility. Each grade of higher civil servant will be responsible personally for the signature of matters in his competence, instead of everything being countersigned and the direct responsibility of the minister as at present : (2) new methods of selection and training along the lines of the French *Ecole Nationale d'Administration* to create a corps of technocrats and managers within the administration; (3) merit to replace seniority as the chief criterion of promotion; and (4) the *Scuola Superiore della Pubblica Amministrazione* at Casterta to be completely reorganized as a permanent college with a full-time staff. The courses will be of fourteen months' duration, of which seven will be spent on a *stage* in a ministry or para-state agency (including IRI) at the end of which each student will have to present a written report for examination in group discussion. The criteria for selection of students will be by ability in service and not on academic qualifications. In the interim, in 1973, salary levels have been raised greatly.

The formulae of the public corporation and the state enterprise have been judged successful by many. Certainly state enterprises have done better in recruiting technically competent personnel; and in one sense this is no surprise, given that IRI runs the only real managerial training school (IFAP – *Istituto Formazione Addestramento Professionale*) in Italy. Thus, in contrast to the higher civil servant, the public enterprise manager is 'seldom under forty years of age, has a university degree, mostly in the technical field, and comes from a family that has lived in northern or central Italy. His father is an executive, a clerk or an independent businessman. He has been working in public enterprises for ten years, but also has worked in other private (more often) or public enterprises' (i.e. he is what is fashionably called a 'technocrat'). It is difficult to make out the same claims of success for the specialized agencies. In fact, it has been argued that state enterprise would have been more successful if the traditional administrative machine had been more efficient and less bureaucratic. For one thing, as Pescatore pointed out, the Southern Development Fund suffered from ministerial compartmentalization and lack of interministerial co-ordination. For another, the specialized agencies have been a particular target for political patronage. They have been the battleground and weapons of the Christian Democrat Party's factional struggles. Half of the eight hundred Christian Democrat leaders surveyed by the Cattaneo Institute had held posts in the various public economic agencies (mainly social security and welfare). Galli and Prandi write:

Giovanni Gronchi, a Christian Democrat and President of the Republic became President of IRI, and the welfare institutes provided positions for members of the unionist faction. While Amintore Fanfani was Minister of Agriculture, with Mariano Rumor and

Luigi Gui as Under-Secretaries, the agrarian reform agencies provided the nursery for Fanfani's *Iniziativa democratica* movement, as they did for other groups. The reform agencies in Apulia and Lucania became the strongholds of Aldo Moro and Emilio Colombo. The political connections of the managerial staff of ENI are well-known. . . .

These political possibilities explain, in addition to the differences of class, mentality, and ideology, the resentment of the members of the traditional civil service at political appointees. In any event, there can be no doubt of the profound differences between the personnel and the style of action of certain special agencies and the ministerial departments. These differences are those of a growing technocracy on the one hand, and a traditional nineteenth century conservative civil service on the other, and even if the Gaspari reforms are successful, will take many years to efface. The limited number of 'technocrats' and the practice of using patronage to pay political debts or to satisfy the demands of private groups anxious to maintain their emissaries in the vital centres of national life, has blurred this distinction in some sectors and accounts for the mixed results obtained. For every Mattei, Saraceno or Ruffolo, how many placemen have been appointed and suffered?

The Decision-Making Process : The Administration's Relations with the Executive and Interest Groups

The decision-making process, like the relationship between ministers and civil servants, is extremely difficult to describe without distortion. The liberal model according to which it is the parties that prepare policy documents which the Minister places before his ministry to use as the basis of the programmes and bills the civil servants draw up for their Minister to submit to the cabinet for presentation to Parliament has always been an improbable description of policy-making in Italy. A recent academic observer remarked :

Only a small part of the bills presented by the government were prepared by the research departments of the majority party or parties, the rest came from the ministries' legislative drafting offices. The latter receive the material from which to draft the text from the respective ministerial directorates which is provided with it by the individual sections. It is these sections which become aware, rightly or wrongly, at a certain moment of the need to take action and so prepare a draft which will be sent, first to the cabinet and then to the President of the Republic before, finally, being presented to Parliament for discussion. Unless the bill has a predominantly political character, in which case amendments to the original text may even be numerous, the draft drawn up by the ministerial drafting offices, and this is what happens in the majority of cases, will become the final text.

Compartmentalization is one of the basic characteristics of the Italian administrative system. It is so strongly institutionalized (Italy had to wait until 1964 before having a unified budget; previously all ministries presented separate budgets) that the government still resorts to special agencies when faced with problems that cut across ministerial lines. Hence there is still a strong tendency to try and deal with problems within a ministry, and even within a directorate. All Director-Generals try to have direct relations with the Minister. This makes the ministerial *cabinets* the nerve centres of Italian ministerial departments. The *chef de cabinet* and his staff spend their time dealing with all the decisions that rain in on them: negotiating with Director-Generals; collecting, collating and passing out information to the various divisions etc. The divisions are primarily concerned with carrying out routine work and under pressure from interest groups, trying to recognize and forecast difficulties that will have policy repercussions; and hence have to be discussed and decided by the Minister.

It is claimed that it is quite possible for a Minister to run his ministry through his own cabinet. Professor Kogan gives the example of Fanfani when Prime Minister and Foreign Minister running the Foreign office in July 1958. Having succeeded Pella, a leader of the opposing right-wing faction of his own party, Fanfani found that all the top civil servants were identified with Pella. In the week of 17 July 1958, Fanfani sent President Eisenhower and Chancellor Adenauer messages that were typed on his own personal typewriter in his own flat. Neither Alessandri, the Secretary-General, nor Magistrati, the Director-General of Political Affairs, knew of these messages nor were their texts known several weeks later. Shortly afterwards Fanfani flew to Washington taking his *chef de cabinet*, Mazzina, a career diplomat, and Bernabei, the editor of the party paper, *Il Popolo*, and secretly negotiated the agreement permitting the installation of US missile bases in Italy. He bypassed the top career men and conducted his own policy through his personal *cabinet* until he could put his own factional supporters into the key posts. His *chef de cabinet* rather than the Secretary-General of the ministry became the distributor and co-ordinator of operations. Professor Kogan adds that this pattern of operations was not unique to Fanfani; he was merely following a long Italian tradition.

Where a problem cannot be resolved departmentally within a ministry, there are two ways of decision taking : the decision can either be handled informally by personal contact between Director-Generals; or by means of working papers. All ministries have Councils of Administration on which the political and administrative heads are represented and a decision can be hammered out on the basis of the working papers. Similarly, each ministry has a number of intra-departmental committees for specific problems, like the legal claims' committee of the Foreign Affairs Ministry or the committee on the revision and publication of pharmaceutical lists of the Health Ministry; or *ad hoc* committees can be created to deal with particular questions when they arise. In addition, it is always open to the Minister to call together meetings of experts on a special subject. For example, the Foreign Minister has made a habit of this with regard to the Common Market; and when questions of urgency arise during negotiations in Brussels, this committee has had to meet at very short notice. Of course, in cases of extreme urgency, this sort of co-ordination is obtained by telephone.

When a question involves several ministries, the mechanism of decision-making becomes more complex. In general, each ministry is competent in a set number of fields, so that when a subject in one of those field interests other ministries, it becomes responsible for co-ordination in that field. For example, the Foreign Ministry is competent on all questions concerning the Treaties of Rome; and the Ministry of the Budget and Economic Planning on questions concerning economic development, or the Ministry of Industry on prices, etc. When the competent ministry is faced with a problem that interests other ministries, it circulates them for their opinions. They can either discuss the matter themselves and make a collective reply, or each can send a separate reply; it is the responsibility of the co-ordinating ministry to take account of all the various opinions in making its decision.

The manner in which the final decision is taken depends on the importance of the question. Minor questions can be resolved by the competent official in the responsible ministry. More important questions require a decision of the Committee of Director-Generals of the interested ministries. The Committee of Director-Generals comprises the Director-Generals of the same Ministries as are represented on the Interministerial Committee for that field. For example, the Committee of Director-Generals for International Action in Political Economy which is responsible for Common Market questions comprises the Director-Generals of the Ministries of the Treasury, Budget, Finance, Agriculture, Industry, Foreign Trade and State-Holdings, as does the Interministerial Committee for International Action in Political Economy. The committee is convoked by the Minister of the responsible ministry, and the Director-General of the same ministry presides.

The most important questions are decided by the relevant Interministerial Committee. The chairman of the major Interministerial Committees, for example, that of Economic Planning, is the Prime Minister. In this case the responsible Minister is Vice-Chairman, and presides in the absence of the premier. Ministers are accompanied to Interministerial Committee meetings by their director-generals. Conflicts of competence can only be decided by the Council of Ministers, which also approves all decisions requiring legislative approval before their presentation to Parliament. Moreover before a bill is presented to Parliament it has to be submitted to the Council of State for its opinion, although its opinion is not binding on the government (the Council of State is concerned principally to ensure good legal draftsmanship and to prevent conflict between different sets of laws). Finally, it is not the cabinet which presents the bill to Parliament, but the President of the Republic who authorizes presentation. This offers him an opportunity (which some Presidents have taken) to comment on its advisability.

Once passed through both Houses of Parliament the bill becomes law as soon as it is published in the *Gazzetta Ufficiale*. However if the measure requires the spending of public funds, it has to pass four hurdles before spending is authorized : (1) verification of the 'legitimacy' of the Parliamentary Act by the Council of States; (2) approval by the General Accountancy office of each of the interested ministries; (3) the agreement of the representative of the Treasury; (4) and registration by the *Corte dei Conti*. As a result there is a long delay between the decision to vote credits for a public project and the work commencing. Jacques Nobécourt claims that the average delay is 900 days; and he quotes the example of the file for the construction of a council house which has to pass 283 obligatory controls, equivalent to a delay of 1014 days before work commences as against the two years required for construction. It is said that claims for compensation for victims of the Messina earthquake of 1908 are still being processed !

This description of the decision-making process raises a number of wider issues. First, who makes the decisions? Second, what is the influence of outside groups? It is difficult to give precise figures, but it is clear that the numbers involved in decision-making are small. If we consider the civil servants in direct contact with ministers (i.e. director-generals, members of cabinets, etc.), the number of important decision-makers is some 3–400, of whom around fifty are politicians (party executive leaders and a few key under-secretaries in addition to ministers). This nucleus forms the policy-making centre in Italy and approximates in size to an estimate made for Great Britain. But the number actually involved in any one crucial decision may be very small indeed.

The paucity of key decision-makers does not exclude the influence of persons outside the charmed circle. In a very real, but paradoxical sense, it increases it. It is a popular theory that Ministers are too busy to have time to think and are in office for short(ish) periods, while civil servants have permanent tenure, familiarity with the administrative machinery, facilities for fact finding and research, and are therefore in a favourable position for long-term reflection and the production of long-term policies. The truth is that top civil servants and officials are just as busy as Ministers; and certainly too busy to think imaginatively. They are in fact, dependent on policy papers originating lower down or outside ministerial departments as Ministers are of the speechwriters in their *cabinets*. Top civil servants, like their political masters, are the focal point for the ideas and pressures of interest groups of all kinds, many of which have better research departments and more staff than the ministries, as well as a whole host of private and semi-public research institutions (*Centri Studi*). The major interest groups have many opportunities to put their views because most ministries have consultative committees on which they get represented. They also have specialists who can be, and are, called in as experts to advise ministers; they are represented on the National Council of Economy and Labour, whose advice the government usually seeks on prospective legislation and major problems; many of them are also represented in Parliament and sit on the respective standing committees, and so are in a position to attempt to amend the government's legislation, if it has not heeded their voice earlier. This institutionalized power of interest groups is a powerful incentive to the government to carry out the widest consultation.

Top Italian policy-making civil servants 'are not – cannot be', as Professor Wilson has said of the British counterparts, 'reflective moulders of ideas; they are the recipients, the collators, the compromisers, among a mass of persuasive influences and persistent people. They do not – and have not the time – to "think"; they respond intuitively, instinctively, to produce decisions often under considerable political pressure, which strike the mean most acceptable to the forces that are struggling to keep the equipoise.' Thus while it is true that politicians are rarely able to question the advice of their civil servants on the major issues of policy – to do so would mean providing an intellectually viable alternative of their own – but are able to push peripheral projects to please their electoral supporters (often what they have most at heart), it is also true that the civil servants largely lack the technical expertise to question the policy proposals of certain interest groups – to do so would mean being able to take the group's proposals apart, extract the information that interests them, and make up a new package. Thus, for example, the late Ernesto Rossi claimed in 1963 that the Interministerial Committee on Prices simply accepted whatever figures were presented to it by the interest groups with which it dealt because it had no research office to analyse prices and costs. Its regulatory power therefore was exercised to the extent of reconciling conflicting groups' claims, and not those indicating a coherent price policy based on informed discussion and independent access to information.

Professor Demarchi concluded an intensive study of Italian bureaucracy with the observation that not only are higher civil servants in general sensitive to requests of interest groups active in their department's field, but become the interest group's representatives and defenders in conflicts with other departments.

The Problems of Economic Planning and Development

The reasons for the move towards economic planning which Italy has taken in the sixties were the opposite to those that affected the similar British decision. Whereas the object of the British National Plan of 1965 was to provide economic growth, it was the very success of achieving economic growth that led the Italians towards planning. The success of their market economy in promoting growth accentuated all its traditional structural contradictions: those between North and South; those between social classes; those between the rival claims of income and leisure; those arising out of the dispute on whether to emphasize on consumption through social benefits or consumption through the market mechanism, etc. The latter was not the least important when one thinks of the primitive state of many Italian social and civic services, like schools, health and recreational facilities, council housing, etc. Planning was a necessity if a start was to be made to resolving some of these economic and social problems, which far from being overcome by growth were taking on new and frightening dimensions. During the forties and fifties there had been a number of exercises in planning, but they remained largely academic. The most notable was the 'Vanoni Plan' of 1955 which was virtually stillborn because of the virulent hostility of the 'centrist' coalitions of those years to any form of 'statism'.

To date Italy has launched one five-year plan (1966–70) and is elaborating a second (1971–5). This concrete commitment to planning (significantly called programmation (*programmazione*) in Italian) poses two fundamental questions. First, how is the plan formulated? Second, how is it implemented? In 1962, the centre-left government made economic planning the central responsibility of the Ministry of the Budget. At the same time it created the National Committee for Economic Planning (CNPE) with the specific purpose of drawing up a plan of economic development; its chairman was the Minister of the Budget; and it was composed of an equal number of representatives of the major employer and labour organizations, and nine experts chosen by the Ministry. A Study Office was established which served as Secretariat for the committee as well as the basic research unit of the organization. The major experts and research institutes that worked in co-operation with the Office were outside the public service. It was assumed that each of the traditional administrative branches would provide the Study Office with whatever assistance it needed, and accordingly co-ordinating committees were set up. This arrangement was not altogether successful, and in 1965 after the first plan had been drawn up the planning process was shifted from the CNPE into the offices of the Ministry of the Budget, which was reorganized in 1967 and took the title of Ministry of the Budget and Economic Planning.

After nine months activity (April 1964), the CNPE published a document, the 'Saraceno Plan', which was the first attempt at a five-year plan. It noted that the general objectives of economic planning had been approved by Parliament and that they were binding on the CNPE group of experts. Moreover it was the CNPE's task to formulate a plan in the light of these general political directives and indicate what needed to be done to achieve its objectives. On this basis the Study Office drew up a draft plan which was to be submitted to the CNPE in June 1964, after which the CNPE quietly expired. It was not discussed because of a cabinet crisis; and a new draft was prepared and submitted to the Council of Ministers in January 1965. On approval it was sent to the National Council of Economy and Labour where it was discussed (March 1965), suggestions were made and incorporated, and it was resubmitted to the Council of Ministers which approved the final draft (July 1965). By this time an 'additional note' had become necessary because of the accumulated delay (October 1965). This was integrated into the original final draft to make a new text, valid for the period 1966–70 (August 1966); it was then presented to Parliament which approved it as a formal law (n. 685) after a long debate on 27 July 1967. Thus three and a half years had passed since the publication of the Saraceno Report; and half the original period (1965–9) of the plan.

It was for this reason that the Ministry of the Budget was

reorganized and economic planning was made the direct responsibility of the newly created Interministerial Committee on Economic Planning (CIPE). In the shake-up, the Ministry was made the clearing-house for economic policy with three directorates, a Central Accounting Office, a Technical Scientific Committee, and a Planning Secretariat. The Study Office was transformed into the Institute of Studies on Economic Planning (ISPE); and the Ministry was flanked by two further committees, one of a technical administrative character containing experts from the various sectors of the public administration, and the second for ensuring consultation between the government, planners and interest groups affected by the plan. Significantly enough, however, monetary and credit policy (the traditional weapons of Italian economic policy) remained the absolute prerogative of the Interministerial Committee for Savings and Credit, and hence firmly in the hands of the Bank of Italy, Treasury and State Accounting Office. Hence, the reorganization of the Budget Ministry was far less decisive than it appeared.

In April 1969 the Ministry published a preliminary report for the Second Plan entitled 'Project 80', which was accepted by CIPE as the basis for the work of preparation in December. In February 1971 CIPE approved the guidelines for drawing up the plan prepared by the Planning Secretariat. In the meantime, technical work on the plan's elaboration had been initiated in October 1970 and was carried out in two phases. First, ISPE set out targets and objectives in the 'Preliminary Planning Document' published in summer 1971. Second, the Minister engaged in a series of consultations with the major economic groups : business, labour, shopkeepers, farmers, artisans, co-operatives and consumers; and the Regional Committees for Economic Planning (CRPE) (winter 1971–2). At the same time, the 'Preliminary Document' was submitted to the National Council of Economy and Labour. At the conclusion of these consultations in July 1972, despite the arrival of a Liberal as Minister of the Treasury, CIPE confirmed its basic agreement with the draft plan and gave instructions for the preparation, by the end of the year, of a revised plan covering the period 1973–7.

The plan is 'indicative' in the French style, i.e. it lays down a number of targets that are expected to be achieved within its lifespan. It recognizes, therefore, that Italy is a 'mixed economy' and that there is no question of imposing obligations on the private sector. However through control of the administration and public enterprise, the government hopes to push the private sector in a certain direction. The task of the public administration is to co-ordinate its activity (public expenditure, fiscal measures and credit, administrative regulations, etc.) in relation to implementing the plan's goals. Public enterprises are obliged to ensure that investment decisions comply with the targets set out in the plan. The law on planning procedure empowers CIPE to control public investment programmes, so that they comply with the plan. Approval is necessary for individual investment programmes, those of a specific sector or of an individual project which modify the original plan. Thus CIPE's approval was sought by IRI in 1967 for the AlfaSud project of building an automobile complex near Naples. In addition, CIPE must approve the five-year plans of public enterprises, defining the objectives and co-ordinating the activities of the undertaking. Finally, CIPE is expected to exercise a further measure of control through the annual review of achievement of investment programmes which enables it to see that estimates are revised if discrepancies have arisen, to bring them back into line with targets for the remaining part of the five-year period. As regards private enterprise, the plan is expected to act through fiscal incentives and credit policy, the major instrument of postwar economic policy. It was clearly not working in 1971 because sanctions were introduced in the form of a payment to the Treasury of 25 per cent of investment by firms who had initiated projects in areas contrary to CIPE rulings, or had failed to notify CIPE of their investment intentions. CIPE was also granted the power of obtaining information from Industrial Branch Associations on development and investment policies; it was believed that by knowing big firms' long-term intentions in advance, it could discuss their compatibility with the plan's objectives.

The first plan was out of date before it could be implemented, hence it failed to meet many of its targets (see Table 7.iv), and this despite under-estimating growth in GNP which averaged 6 per cent instead of the 5 per cent forecast.

The OECD claims that the most important lessons drawn at the official level from the first planning experience were two-fold: (1) that the magnitude and complexity of the problems of econo-

Table 7. iv
The 1966-70 Plan—Targets and Realizations

	Target	Realization	R as % of T
(a) *Public Investment*			
Education	960	339	35·1
Public housing	2,380	700	29·4
Health	360	125	24·7
Transport	4,125	3,007	72·9
of which:			
roads	2,380	1,903	80·0
urban transport	235	97	33·6
Telecommunications	715	927	129·5
Public works	2,270	1,312	57·8
TOTAL	10,810	6,410	59·3
(b) *Public Consumption*			
Education	—	—	92·0
Health	—	—	125·0
TOTAL	25,070	24,442	97·5
TOTAL SOCIAL EXPENDITURE (Billion lire at 1963 prices)	35,880	30,852	86·0

Source: OECD, *Economic Survey, Italy 1972*, p. 33

mic developments in Italy are such as to require strong corrective action through government intervention; and (2) that if the plan is to be an effective instrument of policy, it must not only define general policy directives but lay an important stress on the operative side (i.e. by laying down specific programmes of action). In consequence, a new approach was adopted for the draft second plan. The plan is now conceived as comprising three elements: a *quantitative projection* of the main economic variables, but liable to change in the light of developments outside the control of the planning authorities; a *series of 'programme actions'* on the social and productive sides of the economy to be inserted in the plan as the corresponding decision-making process is terminated; and *annual plans* which test the coherence of the eventual incorporation of the programme actions and link short-term trends with middle-term projections. Thus, as the OECD reported : 'the Plan thus became a framework of co-ordinating a continuous flow of decisions, rather than an immutable set of targets set up once and for all.' Nonetheless, a basic problem remains : it is difficult to see how the government can ensure compliance by large firms determined to pursue development policies incompatible with its targets; it seems that it can just take account of them. Already the precedents are not encouraging. For example, it appears that neither Fiat nor IRI and ENI kept the government informed of their intentions over the Fiat-Citroen merger or the attempted Montedison take-over. Moreover, the *lacunae* of planning are those endemic to Italian policy (shortfall on social expenditure and administrative shortcomings) and nothing decisive has been done to meet them. Finally, the premise of postwar Italian economic activity, sustained growth, has been thrown into some doubt; such a situation does not augur well for the future of economic planning, at least in the short run.

The Military : Organization and Recruitment

The most important single factor governing the Italian military apparatus in the postwar period has been its integration into NATO. Everything – its role, organization, weaponry and activity – flows from that. The Italian army has no operative external role, but quite simply an internal policing one of defending the present socio-economic and political structure of the country. In other words, by joining NATO the Italian government accepted the fact that it was totally incapable of defending its national territory from foreign (defined as Soviet) aggression; and that this would be done, in the event of necessity, by the United States. Its role in NATO was a subordinate one : that of ensuring that American and NATO installations situated on its territory were available to American and NATO troops in case of war by retaining political control of the Italian peninsula.

This stark proposition can be demonstrated by a number of

arguments. First, of all the countries of the Western Alliance, Italy is the one that has been most obsequious to all changes in American Foreign Policy and military strategy; it went to such lengths that two American Professors entitled a book on Italian foreign policy in the mid-fifties *Italy: Dependent Ally or Independent Partner?* Since 1949, it has made loyalty to the USA and NATO the cardinal point of its foreign and defence policies. As General Pasti, one of Italy's commanders in SHAPE, has observed, 'In the Atlantic Alliance, Italy did not participate in any way whatsoever in the formulation of the new NATO strategy in 1963.'

Table 7. v
Composition of Italian Armed Forces in 1967

	Conscripts	Regular Troops	NCOs	Officers	Workers	Civil Servants	Total
Army	213,985	3,724	29,073	20,578	23,147	17,024	307,741
Navy	16,140	7,026	12,514	3,683	21,134	7,666	68,163
Air Force	27,100	1,600	28,600	6,860	6,128	4,340	74,618
Carabinieri	2,700	58,825	17,035	1,940	251	18	80,769
Total	259,925	71,175	87,222	33,261	50,660	29,048	531,291

Source: A. D'Orsi, *La Macchina militare* (Milan, 1971), p. 53

Secondly, only the USA, USSR, China and India have more men under arms. Italy's armed forces number more than half a million men (disposed as in Table 7.v). Moreover Italy does not have a military machine which measures up to the enormous number of soldiers. In 1970, the Minister of Defence, Luigi Gui, admitted to the Standing Committee on Defence of the Chamber of Deputies that 'the Italian armed forces cannot be considered, either from the quantitative or the qualitative point of view, capable of fulfilling the tasks assigned to them by NATO.' This military incapacity is most evident in weaponry which is both out of date and inadequate. The army is still armed with Sherman and Patton tanks; and the German 'Leopard' tanks that it will be receiving are more appropriate for dealing with break-downs in public order than defending national frontiers. The same can be said of the Air Force's aeroplanes (F 104 and G 91) and the Navy's half a dozen ships still in commission. Finally, there is an absolute disproportion in the military budget between the amount spent on personnel, which the Ministry of Defence itself calculates at 65 per cent and that spent on the acquisition of armaments, supplies, transport, naval and aircraft construction and scientific research. Thus while defence holds an important place in the state budget (12.8 per cent in 1970), it is totally unable to provide an efficient military force capable of ensuring the country's defence from outside attack in the case of war. On the other hand, it is adequate, at least in respect of its most efficient element, the *Carabinieri*, for its lesser task within NATO, that of guarding the country from political and social subversion.

Article 87 of the Constitution invests the President of the Republic with the command of the Armed Forces, but the real functions of command are exercised by the Minister of Defence and the Head of the Defence General Staff in the administrative and operative fields respectively. The Armed Forces are directed by three collegiate organs: the Supreme Defence Council, the Higher Council of the Armed Forces and the Committee of the Heads of General Staffs (see Table 7.vi). The Supreme Defence Council comprises the President of the Republic (Chairman), the Prime Minister (Vice-Chairman), and the Ministers of Foreign Affairs, Interior, Treasury, Defence, Industry, and the Head of the General Defence Staff. Other members of the government, industrial and technical experts can be called in in an advisory capacity on the invitation of the Chairman. The Council must meet at least twice a year; and its meetings are secret. Its responsibilities are the examination of the general and technical problems concerning national defence and the determination of the executive criteria to be adopted for its organization and co-ordination. It was conceived of as a consultative body for the government which is, of course, constitutionally responsible for the organization of the country's national defences. The Council has taken on itself responsibility for politico-military policy, acting more as a pressure group for certain policies than as a constitutional consultative body.

Two other committees share with the Supreme Defence Council the control of the Italian military machine. They are very different the one from the other. The Higher Council of the Armed Forces has been called an 'old boys meeting', while the Committee of the Heads of General Staff is the effective military

Table 7. vi
Italian Armed Forces, Scheme of Organization

A. Collegiate consultative-executive bodies	Supreme Defence Council Committee of Heads of General Staffs Higher Council of Armed Forces
B. Supervisory bodies	Ministry of Defence Under-Secretaries of Defence Cabinet
C. Technico-military bodies	Head of Defence General Staff Bureaux of Defence General Staff Inter-Service Agencies Heads of General Staffs (Army, Navy, Air Force) General Staffs of Armed Forces Armed Forces Agencies
D. Technico-administrative bodies	Secretary-General of Defence 5 Central Bureaux 19 Departments (Direzioni generali)
E. Dependent bodies	65 Military Districts Port Harbourmasters (with Mercantile Marine) 67 Military Hospitals Schools and Institutes Training and Instruction Centres Services Factories and Laboratories Welfare Institutes Sports Centres Various Agencies
F. Collateral bodies	Carabinieri Supreme Military Tribunal 13 Military Courts General Military Prosecutor Military Prosecutors Military Ordinance SID (Defence Information Service) Intelligence

Source: A. D'Orsi, *La macchina militare*, p. 39

decision-making centre. It is composed of the four Heads of the General Staffs (i.e. the four military leaders most favoured by the politicians) and the Secretary-General of Defence (a political appointment which requires the confidence of the military). As a result of the recent reform of the Defence Ministry, one person holds in his hands, under the control of the Minister who acts as the guarantor of civil supremacy, all the levers of military power, this is the Head of the Defence General Staff, who is both supreme co-ordinator and chief of all the Heads of the General Staff. These now meet in the Committee of the Heads of General Staff which is under his chairmanship and which is expected to assist him without substituting itself for him as happens in most countries.

The Minister of Defence keeps the Head of the Defence General Staff informed of political developments, consults him obligatorily on the appointment of all officers of field rank, charges him with liaison with the General Staffs of allied military powers and all international military organizations (cf NATO). But the Head of the Defence General Staff is personally responsible for fixing military scientific research programmes and supervises the military information services (SID). The Secretary-General of Defence (who is always a General) is responsible for the technical-administrative sector through five central bureaux and nineteen departments. The control of the military over the Armed Forces is so complete that it is no wonder that d'Orsi, author of the most documented study of the Italian military, has commented that the effect of the reform is the same as appointing a General, Minister of Defence, but with the added advantage of conserving the democratic form of the subordination of the military to the civil power.

Regular Officers, NCOs and troops comprise 38 per cent only of the men under arms; the majority (52 per cent) are conscripts. For several years, however, there has been a crisis in the recruitment of regular officers and NCOs, so that some places available in the military academies are not filled. As with civil servants, officers and NCOs are recruited predominantly from the southern regions and among the middle classes (see Table 7.vii). The reasons for recruitment difficulties would seem to be poor pay (£600/year for sergeants; £800/year for sub-lieutenants; £1500/

year for majors; £3500 for generals); slow promotion (the Army is a gerontocracy and it is difficult to become a general before reaching 55 years of age); and finally a crisis in the military profession brought on by recent social changes. Despite these difficulties, the real weakness of the personnel structure is the disproportion between too few subaltern officers and NCOs (too many leave for a more remunerative and varied occupation in civil life) and too many field officers. In 1970 there were 1016 field officers (generals etc.), whereas the Armed Forces establishment provided for 321 (588 instead of 192 in the Army; 207 instead of 64 in the Navy; and 221 instead of 65 in the Air Force). The same is true of the colonels and staff officers.

Table 7. vii
Social Background of Regular Officers and NCOs, 1965

	Big/Medium Bourgeoisie	Middle Classes	Working Class	Not Known	Total
Officers	31%	59%	10%	—	100
NCOs	4%	61%	16%	19%	100

Source: A. D'Orsi, *La macchina militare*, pp. 182–3

In view of the inadequacy of its weaponry, we may well ask why the country persists with national service. There would certainly be an argument, which technocrats and others have made, for a regular professional army. Three arguments have been advanced to justify conscription. First, it gives the army a popular, and in some sense, democratic basis; the Communist Party has always opposed the ending of national service because it is afraid that a professional army would be more subject to political manipulation. Second, conscription is based on the concept of 'the army: the nation's school'; national service being theoretically the same for all, gives everybody a common experience; this argument was used in the early days of united Italy to create a sense of nationhood. Today it is too often used as a means of inculcating obedience to authority under the name of discipline because it is a useful socialization process for civilian life. Third, the senior military officers have always opposed the ending of national service because they are afraid that a smaller army would mean a smaller military budget; and hence a loss of power.

What then are the relations between civil and military authorities in Italy? The leading military historian Giorgio Rochat claims that political control of the military elite has never existed. Despite many professions of loyalty to the State, government and Italian people, by the various Heads of the General Staffs, General Nino Pasti, one of Italy's most perceptive generals, has written that 'the day in which the military become conscious of their real force and the archaic and undemocratic state of feudal subjection in which they are kept ... that day which is perhaps not too far off ... will be perhaps not too happy.' So far Italy has no history of '*pronunciamientos*', except perhaps Gabriele D'Annunzio's expedition to Fiume in 1919, and even that was carried out by irregulars and repressed by regular troops within a year.

The political leaders have used a number of methods to ensure civil supremacy: flattery – Italian government publications are full of praises for the Army's efficiency (cf *Italy – Documents and Notes*); excessive promotions to field rank; appointment only of officers who have served in NATO posts to the Heads of General Staffs; and rapid turnover of senior officers in key posts. The real limits of the political power of the military in Italy, however, are that the field officers do not form an integrated group but splintered groups with numerous contacts outside. One observer has noted that military power in Italy is based more on persons than office, and the different persons are more integrated with different politicians, economic leaders and top civil servants in their different factions than with each other. This would seem to be the lesson of the so-called coup of July 1964. There seems little doubt that there was a plan for the Carabinieri, the really efficient part of the Armed Forces, to take political power. General De Lorenzo was the promoter, but nobody knows who inspired him. However other military commanders (not all) and various politicians were in the know. It failed because the political situation never developed to the point where the promoters could be sure of success. The suggestion is not that there is no possibility of a coup in Italy; only that if it should occur, it will not be the military who will go it alone, but some may well be party to it in company with political and economic leaders. Moreover it would be contested in the country, not the least by labour leaders, and would probably give rise to civil war.

8 The Judiciary: Archaic Laws and Judicial Confusion

The role of the Judiciary is the adjudication of disputes and the punishment of anti-social behaviour. Of necessity, it is a state institution and, in consequence in most countries, judges are civil servants whose powers are defined and exercised according to law. Thus Article 104 of the Italian Republican Constitution declares that 'The Judiciary is an autonomous order independent of any other power.' Other articles, moreover, enshrine certain further fundamental liberal democratic principles : due process of law (Articles 24, 25 and 27), equal protection of the laws (Article 3), judicial review of legislation (Article 134), etc. The Constitution also expressly protects certain basic civil rights, such as freedom of expression, association and assembly, freedom to travel, freedom and secrecy of correspondence, inalienability of legal status, name and citizenship, etc. Finally, in contrast to most liberal democratic Constitutions, it expressly incorporates a number of social goals. Thus, for example, Article 3 (2) provides that 'It shall be the task of the Republic to remove all obstacles of an economic and social nature that, by restricting in practice the freedom and equality of the citizens, impede the full development of the human personality and the effective participation of all workers in the political, economic and social organization of the country.' The social goals proclaimed include the right to employment, free medical aid to the indigent, eight years of compulsory free schooling, paid holidays for all workers, the right to strike and form trade unions, etc.

Many of these principles, like many of the Italian legal institutions and much of their procedure, are similar to those of other Western European, but more particularly, continental countries, yet their application, functioning and consequences are often very different. Differences due to differences of norms are readily understandable, but differences based on similar norms are less so.

In discussing the judicial system, we shall always have to keep the specific characteristics of Italian legal culture in mind. First, that Italy is one of the major civil law nations, and that the matrix of its legal system is Roman Law. Thus the contemporary legal system is the product of more than twenty-four centuries of more or less continuous legal development. In addition, modern Italian legal science is heir to the work of the medieval glossators. This goes a long way to explaining the weight of tradition, but of a tradition which places greater emphasis on legal doctrine *per se* to the exclusion of problem solving. It is a tradition, moreover, in which law is conceived of as a self-contained discipline that can be understood by systematic study. It is believed that its purity, and so its validity, would be destroyed by the introduction of non-legal elements.

Second, Italy has a code of jurisdiction. Despite the fact that the four codes (Civil, Civil Procedural, Penal and Criminal Procedure are dwarfed today by the bulk of non-codified legislation, the outlook still perpetuates the dogma that the law is complete and coherent. The lacunae and inconsistencies in the law naturally give rise to serious contradictions because of the practical need to bridge the gap between doctrine and reality. Such is the strength of tradition, however, that even the most progressive judges are forced to clothe their interpretative innovations in traditional dress for fear of being disavowed on appeal and overlooked in promotion. In these circumstances, it is little wonder that Italian legal culture has been characterized as abstract and dogmatic, conceptual and culturally agnostic. Nonetheless it is only fair to add that a newer, more modern view of the law, which contrasts with the traditional doctrine, is appearing. The basis of the modern view is the Republican doctrine which 'embodies principles of individual and social justice of the sort which the traditional doctrine rejects as "non-legal". It establishes the institution of judicial review of legislation for the first time in Italy, destroying the dogma of legislative supremacy and increasing the status of the judiciary. It redefines the fundamental legal institutions in terms quite different from those of the doctrine. It provides a basis for theories of interpretation that are more realistic and value-conscious than those of the older model. It provides an alternative source of analogy and general principles of law.' It is, of course, part and parcel of the larger social and cultural changes that we have already outlined.

Organization of the Courts: Dual System of Jurisdiction

Italy has a unified national court system : no regional, provincial or municipal courts exist, with the exception of the anachronistic High Court of Sicily. The system is based largely on the French judicial system and consists of two parallel sets of courts : on the one hand, the ordinary courts which exercise civil and criminal jurisdiction, and, on the other, the administrative courts which are responsible for the judicial review of administrative acts (i.e. the activity of the state institutions).

(a) THE ORDINARY COURTS

At the bottom of the pyramidal organization of the ordinary courts are the *conciliatori* (Justices of the Peace), who are competent only in civil disputes involving less than 50,000 lire. By mutual agreement parties may submit disputes of any value for settlement by a *conciliatore*. Like British JPs, the *conciliatori* are untrained, non-stipendiary magistrates who serve for reasons of local prestige and civic duty. There are altogether some 8000 *conciliatori*, one in every commune. The lowest stipendiary magistrates are the *pretori*, who serve as judges on first instance in about 900 legal districts (*mandamenti giudiziarii*) in civil cases involving less than 750,000 lire and in criminal cases involving a maximum penalty of three years imprisonment. Like the *conciliatori*, the *pretori* sit and adjudicate alone (i.e. without the assistance of an assessor or jury). They are the lowest rank career members of the regular judiciary, and, as such, are entitled to hear appeals from the *conciliatori* on both fact and law.

The court above the *pretore* is the *tribunale*, in which three judges sit on a panel to adjudicate cases. There are approximately 150 *tribunali* located in provisional capitals and some fifty other towns (mainly in the South) which are competent in all civil cases outside the competence of the *conciliatori* and *pretori*; and in criminal cases in which the penalty does not exceed seven years imprisonment. They are exclusively competent in tax cases, in disputes concerning status and capacity of persons or honorific rights, proceedings testing the authenticity of documents, and proceedings levying execution on real property. They also act as appellate courts for cases previously heard by the *pretori*. Owing to the variety of matters within their competence, they are often divided into sections so that they can specialize in particular subject matters. Serious criminal cases are now heard by the Courts of Assizes (*corti d'assise*), which are, in effect specialized sections of the *tribunale*. They are composed of two ordinary judges and six laymen, acting as 'popular' judges, who judge the law and facts together, and not separately as do judges and jury in the Anglo-Saxon system. Moreover all eight vote; and a majority vote convicts, while a tie acquits. There is an educational requirement for laymen of eight years schooling.

Civil and criminal appeals may be taken from the *tribunali* and Courts of Assizes to a Court of Appeal (*corte d'appello*) or the appellate section of the Court of Assizes. There are twenty-three Courts of Appeal located in most regional capitals and a number of other towns (Brescia, Lecce, Catania, Messina, Caltanisetta, etc.) for historical reasons. The court sits in panels of five judges and is competent to decide both law and fact. Normally it has only an appellate jurisdiction, but judges from the Court of Appeal form a number of courts of special jurisdiction which can hear cases in first instance, as, for example, giving domestic effect to foreign judgements, or consensual adoption, etc. In the appellate sections of the Court of Assizes, the panel still consists of two ordinary judges and six laymen, only the laymen in this case must have a minimum of eleven years schooling. Finally, mention must be made of cases involving water rights in public streams, springs and lakes, for which there are special regional tribunals (*tribunali regionali delle acque pubbliche*).

The highest of the ordinary courts is the Court of Cassation (*corte di cassazione*); it has an appellate jurisdiction only, and may reverse decisions of lower courts only on points of law. When it upholds an appeal from a lower court on a question of law, the case returns to the lower court for further proceedings on questions of fact. The Court of Cassation is divided into three civil and six criminal sections, and a panel of seven judges hears each case. As 25 judges are appointed to each civil section and 20 to each criminal section, the Court should comprise some 200 judges in all; in fact, there were 360 in the late fifties. Hence it can undertake a heavy workload. In the most important cases, the civil and criminal sections can each form a united section (*sezione unita*) which would group on the same panel the seven highest ranking judges from the other panels. The chief judge (*primo presidente*) assigns the different cases to the sections, and important cases to the united sections – a very significant power.

Table 8. i
Average Duration (Pending and Hearings) (in days) of Civil Cases Before Courts in 1955 and 1961

| Year | First Instance | | | On Appeal | | | |
	Conciliatori	Pretori	Tribunali	Pretori	Tribunali	Appeal	Cassation
1955	175	320	545	410	478	428	678
1961	288	456	737	653	635	606	711
1968	—	534	892	—	744	670	921

Source: M. Capelletti and others, *The Italian Legal System* (Stanford, 1965), p. 126

The characteristics of Italian justice are readily summarized; it is a crisis situation. First, it stands accused of being slow and inefficient. 'The law's delay' is a truism in the ordinary courts (see Table 8.i). 'Surprisingly,' Professor Cappelletti has commented, 'the increase in the duration of civil proceedings is not caused by an increase in the number of cases. In 1955 ordinary proceedings begun in the courts totalled 538,000; in 1958 the number of new cases was reduced to 503,000; in 1961 458,000 were started; and in 1962 there was a record low of 438,000.' The cause would seem to lie in the productivity of the judges: the number of verdicts at first instance has declined from 6.31 per 1000 in 1901, through 2.81 in 1952 to 2.75 in 1965. Moreover, Nobécourt has noted that while 5576 Italian judges decided some 400,000 cases out of the million and a half pending in 1965, their 4102 French colleagues dealt with some 700,000 cases out of the one million pending. This low judicial output is linked to the multi-judge panels below the appellate level (which is a serious waste of manpower), the lengthy preparation (*istruttoria*) of cases and the much interrupted trials. An explanation of lengthy procedure has been found in the temptation of judges to commit everything to paper, which is responsible for inumerable repetitions, since at every step of the judicial process all judges feel the need to copy out what their hierarchical inferior has written before adding their own observations which, as often as not, repeat what they have already copied out. The result is a fast-growing backlog of cases.

Table 8. ii
The Work of the Court of Cassation and Amnesties, 1958–67

Judicial Year	Appeals referred	Appeals decided	Appeals pending	Amnesties
1958	39,117	18,995	45,460	
1959	30,442	33,113	42,767	11–7–59
1960	24,757	39,273	28,389	
1961	27,503	22,460	33,432	
1962	33,415	27,906	38,941	
1963	22,995	37,175	24,761	24–1–63
1964	23,516	26,910	21,362	
1965	31,013	21,835	30,540	
1966	31,496	27,004	35,932	4–6–66
1967	17,686	39,065	13,633	

Source: G. Moech, *La giustizia in Italia* (Milan, 1970), p. 102

A further explanation is furnished by the advantages which counsel can win from delay because of the periodical amnesties; there is always the possibility that a client can benefit from one before he is condemned if the trial and various appellate procedures can be spun out long enough. Hence counsel are tempted to take cases to Cassation, inventing grounds of appeal if they have not got solid ones. Once an amnesty is pronounced, and they are usually fairly comprehensive (i.e. include a large number of offences), it is much easier for the court to apply its provisions and liquidate a large number of outstanding cases (see Table 8.ii). To this must be added the fact of making a little work go a long way, since there are many more practising lawyers (38,000 in 1967) than can be usefully employed on the work available. Yet another explanation is provided by the bad conditions in which justice is administered in Italy. These range from tumble-down courthouses in out of the way places (courts are often housed in buildings constructed for other purposes, as for example the famous Castel Capuano in Naples) to lack of secretarial assistance.

Second, the law is confused and justice class-biased. Few would deny that the law has got into a complicated state consequent upon the legislators' habit of passing *leggine* (petty laws) but adjourning year after year consideration of general laws. Moreover, recent research has shown that the chances of success in legal proceedings are closely linked to occupation; higher civil servants, professional and businessmen win in 62.5 per cent of cases; middle grade civil service 60 per cent, small businessmen 55 per cent; clerks 40 per cent; artisans, peasants and workers 39 per cent. In consequence, it is hardly surprising that procedure is often arbitrary and verdicts have been judged unsatisfactory in a growing number of cases.

For example, in 1965, three adolescents who broke a shop window to steal some apples were sentenced to two and a half years imprisonment while a schoolmaster who had killed his thirty-year-old daughter's lover received a sentence of two years and eleven months. In 1969 alone there were the Agrigento housing disaster scandal, the Vajont dam disaster and Riva cases in which it was held that either there was no case to answer or minimal sentences were given. Finally, it goes almost without saying that Mafia trials in Sicily end invariably with acquittals for 'lack of evidence'.

(b) THE ADMINISTRATIVE COURTS

Administrative law in Italy serves two major purposes (1) to protect the individual against arbitrary and negligent acts by the administration; and (2) to control the use of public funds. It was believed that the settlement of disputes between the administration and private citizens required, particularly in cases of jurisdiction on the merits, an administrative competence in the judges which the ordinary judges did not normally possess. Hence the Italians have, like the French and Belgians, a system of administrative justice that is separate from the regular judicial system. In cases of dispute with the administration, a citizen may, therefore, bring an action either in the ordinary courts or in the administrative courts. The line of competence between the two sets of courts in this field hinges on the distinction between rights in the strict sense and legal interests, the ordinary courts judge the former whereas the protection of the latter is the task of the administrative courts. When a private person complains of a violation of one of the limits set to the power of the public authorities in his individual interests, the ordinary courts are competent, because these limits impose on the administration duties which are correlative to individual rights in the strict sense of the term, if the person complains of the violation of other limits set in the public interest, the administrative courts are competent. In determining whether a legal interest has been violated, the administrative courts have to decide whether the administrative body issuing the act: (1) was incompetent; (2) exceeded its powers; or (3) violated the law. Finally, in some cases it may have to determine whether an administrative act involved the wise use of discretionary power or not.

The hierarchy of administrative courts is simple: there are two distinct hierarchies, one for adjudicating acts and the other for public funds. If the individual complains of an act by the local administration he can, after exhausting the administrative remedies, seize the Regional Administrative Tribunal (*Tribunale Regionale Amministrativa*). These tribunals were instituted in 1971 as part of the new pattern of regional government and replace the old Provincial Administrative Boards (*Giunta Provinciale Amministrativa*). They are located in the regional capitals, although the larger regions are to have more than one section, the others to be located in other important towns in the regions; and are to be composed of a President and two regional administrative judges. The President is appointed annually by decree of the President of the Republic on the recommendation of the Prime Minister (who must consult the Council of Presidents of Regional Administrative Tribunals) from among Presidents of section of the Council of State or Councillors of State of at least two years standing. A new category of judges, the regional administrative judge, was constituted, and its full complement is to be 220 (46 councillors, 87 first referendars and 87 referendars), of which not less than five will be appointed to each region. Their status is similar to that of the Councillors of State (they are recruited by competitive examination from lawyers and law professors, civil servants and public officials with a legal training

G*

and will have the opportunity to promotion to the Council of State after four years service.

Appeal from the Regional Administrative Tribunals is to the Council of State (*Consiglio di Stato*), which also hears cases in the first instance against the central administration. It is the supreme administrative court and top consultative body of the administration. It is composed of 111 members (a General President, 22 Presidents of section, 74 councillors, 7 first referendars and 7 referendars) appointed by the President of the Republic on the recommendation of the Council of Ministers. Appointments are generally made from higher civil servants and the occasional legal academic, but half the places must nominally be filled from referendars (i.e. civil servants and lawyers selected by special competitive examination). It appears that there were so many vacancies in 1972 that the appointment of the full complement will lead to the political appointments outnumbering those selected by examination by two to one. The Council is divided into six sections: three advisory sections which advise ministries and other administrative bodies on the legality of proposed government bills, general regulations and the codification of legislation (*testi unici*) as well as the legality and merits of proposed contracts, grants of citizenship, etc.; and three judicial sections. The judicial sections consist of about twelve judges, but a quorum in a hearing is seven members. As in the case of the Court of Cassation, if a particularly important case arises, or one that has been decided differently by single sections, the Council of State may hear it in plenary session (*adunanza plenaria*). In this case, the top councillors of each judical section meet together to hear it. The only remedy that the Council of State can give is annulment of the unlawful administrative act; it cannot condemn the administration to make good the damage. In fact the only damages it can award are costs. Actions for damages against the administration must be pursued in the ordinary courts. There is no appeal from decisions of the Council of State, except on questions of jurisdiction which may be taken to the Court of Cassation, and on questions of constitutionality which may be taken to the Constitutional Court.

It remains to add that the aggrieved party may follow another procedure, i.e. he may make an extraordinary application to the Head of State. The responsible minister acting for the Head of

State seeks an advisory opinion from the Council of State. If he does not follow the advisory opinion, the minister must present and have his decision approved by the Council of Ministers. Although somewhat anachronistic (as faintly reminiscent of the traditional appeal to the Royal prerogative), it is both more expeditious and less costly.

The second administrative jurisdiction, totally independent of the first, is that of the Court of Exchequer (*corte dei conti*). It exercises a preliminary control over the legality of government acts, performs a post-audit on the budget and supervises the financial activities of enterprises to which the State contributes capital. It reports directly to Parliament. Many commentators have remarked that, although very thorough in documenting and denouncing abuses, the court's reports rarely lead to judicial action. Indeed, when they do, it is a result not of action taken by the court's General Prosecutor but of action by the ordinary judiciary as a result of newspaper campaigns. It is also responsible for registering all decrees of the President of the Republic and returns them to the government if it considers them illegal. In addition, it must approve all government acts requiring public expenditure, including appointments, promotions and dismissals (and pensions) in the public service.

The Court of Exchequer's jurisdiction is primarily concerned with public money; for example, it is competent for cases of civil liability and accountability of public officials. It had an appellate jurisdiction over decisions of first instance given by the Council of Prefecture as regards the liabilities of the officials of local authorities, and of Income Tax collectors (*intendenza di finanza*) in cases in which the collectors have been held responsible for uncollectable taxes, but, as a result of a recent decision of the Constitutional Court, the Council of Prefecture has been divested of its judicial powers, and these have passed apparently to it directly. Its organization and recruitment are similar to that of the Council of State; eight of its nine sections are judicial, and six hear pension cases exclusively. The Court consists of 523 judges; and judicial sections usually consist of ten members and a quorum for a section is five. Appeals may be taken to the joint sections (*sezioni riunite*) of the Court, which consists of eleven judges from the regular sections. Appeal on matters of jurisdiction may be taken to the Court of Cassation, and on matters of constitutionality to the Constitutional Court. Several writers have noted a procedural peculiarity in its wide powers of decision. In fact the Court enjoys the wide power, not granted to the ordinary courts or the Council of State, to go beyond the original petition or arguments of the parties.

The Constituent Assembly in Article 102 of the Constitution declared its opposition to special courts and jurisdictions, even if it did sanction in Article 103 the continued existence of the administrative courts. Nonetheless, the retention of the administrative courts was against the inclination of an influential section of opinion; and the system so maintained has not been free from criticism, both because of its unnecessary complexity, and because the personnel of the administrative courts are civil servants. It is widely believed in Italy that administrative justice is biased in favour of the administration. This system has not prevented the Council of State from rendering some scandalous decisions. In 1952, it held that restrictions on building in Naples imposed in the 1939 city urban development plan were null and void because it contained no detailed plans – a decision which opened the way to the building speculation under the Lauro administration that has destroyed the face of the city. Again in 1968, it declared null and void a decree of the President of the Republic revoking (on the advice of the Ministry of Public Works) a building licence in Gallipoli (Apulia) because the building concerned exceeded the height limit of 20 metres by 32 metres, and requiring its demolition. Furthermore, the decree of the President of the Republic had been issued originally after the Council of State had given a favourable advisory opinion!

It is true that the administrative judges are civil servants and as such are forbidden to hold other offices while serving on the court. But this prohibition does not seem to be respected. As regards the complexity of the relationship between the two jurisdictions in Italy, perhaps the best statement is that of three Italian jurists writing in an English law review: 'In general,' they wrote, 'one may say that the Italian law proceeds on the principle of admitting a judicial examination of the lawfulness of acts actually accomplished by the administration; but examination by the administrative courts is directed to annulment of the unlawful act, whereas that of the ordinary courts ends in a finding that the public administration is liable to pay damages.'

The Position of the Constitutional Court

Judicial review of legislation was one of the innovations of the Republican Constitution. One of the major differences between it and Italy's previous constitutional charter, the Piedmontese *statuto albertino*, is that it is what the jurists call 'rigid' whereas its predecessor was 'flexible'. This means that it can be amended only by a predetermined and elaborate procedure instead of a simple parliamentary majority. The ease with which Mussolini rode roughshod over the *statuto* without even bothering to repeal it was responsible for this innovation and for the other departure, that of subjecting parliamentary legislation to judicial review to ensure legislative respect of the Constitution. It was believed that the control of legislative sovereignty by certain constitutional principles would afford a greater chance of respect for those principles than had existed hitherto. A further reason advanced to justify the creation of the Court was the form of decentralization with the creation of autonomous regions which the Constitution envisaged. Autonomy did not mean sovereignty, and Italy remains a unitary state without any federal structure. Nonetheless, the regions were granted fairly large powers, legislative as well as excutive. In such circumstances, it was necessary to devise an agency capable of settling disputes between the State and the regions, or among the regions themselves; the Court was made this agency.

The Court's task is to decide on the constitutionality of the laws. Its authority is reinforced by the provision that its decisions take effect *erga omnes*. Some idea of the government's reaction to the potential power of the Court can be had from the fact that it took Parliament eight years to set it up. The antagonism between government, Parliament and the Court has not been dissipated over fifteen years later. The first President of the Court, the former President of the Republic, Enrico De Nicola, resigned after a year because a minister refused to comply with a decision of the Court. His successor, Gaetano Azzariti, made several complaints of a similar nature : specifically that the Court's decisions were ignored by civil servants and politicians. Subsequently, there was a period of pacification. The last two presidents, however, have felt obliged to speak out. Thus Aldo Sandulli complained in September 1967 that Parliament was deaf to its numerous reminders to adapt legislation to the constitution, and yet suspicious of the Court when it attempted to fill the gaps caused by annulment for unconstitutionality. In December 1970, Guiseppe Branca beseeched journalists not to ask of the Court that it do Parliament's job. 'We can destroy the inferno,' he wittily remarked, 'but we cannot build the paradiso and the purgatory out of its ashes; only Parliament can do that.'

What, then, is the position of the Constitutional Court? It is surprisingly limited in point of fact, notably in comparison with other continental Constitutional Courts, like those of West Germany and Austria. First, its jurisdiction extends only to 'disputes regarding the constitutional legality of laws, the "acts having the force of law" of both the State and the Regions; conflicts of attribution between the State authorities, or between the State and the Regions, or between the Regions; charges made against the President of the Republic and the Ministers, in accordance with the provisions of the Constitution.' (i.e. impeachment) (Article 134). To which was added, in 1953, the determination of the admissibility of proposals for referenda (under Article 75). Second, access to the Court is quite limited, since the institution of the constitutional complaint (an arrangement by which any person can question before the Court, any law or regulation which violates his constitutional rights) is unknown in Italy. Indeed the only avenue available to the individual is to secure, during proceedings in the ordinary (or higher administrative) courts, judicial review of the legislation in question for unconstitutionality. However it is up to the ordinary (or higher administrative) courts to decide if a *prima facie* case of unconstitutionality exists to justify reference. This preliminary finding is designed to avoid the raising of constitutional issues for merely dilatory reasons. Unfortunately in the early years of the Court's existence, the ordinary courts, and the Court of Cassation in particular, frequently held that patently legitimate constitutional issues were groundless, thereby foreclosing their consideration by the Court. As it established its position and its prestige grew, reference to it increased, particularly from younger judges in the *pretori*. It has now grown to such proportions that at his annual press conference in December 1970 President Branca felt obliged to draw attention to the fact that this increase was likely to compromise the efficient working of the Court by mobilizing its limited resources to deal with extraneous issues.

The only other procedure for seizing the Court with an action is one that is initiated either by the State against a region, or by a region against the State or another region, on the charge of invasion of the plaintiff's competence. Here the dispute goes to the Court in the first instance, and its competence is not limited to examining the validity of the law (as it is in the case of reference from the ordinary or administrative courts); it extends to any type of act. In addition, the Court may adjudicate conflicts of competence between the fundamental organs of State, which although not named in the Constitution obviously include the President of the Republic, the Council of Ministers, Parliament, the Higher Judical Council and the Constitutional Court itself. Finally, in cases of impeachment of the President of the Republic or ministers, Parliament is charged with the duty of creating a list of persons, sixteen of whom are to be chosen by lot, to serve as additional judges on the Court.

The Court is composed of fifteen judges who serve for nine (originally twelve) year terms. Five are chosen by the President of the Republic, five by Parliament in joint sessions, and five by the highest ordinary and administrative courts (Court of Cassation, Council of State and Court of Exchequer). Appointment runs from oath-taking and taking into account deaths and resignations, etc., creates a staggered basis of membership. Judges are not immediately re-eligible for membership on completing a term on the Court. They are chosen from among senior judges, retired judges, law professors, and lawyers with at least twenty years of practice (the latter are often politicians). It chooses its own president from among its members to serve for a three-year term. The composite mode of selection of judges was a result of a compromise between the various theses debated in the Constituent Assembly as how best to achieve the greatest degree of independence for the Court from Parliament and the government. This mode of selection has been subject to both manoeuvres and controversy. In the enabling legislation setting up the Court in 1953, Parliament inserted a requirement of a two-thirds majority for those elected by Parliament; this was modified in 1967 to a requirement of three-fifths of the members of both Houses for all subsequent ballots after the first three (which still required a two-thirds majority). The government claimed the right to name the five judges appointed by the President of the Republic, on the grounds that all the President's political acts (and it was claimed that this was one) required the counter-signature of the Council of Ministers, and that this gave it the right to name the nominees. The President in office, Einaudi, resisted this interpretation and enabled his successor, Gronchi, to win the right of appointment. After the early difficulties (elections were held twice in 1953, and a third time in 1954, but without success; in November 1955, the first two judges were chosen in successive divisions; and after three more failures, Parliament selected the three remaining judges, at the ninth division) a *modus vivendi* was found of allocating candidatures to certain parties and electing their nominees. Thus in December 1967, Parliament had no difficulty in electing a Christian Democrat, a Liberal and a Communist to the three vacancies that arose on the first ballot. However in 1971, the Christian Democrats took exception to the Socialist nomination of the left-winger, Lelio Basso as their candidate, and refused to vote for him in five successive ballots, so he failed to receive the necessary three-fifths vote required.

The Court organizes its work along similar lines to that of the other courts which have a panel of judges. The president allocates the cases to different judges who act as *rapporteurs*. This gives him considerable influence, as President Branca has admitted frankly. It can be important for one judge to be made *rapporteur* of a certain case rather than another. For example, the giving of successive cases on the attributions of the regions to the Liberal, Giovanni Cassandro, in the early days of the Court's existence, accounts in a large measure for its restrictive interpretation of their competence on the grounds of national unity. In addition, the President fixes the Court's timetable. Again, Branca has confirmed that it can be crucial in the decisions reached that one case be heard before another; or that one case be delayed and another brought forward.

The Court hears the arguments of the parties at the hearing fixed by the President; and the *rapporteur* presents his report on the case for discussion by the plenum of judges at an ulterior date. The number of judges attending the plenary discussion is important. Branca has revealed that many decisions are taken on a majority vote (no dissenting opinions are published) and that the absence of a judge can turn a decision. Since judges are forbidden by law from exercising any other profession during their tenure of office, they study all cases in detail and defend their convictions with passion.

Table 8. iii
Number of Cases Before the Constitutional Court, 1956–65

	Cases of Constitutionality		Conflicts of Competence	
	Received	*Decided*	*Received*	*Decided*
1956	399	231	15	—
1957	124	203	8	15
1958	67	90	13	14
1959	146	77	6	9
1960	108	158	11	11
1961	226	111	15	8
1962	219	242	7	15
1963	268	299	2	4
1964	201	210	9	4
1965	253	139	13	6
TOTAL	2,011	1,760	99	86

Source: *La Giustizia Costituzionale,* ed. by G. Maranini (Florence, 1966), p. 111

Since its inception, the Court has been kept busy (see Table 8.iii). In the first ten years, it received an average of some two hundred cases per year; in the two years 1970–1 this figure has risen to over four hundred per year. Hence President Branca's alarm. On average it decides between a hundred and fifty and two hundred cases per year; and by 1972 the decisions of the Court had already filled some two hundred volumes of law reports. Cases before the Court fall into two broad categories: civil rights and conflicts of competence between the State and the regions. It has upheld the unconstitutionality of the law referred to it in about one fifth of the cases which is larger than in the case of comparable institutions (i.e. the American Supreme Court or the West German Constitutional Court etc.). In the first decade of its existence, the Court was careful to confine its reasoning narrowly to the provisions of the Constitution and showed excessive reticence in going behind the legislative facts. It preferred to insist that its jurisdiction was limited to an examination of the compatibility of the legislation with the Constitution, and to consider itself not competent to pass upon the constitutionality of the Constitutional norms themselves where these conflicted. In practice, this meant that it showed an exaggerated respect for the will of the Republican Parliament, and hence it freely limited its power to annul statutes passed since 1948. Moreover, it upheld the State in almost all cases of dispute with the regions.

In a second period, starting in the later sixties, the Court became bolder in its judgements. It was less obsequious to Parliament, and more inclined to look behind the legislative facts and consider the implications of the Constitution, which it no longer considered as a programmatic document, but as an operative instrument laying down the principles of Italian social life. It also developed its arsenal of instruments for dealing with the growing mass of cases which reached it. It continued to render sentences of annulment, but at the same time, it added '*interpretative di rigetto*' sentences, sentences of partial annulment that rewrote, amended and interpreted the law. President Sandulli clarified the Court's attitude in 1968 when he explained that it had originally attempted to overcome the inconveniences of outright annulment in cases of dubious constitutionality, which created gaps in the law that Parliament was increasingly unable (and often unwilling) to fill by the use of the '*interpretative di rigetto*' sentence (i.e. sentences which do not annul provisions of dubious constitutionality but suggest an interpretation compatible with the Constitution). This ran up against the obstacle of the ordinary judges, who were so jealous of their own independence that they subjected the Court's pronouncements to their own differing interpretations. In response, the Court turned to the use of the partial annulment, which permitted the original legislation to survive amputated of its unconstitutional provisions which were completely reformulated on the basis of principles found in other parts of the law. The inconvenience of this response was that it was unable to deal with (a) cases where the whole law was unconstitutional; and (b) cases where the annulment of the law required replacement by new legislation. There was also still no guarantee that the ordinary courts would accept its interpretations.

At the same time the Court increased its own standing and obviated some of the inconveniences of the above situation by changing its style of rendering its sentences. Instead of persisting with the analytical rendering characteristic of Italian jurisprudence, it developed a synthetic style of sentences which contained a simple declaration of the appropriate constitutional principles. This reinforced the Court's position in two ways. First, it made it more difficult for the ordinary judge to overlook the Court's sentences. Second, it made them more readily accessible to the general public and hence attracted the support of the public towards its activity. The Court also increased its political sensibility. For example, on a number of occasions it delayed considering or rendering sentences in matters under discussion in Parliament so as not to embarrass it. The most obvious example of this was delaying the hearings of cases concerned with the constitutionality of Catholic marriages during the discussion of the Divorce Bill in November 1970. Finally, the Court has not been afraid to re-examine its own jurisprudence when the occasion offered and it employed a more critical spirit than the other Italian courts. Thus, for example, it has changed its attitude towards the position of the regions and interpreted their attributions in a manner more favourable to them than it did initially. In 1970, the regions were successful in six of the eleven cases of dispute with the State. But decisions in 1971–2 suggest that this was no more than an Indian summer. Similarly, it has reversed its position in many areas (family law, private property, penal code, etc.) to bring its interpretation of the Constitution more in line with modern social practice. In this connection, it is worth mentioning that Italian courts are not bound by the doctrine of precedent, as Anglo-Saxon ones are.

As yet the Court has not had to adjudicate conflicts of competence between the fundamental organs of the State. Given the political delicacy of the questions that would be involved, it is difficult to see what role the Court could usefully play in such a dispute. The solution would inevitably have to be political and not juridical. Nor has the Court been called on to judge a case of impeachment. In 1962, Parliament selected for the first (and only) time the panel of forty-five members from which the sixteen additional members of the Court would be chosen, and in 1965 it seemed as though the procedure might, in fact, be used. Senator

Trabucchi, Christian Democrat Finance Minister, escaped arraignment for impeachment before the Court through an unconstitutional parliamentary procedure according to which an absolute, and *not* a simple, majority was required for an indictment (the vote was 451–440 with 49 abstentions).

The vigour of the Court's activity has brought it into conflict with other state organs. These have not been the government or Parliament, as mutual suspicions might have led one to suppose, but the other judicial organs, and singularly the Court of Cassation. Parliament and the government are not really in a position to attack the Court's activity, because to do so would merely highlight their own impotence to act. The gaps, incoherences and obsolescenes that the Court has used its imagination to fill or reform were created originally by the government's and Parliament's inability to act in the first place. The conflict with the Court of Cassation, on the other hand, is more serious, since it places a real limit on the Court's reforming activity. In the present formal state of Italian law, the lower courts are not bound by the Court's decisions. Further, they continue to consider the Court's partial annulment sentence pronouncements 'mere interpretations' of another judicial organ and ignore them altogether.

A most serious conflict has arisen over the legal effect of the Court's judgements and the right of the presence of the accused's lawyer during the instruction of his case. In the first case the Constitutional Court holds that its sentences of unconstitutionality are sentences of annulment (i.e. meaning that the annulled provisions are as though they had never been) and so have retroactive effect. The Court of Cassation, on the other hand, claims that they merely repeal unconstitutional acts, which means that they have no retroactive effects (i.e. the annulled law only ceases to be applied from the date of publication of the sentence). This leads to the paradoxical effect that the person who has brought a case for annulment of a law believed unconstitutional may not benefit from winning the case.

In the second case, the Constitutional Court has held in partial annulment sentences (nn. 190 of 1970, 62 of 1971) it is unconstitutional to exclude the lawyer of an accused during his interrogation while the case is being prepared. The Court of Cassation has ignored this pronouncement, holding that the presence of the accused's lawyer requires specific legislation to this effect, and that Parliament alone is competent to provide it. In all these ways, it has been claimed, the Court of Cassation has demonstrated its contempt for the Constitutional Court.

Despite the various limits on its power, one of the paradoxes of postwar Italian politics is that many observers consider that the Court has been a major influence, both in Italian legal innovation and in the application, and so in the implementation and operation, of the Republican Constitution. Initially this influence was achieved by its example in annulling Fascist, and Fascist inspired, legislation. When the Court was set up, there was strong pressure denying that it had the power to pass on the constitutionality of 'anterior legislation' because the Constitution was silent on this point. In its very first decision, the Court declared that all anterior laws contrary to the self-executing (*provisioni precettive*) provisions of the Constitution were subject to the Court's review. Moreover the Court accepted initially the Court of Cassation's distinction between enforceable norms (*norme precettive*) and programmatic norms (*norme programmatiche*), i.e. between those which were self-executing as a higher law and those which merely set out goals for future governmental and legislative action. In its sentences in the later sixties, the Court buried this as a false distinction and considered all norms as operative norms; it endeavoured to give them as wide an application as was in its power. Such action constituted legal innovation in so far as it brought Italian law and legal thinking into conformity with the postwar reality of Italian society. It stimulated the application of the Constitution in so far as it served as a reminder to Italians, and hence to their representatives, of the Constitution's existence and the chasm separating political and social reality and that sketched in the Constitution.

The Judges and the Independence of the Judiciary

The corps of Italian judges (*la magistratura*) form a career service not only separate from but theoretically independent of other branches of government. Candidates for the judiciary must be law graduates, Italian citizens between the ages of 21 and 30 years, and members of families of unquestionable moral reputation. Since 1963 women have also become eligible. They are recruited by competitive examination which is held annually and is reputed to be one of the most difficult in Italy. In fact, 45 per cent of those successful graduated with the highest possible marks (i.e. 110 *con lodi*). The fact that they perform less well in the competitive examination than at the university suggests that the university legal education does not correspond to that which the judicial administration considers appropriate for the selection of judges. Be that as it may, judges (*giudici*) enjoy, like all civil servants, security of tenure (acquired within five years), a salary in the upper civil service bracket, and substantial pension rights. The prospects are of a safe and respected career with promotion (generally) by seniority, shielded from the stresses and strains of private practice and politics. They appeal above all to the southern intelligentsia of peasant and petty bourgeois origin, who furnish over three-quarters of the five thousand or so Italian career judges (see Table 7.iii).

A successful candidate is appointed to the post of judicial auditor (*uditore giudiziario*); and is assigned to a court of first instance or to a prosecutor's office to begin his apprenticeship, which lasts theoretically two years. Court vacancies are not filled swiftly and a shortage of judges has been the result, despite the high number of judges in Italy compared with similar European countries (6000 in Italy, 4000 in France and 500 in UK). To offset this shortage, auditors are usually assigned to sit on the bench as judges after one year's apprenticeship before they have acquired judicial status. As a further measure to meet the shortage, the government created one thousand new judgeships in 1964. But the real problem is the poor allocation of judges between the various judicial districts. In any event eighteen months after his appointment as a judicial auditor the candidate can apply for the status of judicial adjoint; success entitles him to perform the function of court judge (*pretore* or *tribunale*). On the completion of three years in this position, the District Council of Judges (attached to each Court of Appeal) decides whether he has demonstrated the necessary aptitude to acquire the title of judge (*magistrato tribunale*). If the judgement is negative, he is dismissed; if it is positive, he acquires the title, and tenurial rights which means that he cannot be transferred without his consent, or removed from office without legal cause duly proved. The title of *magistrato tribunale* is misleading in that it does not mean that he will sit in the *tribunale* : he may be appointed to serve as a *pretore*, a judge in the *tribunale*, or as a public prosecutor (*pubblico–ministero*) attached to a *tribunale*.

Promotion beyond this level has been much debated; since 1966 promotion to the Court of Appeal is based primarily on seniority. However there are three routes for judges from the Court of Appeal to the Court of Cassation: (1) by competitive examination (only 10 per cent of vacancies are filled in this manner); (2) and (3) varying combinations of seniority and ability (either investigative, administrative or judicial). The methods of evaluation in the latter two cases are very complex, but the basis is the submission of a number of written judgements for an assessment by a commission of judges appointed by the Higher Judicial Council (*Consiglio Superiore della Magistratura*). In consequence, there is a marked tendency for Italian judges to be prolix and display erudition in their judgements to impress a future commission of their peers, rather than be simple so as to convince the man in the street.

Public prosecutors also form a part of the judicial corps. The rationale behind granting them judicial status is the supposed need for impartiality and freedom from political and governmental pressure. However an understanding of the consequences requires the following points to be taken into account. First, it is the judge, and not the attorney, who carries out the prosecutorial function. Naturally, he works in close collaboration with the public prosecutor. Second, investigation of crimes is the task of a regular judge (*giudice istruttore*) in association with the police. It is the *giudice istruttore* who decides whether to indict or not. Third, judges do not spend all their time on the bench; they can spend part of their career as public prosecutors or *giudici istruttore,* although Professor Cappelletti claims that this happens rarely. Nonetheless this cohabitation between judges, public prosecutors and police raises, naturally, in the mind of a common-law observer, questions about the nature and quality of judicial impartiality. The judiciary may well be free from political pressures in the vulgar sense, but, as disclosures of the distribution of cases between members of the Rome Public Prosecutor's Office have indicated, influence can be used.

Finally, the administrative courts are not staffed by career judges but by civil servants, law professors and lawyers of a certain standing. The *Avvocatura dello Stato* is not part of the judiciary at all; it is an agency dependent on the Cabinet Office which furnishes the legal counsel of the State. State attorneys are career civil servants whose job is to advise and defend the State's interests in law.

The principal weapon of judicial independence in Italy is its supposed total separation from all other government institutions. Judges are appointed, promoted and supervised by judges; it is the principle of the separation of powers taken to its logical conclusion. Prior to 1948, a judge's posting, transfer, career prospects and assignments were fixed by the Ministry of Justice. The Constituent Assembly was afraid that judicial independence and impartiality were liable to be impaired by the weapons available to the Minister and the government. For example, judges who handed down decisions which displeased their political masters could be overlooked when their turn came up for promotion, or posted to a remote province. Similarly, the prospect of living in Rome could be used as an inducement. This fear was in no way theoretical, since interference in the judiciary had been common practice under Fascism. Therefore, the Constituent Assembly proposed to take control of a judge's career out of the hands of the Ministry of Justice and place it in the hands of a special governing body, the Higher Judicial Council which was to be competent in matters of recruitment, appointment, transfers, promotions and discipline. According to Article 104 of the Constitution, it is presided over by the President of the Republic; the Chief Justice (*primo presidente*) and General Prosecutor (*Procuratore generale*) of the Court of Cassation are *ex officio* members; and the remaining members are elected; two-thirds by all the regular judges from among the ranks of the judiciary; and one-third by Parliament in joint session from among University law professors and lawyers of at least fifteen years standing.

The enabling legislation setting up the Council was passed only in 1958; and it has caused a considerable amount of hard feeling, especially among younger judges. In fact Parliament fixed the number of elected members at twenty-one; six are elected from the Court of Cassation; four from the Court of Appeal; and four from the *tribunali*. Moreover it requires a three-fifths majority for the election of the seven members by a joint session of Parliament. Other provisions include : (1) the Council's power to decide on matters concerning a judge's status is dependent only on a request from the Ministry of Justice (this provision was declared unconstitutional by the Constitutional Court in 1963); (2) all disciplinary functions of the Council are attributed to a special section of the Council, composed almost exclusively of the representatives of the higher magistracy, excluding almost all the other representatives, i.e. those of the lower judges and Parliament alike; (3) the right of appeal against the Council's decisions to the Council of State on questions of status, and to the Court of Cassation on questions of discipline; and (4) the traditional practice of awarding higher salaries to the judges of the higher courts.

The consequences of this enabling legislation have been unhappy; it has split the judiciary down the middle. The National Association of Magistrates (the professional association of all the magistrates) came out in opposition to it because the Association was controlled by the mass of younger judges. In consequence, a small group from the higher courts broke away and formed their own exclusive association, the Union of Italian Magistrates. The conflict between the two groups was both political and generational; the younger judges opposed continued hierarchical and political control; and fought for the equality of all judges and the abolition of the hierarchic pyramidal career structure. The senior judges threw their weight behind the maintenance of the *status quo*. Nonetheless, behind the smokescreen of political argument there were two very different conceptions of judicial independence.

The younger judges maintained that the enabling legislation had weakened the framework of judicial independence which the Constitution had established. First, in not clearly defining the spheres of the Higher Judicial Council and the Ministry of Justice, the legislation left open the possibility for political manoeuvre and pressure. Second, in allowing appeals from the Higher Judicial Council, it had undermined the authority of what was intended to be the principal governing body of the judiciary. Third, the elective provisions had also undermined the representativeness of the Council. Fourth, by strengthening the hand of the judges of the higher courts at the expense of the lower, it had perpetuated an outmoded conception of justice, i.e. that the quality of justice is somehow a reflection of the place of the court in the hierarchy of courts. This outmoded view was further reinforced by the differentiation of salaries according to the court in which the judge sat. They argued that it was just as important that justice is good in the lower courts as that it is in the higher courts. Behind the younger judges' arguments lay the assumption that economic inducements are the greatest threat to judicial independence today. They were successful on three points in 1967. A government Act of 1966 abolished competitive examinations for promotion from *tribunale* to Court of Appeal. A further government Act of 1967 reduced the powers of the Ministry of Justice over transfers, promotions and special appointments, which passed to the Higher Judicial Council; in addition, the higher courts' control of the Higher Judicial Council was reduced by changing the mode of election of the judges' representatives : now the fourteen members were to be elected by all the judges from a list of twenty-eight names, nominated by the Court of Cassation (12); Courts of Appeal (8) and *Tribunali* (8); finally, the differences in salary were much attenuated and put on a seniority basis. The continued sensibility of a part of the Italian judiciary to the problems of the independence of the judiciary is obviously in part a legacy of Fascism; nonetheless, it can only be healthy for Italian justice.

The Protection of Civil Rights

The Constitution guarantees specifically not only a detailed list of fundamental human rights but also a number of important social goals. It virtually repeated in detail the provisions for civil liberties that form part of the great Liberal tradition that has come down from the enlightenment, and attempted under the stimulus of the Communists and Socialists to take account of the Marxist critique of civil liberties as abstract rights by establishing a number of economic and social rights. However respect for the new rights was doomed from the outset; putting aside the terrible economic and social situation in which the country found itself in 1948, the Constitution was very vague as regards procedural rights (i.e. what a citizen had to do to seek recognition of his rights and ensure their implementation).

The Court of Cassation attempted to make sure in its interpretation of the Constitution before the creation of the Constitutional Court that the economic and social rights were no more than pious hopes by introducing the distinction between enforceable norms (*norme precettive*) and programmatic norms (*norme programmatiche*). It also subdivided the self-executing norms into those which were complete, and those which were incomplete and required enabling legislation. In the early years, the Constitutional Court accepted this interpretation which naturally reduced the number of civil rights that were immediately enforceable. But, even the incomplete norms had a value, since they were construed by the Court from the start as setting limits to be observed by other state institutions. In general, civil and political rights were self-enforcing; and ethico-social and economic rights were considered programmatic. However in the late sixties the Court buried these distinctions and considered all rights as fully operative norms and endeavoured to give them as wide an application as possible. This view has run up against the reluctance of the Court of Cassation, which is still not prepared to accept the theory or its implications.

Article 13 of the Constitution affirms that personal liberty is inviolable, and declares illegal any form of detention, search seizure, or any other restriction of personal liberty unless supported by an act of the judicial authority; and only then in situations laid down by law. It also provides that police authorities may adopt summary procedures only where law indicates exceptional situations of urgency and necessity. In such situations, the proceedings must be communicated to the judicial authority within 48 hours; and the judicial authorities must approve it within the succeeding 48 hours, otherwise the proceedings are null and void. Similarly, Article 14 protects the inviolability of a man's home; entry, searches or sequestrations require a warrant from the competent judicial authorities. Other articles guarantee the liberty (and secrecy) of correspondence, the liberty of sojourn and travel (which can only be restricted for reasons of health and security); liberty of assembly; liberty of association; liberty of religion; liberty of opinion and press; liberty of instruction; the right to work and to set up unions; the right to judicial process and economic initiative; and the right of asylum.

Political rights are listed in Title IV Part I of the Constitution. In essence they are as follows: the right to the vote (the only limitations are age and civil incapacity (irrevocable criminal sentences and situations involving moral turpitude as determined by law); the right to petition Parliament, but there is no obligation on Parliament to act; and the right to organize politically. Article 49 expressly states that 'all citizens have the right freely to organize themselves into political parties in order to co-operate in a democratic way in determining the national policy.' The only limitations envisaged are on secret organizations of a military character; and the reconstitution of the dissolved Fascist Party. Finally, there is the right to non-elective public offices for which all citizens are eligible on a basis of equality.

The basis of the ethico-social and economic rights are set out in Article 3, which lays down that the task of the Republic is to remove all obstacles of an economic and social nature which, by limiting materially the liberty and equality of citizens, impede the complete development of the human personality and the effective participation of all workers in the political, economic and social organization of the country. Title II Part 1 lists the various principles with social overtones intended to alleviate the citizens' family obligations, to provide for his health needs, and to facilitate his personal maintenance, comportment and education. The economic rights are set out in Title III of Part 1 and requires the Republic to regulate labour in all its forms and applications; specifically: (1) the right to a wage proportional to the quantity and quality of work adequate to the necessities of a free and dignified existence for him and his family; (2) the right not to be subjected to an excessively long working day; (3) the right to weekly rest and annual holidays; (4) the right to adequate insurance in case of accidents, illness, sickness, disability, old-age and unemployment; and (5) the right to collaborate with other workers in the management of business enterprise subject to the methods and limits established by law.

The listing of these principles was intended to give direction to the State in its regulation of production, distribution of wealth and its economic system. This is in keeping with the much discussed Article 41, which starts by stating that economic initiative is free but then goes on to add that it must be conducted so as not to prejudice the security, liberty and dignity of all citizens. It further states that legislation will determine the plans and controls necessary to ensure that economic activity is directed and coordinated for social ends. As more than one commentator has noted, it 'seems to favour a planned economy, rather than a free one, and requires implementing legislation'. On the other hand, Article 42 recognizes and guarantees private property but indicates that appropriate legislation will determine the methods of acquisition, enjoyment and inheritance, and other limitations so as to ensure its social function and render it available to all.

In spite of a certain lethargy, Parliament has attempted to translate the various programmatic norms of the Constitution into reality over the years, and legislation has been passed giving substance to a number of the social and economic goals. Perhaps the most important of the latter was the approval of the so-called 'Labour Charter' in May 1970, which gave legal backing to the sections of the Constitution concerned with the dignity of workers, labour accident safeguards and trade union activities. It did not deal with individual dismissals, because this had previously been regulated by Act No. 604 of 1966. Among other things the Labour Charter gives workers the right to control the enactment of regulations regarding accident prevention, occupational diseases and research into them; forbids all political, union and religious discrimination when hiring workers and during employment; and amends Article 2103 of the Civil Code on the duties of workers. A worker may now be employed only to do a specified job; and if he is used to do another he must be paid the higher rate of the two. Finally, Italy has ratified both the European Charter of Human Rights and the European Social Charter, which now form part of Italian domestic law. However where Parliament has not acted, the pre-Constitutional legislation remains in force – and this means a large mass of Fascist legislation and the legal codes – and it requires litigation taken to the Constitutional Court, which is often expensive, to get it declared unconstitutional and hence void.

It is clear that the Constitution affords the Italian citizen a large measure of protection. In practice, unfortunately, the situation is much less satisfactory. The Fascist Rocco Penal Code (devised to outlaw all political activity) is still in force; and is applied from time to time. Among crimes it includes, *inter alia*; the membership of 'subversive' and 'anti-national' associations (arts. 270–1); the constitution or membership of international associations without the government's permission (273–4); 'subversive' and 'anti-national' propaganda and apologetics (272); political conspiracy by agreement and association (304–5); the inciting of military personnel to disobey the law (266); *vilipendio* (defamation) of state institutions (308); apology for crime (414); the inciting of 'class hatred' (415); spreading false and tendentious news (656). What is worse, these crimes are defined in such a way that a critical or anti-Fascist act falls within their definitions. The courts have interpreted the code so that the commission of any of these acts in private is a crime, as is the association with anyone who has committed one of them, even if the accused was unaware of the facts. It is hardly surprising that many jurists have considered the code 'one of the most severe and complete systems of repression of political activity in its fundamental forms of association, propaganda and proselytism that has been devised'.

An Italian citizen does not have the faculty of making constitutional complaints. If charged under the Rocco Code he must ask his counsel to refer the matter to the Constitutional Court on the grounds that the decision involves a constitutional right; and it is for the ordinary judge to decide if there is a *prima facie* case for reference. While the majority of lower judges are now quite prepared to do this (thus decision No. 87 of 1966 declared the second paragraph of Art. 272 making 'anti-national' propaganda a crime, unconstitutional), the Court of Cassation has been much less ready. It has referred less than five cases concerning the Rocco Code; and none as regards the political articles.

Even if an issue is referred to the Constitutional Court and the litigation is successful, there is still the obstacle of acceptance by the lower courts that the sentence is immediately operative. In April 1972, the Anarchist Pietro Valpreda, accused of the Milan Bank bomb attack of 1969, was unable to benefit from the fact that the Constitutional Court declared that the manner in which the case against him had been drawn up was unconstitutional. The Court of Cassation held that the higher Court's ruling did not effect this particular prosecution because it was anterior to the declaration of the principle which made it unconstitutional.

Despite some obvious limitations, freedom of speech and expression has been reasonably respected in Italy. Although Communists and Leftists have complained rightly at different times of discrimination, particularly in employment, both Communist and Neo-Fascist Parties, not to mention the numerous Leftist groups, have been permitted. As regards freedom of the press, Italy's record is better in recent years than that of neighbouring France. Both the editors of *Potere Operaio* and *Lotta Continua* have been successfully prosecuted for 'incitement to hatred between classes' under Article 415 of the Rocco Code, but no Leftist journal has been systematically persecuted like *La Cause du Peuple*. On the other hand, the Communist philosopher Braibanti was sentenced to nine years imprisonment (reduced to four years which he had already served awaiting trial on appeal) for the medieval crime of *plagio* (i.e. possessing another man's soul) revived by the Fascists. Similarly while few Italians were prosecuted before 1968 under Article 656 of the Rocco Code, which was considered to have fallen into desuetude, it has been used with a frequency reminiscent of the Fascist years since the appearance of student contestation and the 'Hot Autumn' of 1969. Thus in 1970 three workers were fined 10,000 lire each by the *pretore* of Borgo Valdi Tauro (Parma) for having distributed a pamphlet which began : Workers, citizens, serious dangers hang over the country's institutions.' It was as though the public authorities had suddenly become frightened that subversive ideas could undermine their power. Finally, slander, libel and defamation are still treated as crimes and not civil law offences; and the police have the power to make emergency seizures of publications on the grounds that they are violating or are about to violate the law. Article 21 of the Constitution lays down that the authorities 'must immediately and in any case within not more than 24 hours present charges before the courts. If the judicial authorities do not sustain the charge ... the distraint is understood to be revoked and without effect.' However this is not necessarily a valid safeguard because it is clear that it would not be difficult for a prefect to find a compliant judge. It is only fair to add that it has not been invoked very often : one such occasion was in April 1972 when the police raided the offices of the conservative *Corriere della Sera* in Milan and seized some documents after the paper had criticized the police in the Feltrinelli affair. Even more unsatisfactory is the crime of *vilipendio* or contempt with particular reference to the State, Head of State, Armed Forces, Judiciary, Police, Catholic Church, Pope etc. In view of the open partisan position taken in Italian politics, not only by all state office-holders, but by the hierarchy of the Catholic Church, it is hardly surprising that cases of *vilipendio* have been not uncommon. It has been used to punish the critics of presidential and Church action; and more recently the Leftists for their denunciation of police repression and military violence. In 1971, it was even invoked against a judge for his Marxist critique of the legal system.

Three other areas where the situation of civil rights is not good are religious freedom, sex discrimination and relations between the State and the citizen. Religious freedom is recognized, but the Constitution also accords the Catholic Church the privileged position recognized by the Lateran Pacts as the state religion. The Church has presumed on the State to support its position; and there are numerous cases where the courts and police have acted as the secular arm of the Church, whether it be in harassing fundamentalist protestant sects for prosetylizing or in the banning of Hochhuth's celebrated play *The Deputy* in Rome in 1965. This is to be expected in a country which has been governed by a Catholic Party throughout the postwar period; it has meant that non-Catholic religious groups have had short shrift if they took their grievances to the courts. As regards sex discrimination, family law is one of the areas of the Constitution in respect of which the Constitutional Court has complained of Parliament's inactivity. In its early decisions the Court appeared to approve of sex inequality by, for example, accepting that adultery was a different crime when committed by women. This was because it was expecting Parliament to carry out a fundamental reform of family law. In 1968, this expectation was disappointed so it reversed this view and severely criticized the punishment of women who were guilty of adultery and not their husbands if they were. However it remains true that despite the ratification of the ILO Convention on equal pay, discrimination against women in employment continues. Certain professions, like the legal profession, have been opened to women in the sixties, but the courts have shown little enthusiasm for applying constitutional and international provisions in this field.

The last problem area, that of State-citizen relations, is not properly one for the courts. It is really one of political culture, and as such, has already been touched on. Hence, it is only necessary to recall the basic antagonism between the two components: the distrust of the individual citizens for the State; and the scorn of the public official for the individual citizen. It does reach the courts, however, in the problem of law and order. The Italian government's preoccupation with maintaining law and order has been a continuing one since the Risorgimento. It had its origin in the fact that the unification of the country and the establishment of the national State was a minority movement. It was not, moreover, helped by the Fascist interlude. Together they created the mentality which is responsible for the continued application of the 1931 Fascist code of Public Security. Its effects were seen most recently in the 'hot autumn' of 1969. Free assembly and demonstrations are guaranteed by the Constitution, but police repression is fast and furious; 13,000 industrial and agricultural workers, as well as students, were either arrested or charged with offences under the 1931 code between September and December 1969. In such circumstances, the courts act as a natural extension of the police, as the Pinelli and Valpreda affairs arising out of the Milan bomb incidents of December 1969 amply testify. In the final analysis, the defence of civil rights in Italy is only as good as the courts are prepared to make it. Moreover, although there is plenty of evidence of a new spirit abroad in some sections of the Italian judiciary, above all in the lower echelons, the top echelons and the Court of Cassation still cling to the authoritarian attitudes inculcated in them in their youth.

9 Local and Regional Government: Political Autonomy or Regional Decentralization?

Local autonomy has a long and glorious tradition in Italy that goes right back to the Middle Ages. The commune, that symbol of autonomous municipal government, had its origin in Italy, and it is fitting that it should remain the most important type of local authority today. However its status and functions are very different from what they once were. The communal movement of the Renaissance was an assertion of the right to municipal independence and self-government against feudal suzerainty. Although the movement was never totally successful, many towns in northern and central Italy enjoyed a practical measure of political and administrative autonomy, based on a *statuto* in the hands of an elected oligarchy, which many of them managed to preserve when the country fell under the absolutism of a plurality of petty princes and foreign rulers in the fifteenth century and which lasted up to the Napoleonic conquests. This experience supplied one basis for the tradition of local autonomy which triumphed in the Constituent Assembly of 1946-7 and led to the incorporation of the principle of regional government in the Republican Constitution.

The status and functions of the commune owe more today to the other tradition, that of the centralized state of uniform law and institutions introduced into the peninusla by Napoleon in the aftermath of the French Revolution, and which triumphed politically on unification in 1861. In this tradition, not only were the powers granted to local government extremely limited, but they were subject to the immediate and direct control of the central government. Today both traditions coexist in forced cohabitation.

The Italian state system is, in the words of one student, 'a unitary system characterized by regional autonomy'. The powers and structures of local government are those of the Napoleonic tradition, but those of the regional governments (created after some twenty years delay in 1970) are ones of political autonomy and administrative decentralization. It is too early to say what the consequences of regional government are likely to be on local government, but the principal features of the latter, namely over-centralization and uniformity, are likely to be alleviated.

Local Government

(a) THE STRUCTURE OF LOCAL GOVERNMENT

The basic unit is the commune; it is typically a city, town or village and the surrounding area up to the boundary of the adjoining communes. There are some 8000 communes in all, and their area and size of population vary considerably. On the one hand, there are the metropolitan cities like Milan, Rome or Naples, with over a million inhabitants and an area of perhaps fifty square miles; and, on the other hand, there are small villages with less than five hundred inhabitants and an area of a few square miles only. Similarly, communal resources vary : some are wealthy and others are so poor that they cannot even finance the minimal essential community services. Despite these disparities, they are all communes; and all communes have roughly the same powers and must perform roughly the same functions, irrespective of their different economic and social conditions. This is because they still depend on the Fascist legislation of 1939 which requires absolute uniformity. Postwar amendments which do, in some cases, make different provisions for different communes according to population and financial resources are 'not substantial enough to alter the general picture of uniformity'.

Municipal self-government is achieved by the election of the communal council every four years. The voting system and the number of councillors vary with the population size of the commune. In communes of less than 10,000 inhabitants, the electoral system favours the choice of individual candidates irrespective of their party affiliations, because each elector is entitled to vote for a number of candidates equal to four-fifths of the seats on the council. By this method, the minority is ensured of at least one-fifth of the seats on the council. In the larger communes the Proportional Representation system of lists with preference voting as in General Elections is used. Parties are, however, permitted to present common lists (*apparentamento*) to avoid the dispersion of votes. The number of councillors varies from a minimum of fifteen in communes with less than 3000 inhabitants to eighty in communes with a population of over half-a-million. The widespread use of the Proportional Representation electoral system means automatically that the number of communes dominated by one party majorities are limited (see table 9.1). Hence local government, like national government, is also an arena of party alliances and the style of politics which the negotiation of party alliances brings in its wake. Some of the major Italian cities, like Rome, Naples, Bari and Venice, have been continually prey to this kind of factional politics because their electorates are so fragmented that only exceptionally has a party, or alliance of parties, been able to form a coherent majority on the Council.

Table 9. i
Types of Municipal Majorities in Provincial Capitals in 1967

Single Party Majorities		Coalition Majorities							
DC	PCI	DC/ PSU	DC/PSU PRI	DC/ Various	PCI/PSU PSIUP	PCI/ PSU	PCI/ Various	Gov't Comm'r	Total
11	2	42	14	9	4	4	2	4	92
13 (15%)		75 (80%)						4 (5%)	92 (100%)

Source: elaborated from *Annuario politico italiano* (1967), pp. 2195–9

The Council is responsible for elaborating the main policies of the commune; it enacts municipal legislation, approves the municipal budget, and controls the activity of the Junta (*Giunta*) and the Mayor (*sindaco*). The Junta is a collegiate body of from two to fourteen councillors (*assessori*) depending on the size of the commune, which acts as an executive committee presided over by the Mayor. Each *assessore* is responsible for one or more of the municipal services, as, for example, public works, public health, personnel, finance, etc. The Junta directs the municipal administration, prepares the budget for approval by the Council and submits most of the municipal laws and statutes to the Council for consideration. When the Council is not in session – according to law the Council must hold at least two sessions a year; one in the spring, the other in the autumn – the Junta may act in its place if it is necessary to make an urgent decision. Such decisions have to be ratified by the Council as soon as it can be convened. If the Council rejects the decision, the Mayor and Junta are personally responsible for it.

The Mayor is the head of the commune; he directs the work of the Junta, presides over the Council, represents the commune both ceremonially and in relations with third persons, and signs all orders, acts and contracts made by the commune. In these tasks he has the collaboration of the Municipal Secretary (*segretario comunale*), the top communal official, who gives him legal advice. The Municipal Secretary is responsible for the legality of all the activities of the commune and the keeping of records of all acts and decisions of the municipality. In the small communes where the Mayor usually knows 'little about the law and administration, the Municipal Secretary is often the *deus ex machina* of the situation'. Nonetheless whatever relations between the Mayor and the Municipal Secretary, the Mayor is responsible to the Council for his acts. Generally, however, he enjoys a position of substantial power. His power is, of course, a function of the political complexion of the commune. It is greater in communes with a stable political majority, and in the small rural communes where the Council seldom meets and the Junta leaves most things in the hands of the Mayor who is often a local notable. In the large urban communes where the Junta is formed from a heterogeneous majority, each act of the municipality can require long and often fruitless negotiations. A breakdown, resulting in the impossibility of finding a majority to form a Junta, leads to the intervention of the Prefect and the appointment of a Government Commissioner to carry out routine administration until the holding of new elections (in law within six months). Since the office of Mayor and local councillor form part of the career pattern of party officials and Members of Parliament, it comes as no surprise to learn that they are recruited from the same social area, the various sections of the middle classes (see Table 9 ii).

At the intermediate level between communes and regions are the provinces, of which there are ninety-two. As Professor Cappelletti has remarked, these are more significant as geographical or field areas for the central administration than as a form of local government. This has two causes : first, the provinces are artificial constructions without traditions or distinctive economic and social conditions to justify their separate existence; and second, their powers are very modest. The organization of provincial government follows that of the commune very closely. A Provincial Council is elected once every four years using the proportional representational electoral system (since 1960); the number of councillors varies from 24 to 45 according to population. The Council elects a Junta (size dependent on population) of *assessori* responsible for the various departments of the provincial government. Party alliances are the essence of provincial government, as they are of all levels of Italian government; but the power struggle is less bitter because there is relatively little at stake.

Table 9. ii
A Social Background of a Sample of Communist and Christian Democrat Mayors (1946–63) and Communal Councillors (1963)

Class	Mayors		Councillors	
	PCI	DC	PCI	DC
Upper and middle bourgeoisie	15·6	35·4	10·8	20·5
New middle class	25·3	32·2	38·4	38·1
Old middle class	20·3	6·8	21·4	27·0
Working class	9·8	2·0	21·7	7·9
Pensioners and other occupations	13·4	12·4	5·9	5·5
Not known	15·6	13·2	1·8	1·0
	100·0	100·0	100·0	100·0
No.	(276)	(858)	(3,148)	(6,158)

Source: adapted from G. Galli and A. Prandi *op. cit.*, pp. 250–1

(b) THE FUNCTIONS OF LOCAL GOVERNMENT

The fundamental law governing the functions of local government is still the comprehensive Fascist act of 1934. Although it has been amended in the postwar period to repeal the more obviously unconstitutional provisions, these amendments have not altered its basic features. Its chief characteristic is to lay down in great detail the functions and activities of local councils and, hence, to leave, very little margin for local initiative. The functions of communes are similar to those carried out by the Municipalities of most other European countries. They are responsible for the registration of births, marriages and deaths, and the records of real property ownership. They provide sanitation facilities, fire service, certain social services, street-lights and roads, etc. Contrary to the British situation, local government is not responsible for either local police (except for traffic control) or education (except for the maintenance of land and buildings of primary schools). Law and order in Italy is a central government responsibility, and all police forces are nationally organized. The educational system is also a central government responsibility. Teachers are appointed and paid by the State, and the Ministry of Education establishes a uniform national curriculum and related syllabi for all types of school from the primary school to the university.

Although the functions asked of all communes are uniform, differences arise because some functions are mandatory, others optional. And it is only after meeting the obligatory functions that a commune can consider undertaking some of the optional functions. It is only the wealthier communes, which are generally the larger communes, that have the resources to consider providing some of the voluntary services. If a commune does not perform one of the mandatory functions, the Prefect may appoint a civil servant to carry it out in place of the municipal authorities. The limiting factor is naturally financial resources. In Italy, municipal income comes from a variety of local taxes, and is woefully inadequate. Moreover the central authorities can keep a tight control on municipal spending because present legislation requires : (a) that the communal budget is not too unbalanced; and (b) that additional burdens on local taxpayers do not pass a stipulated ceiling. The most important of the multitude of local taxes are the family tax, the *dazio* or excise tax, and the *sovraimposta* or additional tax.

The family tax is a tax on each family unit resident in the commune; it is supposedly proportional to the family's 'ability to pay', but is actually assessed according not only to ascertainable income, but on such income together with all other outward signs of wealth (type of house, car, servants, etc.). The rate varies according to the resources of the commune, but within limits laid down by the government. In general, it is higher in the larger communes. In any event, it has been the subject of much criticism. In the first place, reliance on outward signs of wealth is often deceptive as to true ability to pay. In the second place, not only are assessments uneven, but many taxpayers succeed in evading them entirely, especially in big cities. In 1961, it was claimed that the loss in municipal revenue in Milan due to family tax evasion was over £750,000 annually. This is not surprising when one realizes that the muncipal tax collecting service is inefficient and staffing and facilities inadequate.

The excise tax is a tax imposable on almost all goods sold within the communal boundaries. They include food, beverages, electricity, building materials and stationery, gas and cosmetics, etc. Since many of the items are products of popular consumption, it is, in fact, a consumer tax, because although it is levied on the sale from wholesaler to retailer, the latter naturally passes it on to the consumer. Local manipulation of this tax can have regressive effects on trade because it impedes the co-ordination of a national fiscal policy. Furthermore, collection of this tax is often farmed out by the commune to a licensed private firm, which takes a percentage. Farming is still the practice in smaller communes; and it is claimed that the cost of the collection in the South amounts to more than 60 per cent of the total money collected. It was to overcome inefficiency and possible corruption that a public body INIGIC was created in the pre-war period to collect the excise tax. In 1954, however, INIGIC itself became the subject of a scandal involving 1 billion 500 million lire contributed to party funds, 1182 defendants, 15,000 witnesses, seven tons of documents and 3000 pages of judgement, which sent six hundred people to stand trial. Finally, the *sovraimposta* is an addition which local authorities are allowed to add to certain national taxes. The commune is permitted to add a fraction to national taxes on real estate, business, industrial and professional transactions. Recently, this source of revenue has lost importance because the government has granted substantial exemptions on real estate taxes.

The consequence of the above situation is simple : local finance is in a sorry state. It was claimed that 3842 of the 8095 communes were in debt in 1970 to the tune of 8520 billion lire, which was equivalent to half the annual national budget. Rome, the national capital, is perhaps the most notorious case: the annual income of the city is just sufficient to pay the interest on the city debts, currently running at more than 1500 billion lire annually.

Table 9. iii
A Territorial Distribution of Outstanding Debts of Municipalities and Provinces on 1 January 1968 (in millions of lire)

	Current Account	Capital Account	Total
NW Italy (Industrial triangle)			
Provinces	51,729	236,229	287,958
Communes	169,271	1,003,771	1,173,042
Total	221,000 (6·7%)	1,240,000 (42·1%)	1,461,000 (24·4%)
NE and Centre (Red and White provinces)			
Provinces	166,738	225,843	392,501
Communes	1,068,878	1,027,364	2,096,242
Total	1,235,616 (37·3%)	1,253,207 (42·6%)	2,488,743 (39·9%)
South and Islands			
Provinces	339,083	108,945	447,983
Communes	1,514,793	340,226	1,855,019
Total	1,853,831 (56·0%)	449,171 (15·3%)	2,203,002 (35·7%)
Total			
Provinces	557,505	571,017	1,128,522
Communes	2,752,942	2,371,361	5,124,303
Grand Total	3,310,447 (100·0%)	2,942,378 (100·0%)	6,252,825 (100·0%)

Source: G. Pianese, 'Local Finance' in *Economic Conditions in Italy* (1969), p. 39

In addition 71 of the 92 provinces were in debt in 1968. Not surprisingly, moreover, the distribution of municipal debts is related to national economic development. For example, 145 only of the 3062 communes of the industrial triangle are in debt, as against 1340 of the 2482 communes in the North East and Centre and 2223 of the communes in the South and the Islands (for the nature of the debts, see Table 9.iii). The inadequacy of the traditional systems of local revenues to cover current expenditure, much less capital investment, in so many communes explains why the social, educational and recreational services of many of them are so pitiful. Public libraries are few, and sports' and recreational facilities are seldom provided by the municipality. Indeed, where

H*

they exist at all, they are often left to political parties and other voluntary associations to provide. Moreover, to meet the cost of essential capital works, the communes are forced to borrow from special government credit institutions (*Cassa Depositi e Prestiti, Consorzio di credito per le opere pubbliche,* etc.), or the banks. For obvious political reasons successive governments have deemed it wiser to allow municipalities to secure increased revenues from borrowing rather than force them to raise taxes. This borrowing is subject to close control by the central government authorities. Where credits are insufficient, as has been the case with Rome, Naples and many other large southern cities, the government has been forced to step in with special legislation to provide grants of funds from the State Treasury. The result has been further to curtail local autonomy.

Not only are the functions of local government limited, but the area of real local self-government is restricted by lack of financial independence. The greater the direct contribution from the State Treasury to the local authorities – and most of the larger communes are unable to meet their obligations from their own resources today – the closer the control the central authorities claim to exercise, a control which is subject to political influence and partiality (the relations of the local Mayor with a political protector in Rome, and the latter's power). In addition, the government has preferred to intervene, and transfer financial responsibilities to the State Treasury when its hand has been forced by the inability of a growing number of municipalities to cope, rather than completely to reorganize local government finance on a more rational basis.

Finally, it needs to be noted that municipal authorities do not appear to have used such autonomy as they do have in the financial field to pursue specific taxation policies. A Cattaneo Institute study of municipal budgetry policies indicated that it is not possible to distinguish Communist taxation policies from those of the Christian Democrats. Table 9.iv shows that a heavy reliance on family tax (considered an instrument of progressive fiscal policy) has not been the prerogative of communes controlled by left-wing administrations, nor that reliance on excise taxes (considered an instrument of conservative fiscal policies) has been that of communes controlled by the Christian Democrats and their allies.

The powers of provincial governments are extremely limited.

They may legislate and perform administrative functions only in a few minor fields, rigidly determined by law, such as highway construction (but only those highways not the responsibility of either the State or the Commune); public assistance (with special regard to paupers; orphans, the disabled and the mentally ill); public health (prevention of contagious diseases and control of communal sanitation). Recent legislation has also given them extended powers for the conservation of game and fish. Their financial situation is worse than that of the communes; they are wholly dependent on the State Treasury and in consequence heavily in debt. They touch a small share of certain national taxes collected by the State revenue officials (*Intendenza di finanza*).

Table 9. iv

Family and Excise Taxes as Proportion of Total Revenue of Thirteen Large Communes in 1952 and 1962

Commune	Region	Maj.y	1952 Family	Excise	Maj.y	1962 Family	Excise
Alessandria	North	PCI/PSI	6·4%	39·0%	PCI/PSI	12·3%	25·6%
Ferrara	Centre	PCI/PSI	13·5%	33·6%	PCI/PSI	16·4%	25·7%
Modena	Centre	PCI/PSI	13·5%	40·0%	PCI/PSI	16·1%	28·2%
Parma	Centre	PCI/PSI	16·8%	36·0%	PCI/PSI	16·4%	28·4%
Reggio Emilia	Centre	PCI/PSI	14·0%	32·4%	PCI/PSI	14·0%	26·3%
Foggia	South	PCI/PSI	3·7%	43·2%	DC	8·7%	34·4% * (1961)
La Spezia	North	PCI/PSI	4·9%	30·2%	DC/PSI	11·7%	33·5%
Bergamo	North	DC	11·1%	42·0%	DC/PSDI	18·3%	26·5%
Brescia	North	DC	12·9%	45·6%	DC/PSDI	12·9%	26·9%
Vicenza	North	DC	10·0%	44·1%	DC/PSDI	14·0%	28·6%
Padua	North	DC	16·4%	43·4%	DC	16·3%	24·7%
Reggio Calabria	South	DC	5·1%	14·2%	DC	7·1%	35·2%
Salerno	South	DC	10·5%	27·6%	DC	5·3%	30·7%
National Average			10·0%	29·8%		Not known	

Source: adapted from G. Galli and A. Prandi, *op. cit.*, pp. 241–3

(c) CONTROL OF LOCAL GOVERNMENT : THE PREFECT

The Prefect is the central government's chief agent in the provinces. He is a career civil servant appointed by the President of the Republic on the advice of the Council of Ministers. There is no prefectoral corps in Italy as there is in France and prefects have no tenure of office. They are promoted, demoted, and transferred at the government's pleasure and at a moment's notice. The appointment is essentially political, and although the Prefect is the local representative of the State, his tour of duty is judged in strictly partisan terms, i.e. the extent to which he has promoted the particular government's, or even that of a specific government party's, interest in his province. Electoral results often figure prominently in his appreciation. The government is free to appoint whomsoever it will; and occasionally it appoints a politician or military officer. In general, however, the majority of prefects are appointed from career men in the Civil administration of the Ministry of the Interior; from men who have made their way up the hierarchy of the prefecture (through the grades of Councillor and Sub-prefect). Professor Fried found in 1961 that 'most of them came from southern middle-class families of modest means and retain(ed) the conservatism of that milieu ...' (see Table 7.iii for region of origin). He further observed that 'although all of the prefects entered and rose in the career service under Fascism, they made the transfer of allegiance to the post-Fascist regime with ease ...'

The active powers of control of the Prefect over local government were until recently very substantial. It has been claimed that the difference between Italian and Anglo-American local government is not so much in the functions exercised but in the powers of control exercised by the central government. First, every act or decision of the municipal authorities (Mayor, Junta or Council) had to be communicated to the Prefect within eight days, and the Prefect had twenty days in which to annul it as being not in accordance with law or central government instructions. Second, the Prefect's approval was required for all local government contracts, and he could take into account the merits of the contract as well as its legality. All contracts of a certain size (sums fixed according to population of commune or province) had to be submitted for approval in principle before negotiation Third, the Prefect could order inspections of communal operations where he suspected mismanagement or irregular administration. Furthermore, where the municipal authorities did not perform some mandatory functions, he could send civil servants to perform the function in place of the defaulting authorities. Fourthly, the Prefect could recommend the dissolution of the communal or provincial administration. The power of dissolution belongs to the government, and is given effect by a decree issued by the President of the Republic. Normally dissolution is used when a Council refuses to meet, cannot form a stable majority, or is guilty of irregular administration. The decree of dissolution appoints a special government commissioner (*commissario prefettizio*), who is generally a prefect, to carry on the ordinary administration until new municipal elections can be held, which legally must be within six months. However this is a stratagem to which prefects can resort in complicity with the government for reasons of political expediency as much as on sound legal grounds. But it must be admitted that postwar governments have not employed this stratagem with anything approaching the systematic nature of their Liberal and Fascist predecessors (see Table 9.v).

Table 9. v
Dissolutions of Communal and Provincial Councils Before and After Fascism

Year	Communal	Provincial	Year	Communal	Provincial
1913	155	3	1947	13	
1914	172	1	1948	18	
1915	72		1949	10	
1916	70		1950	8	
1917	106		1951	7	2
1918	131		1952	1	
1919	134		1953	4	
1920	284	3	1954	3	
1921	365	8	1955	4	
1922	281	16	1956	30	3
1923	561	26	1957	18	
1924	278	10	1958	18	1
1925	228	5	1959	12	1
1926	126	9	1960	8	
TOTAL	2,963	81	TOTAL	154	7

Source: A. Spreafico, *op. cit.*, p. 104

From Summer 1972 the Prefect is to be partnered, if not totally replaced, in his supervision of local government by the new Control Committee on the Acts of Provinces and Communes (*Comitato di controllo sugli atti delle provincie e dei comuni*), composed of five members appointed by the Chairman of the region. Three members must be administrative experts elected by the regional council, one member will be named by the Government Comissioner of the region, and one must be a Regional Administrative Judge selected by the President of the Regional Administrative Tribunal. The committee will elect its chairman from among the three elected members. Each region will decide whether to have one regional Control Committee or a number of decentralized Control Committees with the same kind of membership for each individual province. In future, the distinction between the control functions of the Control Committee and the Prefect will be that the former will be responsible for the control of local government acts, whereas the latter will be responsible for the supervision of all local public and semi-public agencies (*Enti pubblici comunalie provinciali*). Thus the acts and decisions of the municipal authorities must now be transmitted to the Control Committee, but the Prefect still retains the right to order inspections in cases of suspected mismanagement and irregular administration as well as the authority to appoint civil servants to perform mandatory functions in place of defaulting municipal authorities. But the Control Committee will now exercise administrative control over communal and provincial budgets and all aspects of local government finance. Its control will be more restrictive than was that of the Prefect, because while he had to limit his judgement to the legality of actions, the Control Committee will be able to pass judgement on the administrative soundness and usefulness to the community of the financial activity of local government. If the Control Committee rejects the budget or other financial acts of a local authority as illegal or administratively unsound, it must return them to the authority, which can either modify or abandon them. In no case can the Control Committee substitute itself for the local authority by directly modifying the latter's decision. It can annul decisions and return them, but it is for the local authority to take the necessary corrective measures.

The Prefect and Control Committee also have more or less direct control of certain local institutions such as orphanages, hospitals, Chambers of Commerce and Communal Relief Agencies (ECA) as well as some charitable institutions. The same distinction between control of acts and supervision of agencies applies. As regards welfare and charitable institutions, the Prefect may not veto appointments made by local councils but he can dissolve the appointed boards and place them under special commissioners and allocate most of the funds.

The use by the Prefect of his very substantial powers depends, naturally, on the political physiognomy of the province. In case of control by government (and right-wing) parties, mutual understanding is forthcoming not only because it is in keeping with the conservative temperament of most Prefects but also because many government-party local leaders have powerful friends in Rome whom it would be unwise for the Prefect to antagonize if he does not wish to jeopardize his career. On the other hand, intervention and stern control are weapons that the Prefects can use against the opposition parties, as they were against the Communist Party throughout the Cold War. More recently, this antagonism between the Prefects and Communist administrations has been replaced by a greater spirit of co-operation.

In general, given the limited opportunities for the exercise of political initiative in local government, all parties have conceived control of local authorities in patronage terms. The share-out of departments (*assessorati*) in the Junta depends on the type of alliance formed and the power relations of the local constituent parties. The dominant party makes sure that it keeps control of key financial departments like Public Works and Welfare. Commissions on contracts where public money is involved are an important source of local party finance. In their allocation, the party achieves a double aim : that of favouring party members by awarding them contracts where possible; and that of collecting large contributions to be credited against the cost of local organization. Parties outside the Junta but hopeful of forming one in the near future can expect smaller contributions from entrepreneurs who wish to insure against a change of Junta. In addition, party members can be put on the pay-roll of agencies and institutions in the gift of local authorities.

Regional Government

(a) THE STRUCTURE OF REGIONAL GOVERNMENT

There are two types of regional government in Italy : special and ordinary. Structurally both types are alike, but their powers differ in as much as special regions have greater powers than ordinary regions. There are five special regions: four (Sicily, Sardinia, Val d'Aosta and Trentino-Alto Adige) were set up between 1946 and 1949, and one, Friuli-Venezia Giulia, was created in 1963. They are either islands or frontier zones, and all have either special social and economic problems, the case of both Sicily and Sardinia, or linguistic and cultural ones, the cases of Val d'Aosta, Alto Adige and Venezia Giulia. They were all areas where the demand for regional self-government was particularly strong in the early post-war years.

The Constitution also named fourteen ordinary regions (Piedmont, Lombardy, Liguria, Emilia-Romagna, Venetia, The Marches, Tuscany, Umbria, Abruzzi-Molise, Latium, Campania, Apulia, Basilicata and Calabria), which were increased to fifteen subsequently with the separation of Molise from the Abruzzi, but these were not established until 1970 after twenty-two years of struggle, polemic and parliamentary debate. This delay occurred in spite of the fact that the Constitution explicitly recognized in Article 114 that regional government formed an integral part of the new organization of the Italian State. The reason was due to the fact that it left the modalities of the establishment of regional government to Parliament, and successive Christian Democrat-dominated government coalitions were afraid that some regional governments, above all in the Centre, would fall under Communist control, and that the Communist Party would use regional power as a basis for subverting the Italian political system. Indeed the eventual decision to implement the regions was one of the Socialist Party's demands for collaboration in the 'centre-left' alliance, and one which took more than six years to achieve.

The institutions of the regional governments, both special and ordinary, are similar, and resemble those of local government. They consist of a unicameral legislature, the regional Council, which sits for a five-year term. The size of regional Councils varies according to population, ranging from eighty members for regions with over six million inhabitants to thirty for those with less than one million. The electoral system adopted was similar to that of the Chamber of Deputies: the list system of Proportional Representation with preference voting to designate successful candidates. The regions are divided into a number of multi-member constituencies formed from the individual provinces in the region, and each one has a number of seats proportional to its population.

Successful candidates are those in each list with the highest number of preference votes according to the number of seats attributed to the list (for party distribution of seats, see Table 9.vi)

Table 9. vi
Distribution of Seats on Ordinary Regional Councils 1970

	PCI	PSIUP	PSI	PSU	PRI	DC	PLI	MSI	Total	Maj.y
Piemont	13	1	5	4	1	20	4	2	50	DC/PSI/PSU/PRI
Lombardy	19	2	9	5	2	36	4	3	80	DC/PSI/PSU/PRI
Veneto	9	1	5	3	1	28	2	1	50	DC
Liguria	13	1	4	3	1	14	3	1	40	DC/PSI/PSU/PRI
Emilia-Romagna	24	2	3	3	2	14	1	1	50	PCI/PSIUP
Tuscany	23	1	3	3	1	17	1	1	50	PCI/PSIUP/PSI
Marches	14	1	3	2	1	14	1	1	40	DC/PSI/PSU/PRI
Umbria	13	1	3	1	1	8	1	1	30	PCI/PSIUP/PSI
Latium	14	1	4	3	2	18	3	5	50	DC/PSI/PSU/PRI
Abruzzi	10	1	3	2	1	20	1	2	40	DC/PSI/PSU/PRI
Molise	5	—	3	2	1	16	2	1	30	DC/PSI/PSU/PRI
Campania	13	1	8	4	2	13	2	5	60	DC/PSI/PSU/PRI
Apulia	14	1	5	2	1	22	1	4	50	DC/PSI/PSU/PRI
Basilicata	7	1	1	2	—	14	1	1	30	DC/PSI/PSU
Calabria	10	1	6	2	1	17	1	2	40	DC/PSI/PSU/PRI

Source: *Italy – Documents and Notes* (1970), 4–5, pp. 397–9

Studies of the social background of regional councillors indicate that they are similar to those of Members of Parliament and Communal Councillors, i.e. that they are recruited from the middle classes.

The regional Council elects an executive committee, the regional Junta, and a Chairman or President (*Presidente della regione*) from among its members. The size of the Junta depends on the size of the region, but is determined by each according to its regional statute, which was the first legislative act that the regional governments had to undertake. All regional Councils were free to determine their own statutes (i.e. provisions relating to internal organization and operation of their institutions) within the limits laid down in the Constitution and the enabling legislation; their approval by Parliament was a formality to give them greater solemnity. The members of the Junta are *assessori* and responsible for a specific department or regional service. The regional governments are empowered to establish their own administrative services, although the Constitution indicates that they are expected to work through the existing offices of the provincial and communal services. Moreover the central government has authorized the transfer of some of its services to the regions, above all in agriculture and public works, so that they can carry out the functions specified in Article 117 of the Constitution. However the modalities of the transfer have not yet (autumn 1972) been completed, so it is difficult to get an informed view of the new arrangements. When it is completed, it is expected that some 15,000 state employees will be moved from the capital to the regions. One of the reasons for the constitutional clauses promoting decentralization was the desire to reform and limit the size of the public service. The experience of the special regions which have built up ample, and often overlapping, administrative organizations makes the constitutional suggestion seem likely to be no more than a pious hope. This scepticism is reinforced by the riots in L'Acquila and Reggio di Calabria in 1970 over the location of the regional capitals of Abruzzi and Calabria and the jobs it was anticipated that the privilege would bring.

(b) THE POWERS OF REGIONAL GOVERNMENT

The legislative powers of the regions are of three kinds. The first has been called 'limited exclusive legislative power', i.e. areas of competence defined by the Constitution or constitutional statutes where the regional Council may legislate for the area of its jurisdiction unhindered and to the exclusion of national legislation. The second has been called 'complementary legislative power', i.e. areas where the regional Council is limited to legislating within the framework of national legislation in certain fields. A framework of principles governing legislation in a certain field may be established by national 'framework laws' (*leggi cornici*) enacted by Parliament, or may be deduced by the regional Council from the existing body of national legislation in the field concerned. The third has been called 'integrative legislative power', i.e. the power which permits the regional Council to adapt the details of national laws to the specific needs and conditions of the region.

The importance of this distinction between these three types of legislative power is that it is what distinguishes the different types of region. The special regions alone possess all three types of legislative power, whereas the ordinary regions possess only the latter two, i.e. 'complementary' and 'integrative' legislative powers. In addition, ordinary regions are inferior to special regions in the field of 'complementary' legislative power because their competence is more modest. For example, all regions have 'complementary' legislative powers regarding organization of regional offices, communal boundaries, local police, fairs and markets, public charities, health and hospital services, vocational training and aid to schools, local museums and libraries, town planning, tourist trade and hotel industry, tram and motor coach services of regional interest, roads, aqueducts and public works of a regional interest, lake navigation and ports, mineral and spa waters, quarries and peat bogs, hunting and fishing, agriculture and forestry, and arts and crafts. All these matters were attributed to the regional governments by Article 117 of the Constitution. However all regions have attributed to themselves a similar competence in the field of regional planning, an area where the Constitution said nothing (*et pour cause!*); and since Parliament has subsequently ratified the regional statutes, we may take it that it has accepted this new attribution. In addition, the special regions have 'complementary' competence over local and regional banking, mines, expropriation in the national interest, public health, publicly-owned housing, fire-services, labour relations, social insurance, industry, commerce, and land reclamation. Furthermore the areas of 'limited exclusive' legislative competence of the special regions include (although they differ a little between special regions) agriculture and forestry, communal boundaries, public works, hunting and fishing, town planning, civic customs, tourism, artisanship, museums and libraries of regional interest, local and regional roads, regional markets and fairs. The Constitution did not outline the fields in which the regions are to exercise 'integrative legislative power; it preferred to give Parliament the right to delegate the power to issue norms for the execution of any legislation it so desired. Regional governments enjoy two further rights : (a) they are authorized to initiate proposals for submission to Parliament concerning matters of regional interest which are outside their own legislative competence : and (b) the Chairmen of the special regions are permitted to attend the Council of Ministers when matters concerning the regions are being discussed and to put the regions case, but they cannot vote; the Chairmen of the ordinary regions have no such right.

The transfer of the powers and responsibilities of the State to the ordinary regions outlined in Article 117 of the Constitution was carried out on 1 April 1972, but it is incomplete. It was only effected after an exhausting trial of strength between the regions and the State as a result of endless negotiations during which the former struggled, often without success, against the jealous resistance of the Roman ministerial bureaucracy, unflinching in its determination to hold on to its prerogatives and functions. For this reason, it has been called 'more of a sharing out than a transfer of power'. Thus, in the health sector, for example, the State has refused to hand over to the regions jurisdiction on the production and sale of medicines, on transplants, on the prevention of accidents, and on industrial health.

The key to the powers of the regional governments is, in any event, to be sought in the degree of financial autonomy which they have been accorded. Article 119 of the Constitution states somewhat sibyllinely that the 'Regions have financial autonomy within the forms and limits established by the laws of the Republic which coordinate it with the finances of the State, the Provinces and the Communes. This has been interpreted as meaning that the regional governments only have as much financial independence as the central government is prepared to give them. Certainly this was the opinion of the Chamber Standing Committee on Home Affairs on the Regional Finance Bill adopted 16 May 1970; it wrote that 'one can observe in the bill a tendency to align regional government finances on that of local government, and hence to orient them towards a regime of integral participation, abandoning purely and simply the idea of a real regional fiscal power'. In effect, regional governments may not levy import, export or transit duties, nor adopt provisions which in any way hinder the circulation of goods between the regions, while regional financial policy and practices must be in accord with those of the national government.

The Regional Finance Act of May 1970 conceded the regional governments revenue from two sources: regional taxes (specifically, public land and property, regional concessions, road traffic taxes, rents on public property; quotas on the regional yields of national taxes (specifically 15 per cent of government receipts on taxes on petroleum products, together with 75 per cent of government revenue from excise duties on beer, spirits, and sugar and 25 per cent tobacco tax); it also permitted them to contract loans and issue their own bonds to raise investment capital. This apportionment was not very generous. The first source, which alone can be considered as the regions' 'own' resources in the terms of Article 119 of the Constitution, accounts for only 120 of the 700 billion lire accorded them. The second source, which represents almost six-sevenths of the total sum made available, is the quotas which supply a common fund (*fondo comune*) with complex rules for its distribution between the different regions (see Table 9.vii).

Table 9. vii
Distribution of Financial Resources Between Regions in 1970 (in mill's of lire)

Regions	Own Resources	Common Fund A	B	C	Total	Total Resources	%
Piedmont	14,700	32,872	6,498	5,093	44,463	59,163	8·4
Lombardy	27,900	62,707	6,096	9,715	78,518	106,418	15·2
Venetia	9,650	31,081	4,702	14,448	50,231	59,881	8·6
Liguria	6,800	14,344	1,384	2,223	17,951	24,751	3·5
Emilia-Romagna	12,250	29,291	5,658	9,067	44,016	56,266	8·0
Tuscany	9,850	26,343	5,881	8,155	40,379	50,229	7·2
Umbria	1,800	6,049	2,164	3,745	11,958	13,759	2·0
Marches	3,100	10,460	2,479	6,478	19,417	22,517	3·2
Latium	14,730	34,722	4,400	10,751	49,873	64,603	9·2
Abruzzi	2,010	9,367	2,760	8,697	20,824	22,834	3·3
Molise	510	2,637	1,136	3,267	7,040	7,550	1·1
Campania	8,000	39,336	3,479	36,547	79,362	87,362	12·5
Apulia	5,450	27,828	4,950	27,848	58,626	64,076	9·1
Basilicata	830	4,938	2,555	7,642	15,135	15,965	2·3
Calabria	2,420	16,025	3,858	22,324	42,207	44,627	6·4
Total	120,000	348,000	58,000	174,000	580,000	700,000	100·0

$A = 6/10$ according to population. $B = 1/10$ according to the territorial area of the region. $C = 3/10$ according to a socio-economic coefficient based on rate of emigration, unemployment and *pro-capita* tax charge (Art. 8C of Law n. 281 of 16 May 1970)

Source: P. Ferrari, *Les régions italiennes* (Paris, 1972), p. 62

The object of these rules is to attenuate the existing disequilibria between regions. The nobility of this gesture is rather tarnished when one compares the total of 700 billion lire accorded to the fifteen ordinary regions in 1970 with the resources of the five special regions in 1969, which amounted to 424 billion lire. Against this

the regions have received quite a number of sums for specific purposes: 1300 billion lire to spend on housing and around 1100
billion lire for school building. They have also been allocated
116,000 million lire for special measures for mountain areas, an
initial 20,000 million lire for the implementation of regional planning; and finally, the execution of the law of 29 September 1971
for the South with its substantial financial provisions is entrusted
to them. Thus the regions are called on to administer extremely
large sums of money which raises the question, will they assume a
position of economic importance?

The economic powers of the regions have been divided into two
main categories, one covering matters of primary economic interest, and the other matters for socio-economic intervention (i.e.
indirect economic powers). The first category covers agriculture,
the tourist and hotel industry, and arts and crafts: sectors in
which the regions can exert influence through the classic instruments of economic policy (except that agriculture is subject to
EEC policy). In general, the regions have been left little room for
manoeuvre in the productive sectors, although it is claimed that
they are developing a policy that could have far-reaching consequences in the long term by filling in the gaps left by the central
government's economic policy.

Potentially more important are the indirect economic powers of
the regions. They are endowed with wide powers in the fields of
territorial, economic and structural planning, and in the social
services, but their activity is likely to be hampered in the foreseeable future by the lack of general administrative instruments at
the regional level, and in some fields, even at the national level. It
seems likely that they will be more successful, at least initially, in
micro-territorial organization, where most of their social welfare
powers are concentrated, than in macro-regional development,
which, to a great extent, escapes their control.

The regions are still largely political bodies and, despite their
aspirations to a voice in the social and economic development of
the country (written into most of their statutes), they have had as
yet little impact on economic decision-making. Indeed it is clear
from what has been said that they have not been given a position
of autonomy in the economic and financial field on a par with
their political status.

(c) THE CONTROL OF REGIONAL GOVERNMENT

The central government's powers of supervision and control over regional government are exercised by a Government Commissioner residing in the regional capital, backed by a regional Control Commission (*Comitato regionale di controllo sugli atti della regione*). The Commission is composed of seven members and is presided over by the Government Commissioner. The members are appointed by decree of the President of the Republic on the basis of a proposal from the Prime Minister and the Minister of the Interior. The members, in addition to the Government Commissioner, who sits *ex officio*, must comprise one judge from the Court of Exchequer, three civil servants, of whom two must be from the administrative personnel of the Ministry of the Interior and two must be experts in administrative questions selected from two lists drawn up by the regional Council. For each of these three categories, with the exception of the Government Commissioner, the decree of appointment must name three replacements to serve in cases of the indisposition of members. The presence of five members constitutes a *quorum*, and in the case of a tie, the chairman has a casting vote.

All regional legislative and administrative acts must be ratified by the Control Commission. It has twenty days from the reception of the *procès-verbal* to annul the act; and all acts not annulled within that period become executive. They may annul acts on the grounds that the Council has exceeded its statutory authority; or that the act in question in contrary to the national interest; or that of other regions. It also has the power to investigate the merits of a certain number of acts, specifically, the regional budget, long-term expenditure, the cession of real property to cover public debts and borrowing, the acquisition of shares and bonds, long-term leases; the management of public services, and any matters which Parliament so directs. If the Control Commission refuses to ratify the act, the Government Commissioner must return it to the regional Council stating the reason for refusal; if it is re-enacted by the Council by an absolute majority, and the Commission again refuses to ratify the act, the issue must be submitted to the Constitutional Court, if the dispute is one of legality, or to Parliament, if the dispute is one of interest (i.e. merit).

It is clear that control of the legality of regional legislation is a straightforward judicial process (despite the fact that the Constitutional Court has been very restrictive in its interpretation of regional powers), but control of merit is a political control which the central government could exploit to limit regional autonomy. After all, it is the central government (and its majority) which decides what is the 'national interest' or the 'interests of other regions'. This has become more than a theoretical possibility because three of the ordinary regions are controlled by Communist-dominated left-wing alliances. However the peculiarly delicate political situation in the country since the institution of the regional governments in 1970, and the general climate of co-operation on the part of the regional governments, and not the least on the part of those controlled by the opposition, has not so far made conflict between the central government and the regions an issue in Italian politics, although the increasingly hostile attitude to the regions demonstrated by the Centre-Right cabinet formed by Andreotti in summer 1972 could well, if not corrected, bring a latent situation to a head.

The Control Committees were not set up until April 1972. In the transition period between June 1970 and April 1972, the Government Commissioner exercised the government's control function alone. An indication of how it may be used in future is provided by the action of the Government Commissioner for Lombardy. On 5 August 1971, he informed the Chairman of the region that while according to the regional statute 'the region has its own flag and coat of arms determined by regional law', the region was in fact not free to determine its coat of arms as it wished by virtue of two royal decrees of 7 June 1943 which regulated the attribution of coats of arms to provinces, municipalities and other officially recognized bodies. Again on 6 September 1971 he returned to the regional council the regional law concerning 'popular legislative initiative' provided for in the regional statute. At the same time, he raised objections to a proposed regional inquiry into the activity of the Neo-Fascists in Lombardy on the grounds that (1) the sum allocated by the State to the regions was not intended to cover such purposes; (2) the decision to hold the inquiry would have to be approved by the Control Committee which had not yet been constituted, (3) the problem of the struggle against Neo- Fascism was a national one and did not concern the regions.

The central government has the power to dissolve regional Councils in certain circumstances. These circumstances are set out in Article 126 of the Constitution; they are acting unconstitutionally, grave violations of the law, failure to replace its Junta or Chairman at the request of the central government when they have perpetrated similar acts or violations, inability to function because of resignations or failure to produce a working majority, or reasons of national security. The President of the Republic is responsible for issuing the decree of dissolution which must be supported by a statement of the reasons. At the same time, the inter-Parliamentary Committee on Regional Problems (which comprises fifteen deputies and fifteen senators) must be consulted whenever a dissolution is proposed, but its opinion is not binding on the government. Elections for a new regional Council must be held within three months of a dissolution. In the meantime, the regions are administered by a three-man commission appointed by the government; their major responsibility is, of course, the preparation of new regional elections within the three-months period. It is clear also that the power of dissolution, like that of annulling regional government acts, is potentially a weapon in the hands of the central government which it could use against the regional governments, either collectively or singly, for political ends. Constitutionally, the regional governments are defenceless against the central government supported by a determined parliamentary majority, but this is merely to repeat what has been clear from the outset : that Italy is a unitary state. Of course the central government's use of its powers would depend on the political situation. At the present time (autumn 1972), it is impossible to see it taking such action without provoking the most serious political situation in the country.

The Regional Debate: Political Autonomy or Administrative Decentralization?

In presenting the draft Constitution to the Constituent Assembly, the reporter of the Drafting Committee, Meuccio Ruini, wrote that 'the most profound innovation introduced by the Constitution lay in the organization of State institutions on the basis of the principle of Autonomy', and he went on to prophesy that the principle of autonomy 'could be of decisive importance for the history of the country'. His prophecy has not been realized to date; but it still remains open. To appreciate what is at stake it is necessary to consider briefly the nature of the postwar debate on regionalism in Italy. The hopes of the regionalists were centred essentially on the belief that the creation of politically autonomous regional governments would be responsible for a radical social and political renewal of the country. They thought that regional political autonomy would be instrumental in destroying political clientelism because they were convinced that the latter thrived in a centralized administrative system. They argued that the existence of regional government would rapidly promote a high level of political participation, because it would necessarily be dealing with problems nearer the hearts of the mass of the population than those that the national government habitually dealt with. They also claimed that the weakening of the centralized power structure of the Italian state system was a necessary prerequisite for overcoming regional inequalities. Finally, they maintained that by multiplying the number of effective decision-making centres by twenty, politically autonomous regional governments would act as a corrective to the concentration of Italian industry which they judged excessive.

The argument of the anti-regionalists was simply the traditional one that local political autonomy would only disperse and fragment political power in the State without bringing any of the advantages that the regionalists promised; indeed, many resolutely denied that these were advantages. They had a relatively facile task in pointing out that political power was dangerously dispersed already; although, of course, they rarely went one step further to ask why it was so. This traditional argument that the State was the proper entity for the exercise of political power received additional support from planners and technocrats, who claimed that it was the only level (in default of supranational structures) at which to get a global view of national economic problems. In consequence, for them local political autonomy could have as its effect the undermining of national policies by aggregating mutually contradictory cross-pressures instead of promoting a synthesis.

None of the major hopes of the regionalists have been achieved. This disappointment has not been altogether the fault of the regions, although the experience of the special regional governments has been very mixed. The action of successive Christian

Democrat-dominated coalition governments has been one of procrastination, when not actively hostile. Their attitude has ensured that there has been little or no decentralization or devolution of powers and functions from the central to the regional governments. As a direct consequence, 'the relationship between the central government and the regions has been at best uneasy and at worst a bitter contest for ascendancy; the central government trying to dominate the regions, the regions trying to maintain and extend their autonomy . . . Sicily more than any other region has quarrelled with the central government.'

Such energy as successive governments have devoted to the regions has been employed in undermining their political autonomy as laid down in the Constitution. This was notoriously the case of the so-called Scelba Law (No. 62 of 10 February 1953) which formed the first part of the implementing legislation. It laid down contrary to Article 123 of the Constitution very precise regulations governing the operation of regional Councils (Articles 14, 15, 19 and 22) and Juntas (Articles 23, 26 and 27). Indeed it went so far in this direction that the Tupini Committee set up by Parliament in 1962 to study the implementation of the ordinary regions reported as follows : 'Law No. 62 imposes on the regional legislatures the adoption of undifferentiated structures similar to those of the communes and provinces; it takes no account of the diversity of the regions, and violates their statutory competence established by Article 123 . . .' It also fixed limits on regional legislative initiative and the use of referenda, and extended the control powers of the Government Commissioner far beyond anything contemplated by the Constituent Assembly. Moreover, if the Scelba Law was the most far-reaching attack on regional political autonomy, it was not the only legislation passed which had this effect. Law No. 281 of 16 May 1970, on regional finance, imposed similar restrictions : 'Of the two elements which compose regional financial autonomy,' Ferrari has commented, 'it establishes that of payment but reduces that of perception to nothing.'

Similarly, the legislation on economic planning rides roughshod over regional autonomy by virtually excluding all forms of regional planning, either global or sectoral. In addition, various measures, and specifically the bill patronized by the young left-wing Christian Democrat Ciriaco De Mita, when Under-Secretary of the Interior in 1968, which were never passed, were aimed at cutting down regional political autonomy even further by imposing rigid uniformity. The reasons for this consistent hostility to regional political autonomy are not hard to find. In addition to the fear which the spectre of Communist control of a number of regions of central Italy raised in the hearts of members of the government coalition, the central government had a specific problem : that of a serious crisis in the state administration and the latter's inability to solve a number of pressing social problems (health, education, town planning, etc.) It was natural in these circumstances that it should look to the possibility of an administrative decentralization in a regional framework as a solution. Such an operation would have had the political advantage that, by transferring administrative responsibility but retaining political control, the government would remain the master and so be in a position to blame any shortcomings on the regions and claim any political successes as its own.

It would seem, however, that the creation of the ordinary regional governments in June 1970 has reversed this climate of opinion. All the regions in their statutes stressed their own political autonomy, and their role as instruments of political participation in the exercise of both political and economic power. They also affirmed their right to establish economic and social regional plans as well as to participate in the elaboration of national planning. Parliament, by ratifying the regional statutes, has underwritten this new situation. Moreover the Minister responsible for Regional Reform was at pains, when presenting the statutes to the Senate in March 1971, to claim that they 'had been elaborated with the greatest respect for the political autonomy of the regions'. This suggests that the government is prepared to accept, if only half-heartedly that the Italian system of regional government is a feasible solution to the problem of how to secure devolution and decentralization in a unitary state without endangering its unity; and that some of the hopes of the regionalists are achievable.

Conclusion: Republic Without Government?

Son livre devait être l'*Esprit des Lois* des gouvernements successifs de l'Italie, et il y a eu dans ce pays-ci beaucoup plus de gouvernements que de lois, et le gouvernement y a toujours eu la couleur du gouvernant.

Stendhal

Conclusion:
Republic without Government?

The foregoing chapters have outlined the major components of civil society and the State in Italy and their political activity in the process of government. On the one hand, civil society appears in the image of the party system characterized by dualism and discontinuity, fragmentation and dispersion. On the other hand, the State's image is furnished by the government beset by instability and delay, contradiction and inefficiency. If these are appropriate images, it is no wonder that Italy lurches from crisis to crisis; the marvel is that the political system operates at all. In these circumstances, we can understand the heartfelt cry of an Italian banker during the cabinet crisis of spring 1970 when he exclaimed: 'We're better off without a government. Workers don't strike and students don't protest when there is nobody in power to listen to them.' That such a view is likely to be superficial is clear from the fact that one of the paradoxes of postwar Italy has been the flourishing state of the economy. In fact it is difficult to imagine a greater contrast than that between the dynamism of the economy for many of the postwar years and the immobilism of the polity. Such a paradox raises the question how was it possible and what are the prospects of its continuance?

In answering this question we need to examine the image of civil society. It is true that it is characterized by duality and discontinuity, fragmentation and dispersion, but within basic limits that have conferred a unity on it. It has been conditioned by the international situation which has imposed certain parameters. It is not only that advanced capitalism, in whose cultural area Italy has been in the postwar period, has its own international culture complete with its own language, procedures and organizations, but all groups, including the major opposition groups, accepted the consequences of Italy's place in the international situation. Thus, for example, the fundamental features of the postwar economic and political system – capitalist economy and parliamentary democracy – were not seriously disputed, not even by the opposition; recent attacks on the whole economic and political system, although symptomatic of a wider malaise, have been restricted to limited groups.

The poverty of civil society in Italy until the sixties meant that much social experience was not articulated and hence rarely found coherent and durable political expression. Before Fascism the State was manipulated by a small oligarchy through its chosen instruments, the administration, police, army, and judiciary. During the First World War big business entered the traditional centres of power; and under Fascism the Catholic Church with its network of ecclesiastical organizations was integrated into the power structure. The strength of the oligarchy and the weakness of civil society explain the failure of the Resistance to effectuate major reforms and the ease with which its political organization, the CLN, was liquidated at the end of the war.

The overwhelming consensus of civil society in favour of the basic orientations of the economic and political system throughout the postwar period is less than surprising when one considers the virtual monopoly that the ruling class and its supporters enjoy over the material means of ideological production (i.e. creation and diffusion of ideas): education, press, publishing, radio and television. It has used them to define the frame of reference of postwar politics and the terms of the ideological debate. These significantly enough were founded on an economic definition of reality: the reconstruction of the economy in the late forties and the god 'Growth' thereafter. The hegemony, or ideological domination of the ruling classes over civil society, despite the obviousness of its achievement, has been critical in securing the basic consensus towards the present system. Of course, the development of civil society in the sixties has introduced changes but the situation remains more one of potential than achieved articulation and, hence, substantially the same. After all, it must be remembered that Italy still remains 'a semi-literate nation'. One should perhaps add that consensus achieved in this manner (i.e. through the orientation of the major institutions of the state system) is somewhat superficial, and so fragile, to the extent that it is founded on conformism towards imposed norms rather than internationalized experience. It can, therefore, be swept aside by a new conformist consensus, if articulate groups manage to persuade the major institutions to change their orientation, as occurred once earlier in this century. While it is difficult to determine the exact conditions in which this might recur (type of economic and social crisis, etc.), we can be sure that the present Neo-Fascist groups do not represent such a threat as they are too marginal to Italian life.

The great majority of the leadership personnel of organizations of civil society in addition to that of the state institutions is recruited from the middle classes (see Table 10.i).

Table 10. i

Family Background of Civil Society and State Leadership Personnel 1962

	Upper and middle bourgeoisie	New middle class	Old middle class	Working class	Total	(N.)
Political leaders	26·7%	36·3%	16·9%	7·1%	14·6%	(142)
Economic/administrative leaders	47·9%	32·0%	18·9%	0·6%	49·9%	(483)
Ecclesiastical leaders	10·5%	10·5%	39·5%	39·5%	3·9%	(38)
Artistic/liberal professions	57·0%	29·0%	11·6%	1·2%	26·6%	(258)
University teachers	42·9%	49·0%	—	8·1%	5·0%	(49)
Total	44·5%	31·7%	16·7%	3·6%	100·0%	(970)

Source: adapted from *Inchiesta Shell* No. 3, p. 34

One of the characteristics of the middle classes is that they are a largely parasitic strata because they lack an autonomous economic position in society. An Italian observer has commented that 'although the middle classes do not constitute a class properly speaking, they possess like certain saints the gift of ubiquity. Even the interests of the working class are managed in large part – at least on the political and trade union level – by members of the middle classes who enjoy, in contrast to wage-earning-workers, among other privileges those of more free-time and a higher level of education. 'While they administer public bodies and party machines and condition, to a large extent, taste and social aspira-

I

tions, it is not possible to say that "power" is in the hands of these strata. In advanced industrial nations, the middle classes are the universal administrators : they condition the basic decisions – even to the extent of having a power of veto in many cases – but they do not make them.' 'Power' (i.e. the power to make basic decisions) is in the hands of the ruling class.

Professor Meynaud concluded the most detailed study of the Italian ruling class to date with the assertion that 'the higher direction of Italian life is assured by a coalition, more or less coherent according to the period, of economic, political or religious forces, whose identification does not raise difficult problems. However, if the centre of gravity of this oligarchy can easily be discovered, the situation of the different categories raises delicate problems.' For my part, I would put the dyarchy of the Roman Catholic hierarchy and the big economic groups at the centre of the Italian ruling class, and the political and administrative leaders behind them as their agents, but with a wide area for manoeuvre. The power of the Church is logical in a predominantly Catholic country, which is the home of its temporal seat, and in which the Catholic party has been in power for close on thirty years, largely thanks to the Church's electoral influence. The big economic group leaders can be defined as the small circles of Chairmen and Managers (technocrats) of the major private and public corporations grouped round the big four of Fiat, ENI, IRI and Montedison, which dominate the Italian economy. They spring generally from the northern bourgeoisie and their career patterns are being characterized by greater interchangeability. Their economic influence derives from their relative weight in relation to the fragmentation of the greater part of the Italian economy. Their political influence is founded on their ability to determine large areas of economic activity and to manipulate parties and pressure groups. Co-ordination between them was achieved externally through Confindustria (until the withdrawal of the state-holding companies) and internally through reciprocal share-holdings in the major financial corporations (cf. Bastogi, Mediobanca, etc.). In fact, Italian capital is very concentrated and the ramifications between the major corporations are endless. In addition, there has been a tendency in recent years for these groups to extend their international ties (Fiat with Citroen, and in the USSR Pirelli with Dunlop, ENI with local consortia in oil-producing countries, etc.)

to reduce their dependence on the Italian economy. The Vatican has also tended to diversify its investments in recent years, selling its stake in some Italian companies and buying interests in multinational (principally American) companies. The economic difficulties of the sixties have led to an accelerated expansion of the public sector and of foreign capital in Italian industry, and to a corresponding decline of private capital. In consequence, the new economic planning machinery has become more important than *Confindustria* as a mechanism of external co-ordination.

Co-option, is as it always was, the main form of recruitment to political and administrative leadership. Accession to posts of public responsibility, whether elective or appointive, is dependent not only on broad ideological sympathy for the *status quo* but often on personal loyalty to specific politicians. It is here that a number of specific facts assume their full significance: first, the increase in the proportion of full-time professional politicians in Parliament and party positions; second, the dependence of parties on public and private funds because income from membership dues and party activity in no way covers current operating expenditure, much less campaign expenses; third, the low pay and lack of technical and management expertise of the predominantly 'southern' higher civil servants; fourth; the dependence of business on the State for many things: protection from foreign competition and the disciplining of the working classes, the channelling of government purchases and public utility franchises, etc. In consequence, politicians are subject to the wire-pulling influence of interest groups (specifically, the Church, big business and parasitic interests), and civil servants are no match for the sophisticated lobbyists of interest groups determined to get what they want out of the government machine. There can be little doubt, therefore, of the general sense of the activity of the influential leaders of civil society and the State: the preservation of the *status quo*. It does not preclude conflicts of interest between different factions of the ruling class, nor that opposition groups, like trade unions, are devoid of influence. It is simply that the disagreements which there are, and they can be violent, do not question the basis of the social system, but rather the best way of reinforcing it, or defending specific interests within it. Nor are the disagreements without political significance. On the contrary, they are often important; and can have more far-reaching consequences for the operation of the system than the insufficiency and inadequacy of many of the organizations and institutions.

The framework of the economic and political system in the immediate postwar period, was established by the government under the pressure of external events. In this the De Gasperi-Einaudi package was as important for the economy as the writing of the Constitution was in creating the political institutions. In fact it is no paradox to say that the so-called Einaudi line had a more direct influence on the operation of the economy than did the Constitution on postwar politics. The Einaudi reforms provided the basis for economic growth and the instrument for imperative co-ordination of all sectors of the economy by the Bank of Italy. In conjunction with other favourable circumstances, the Bank's skilful management of monetary policy enabled it to play a role similar to that of the *Société Générale de Belgique* or *Union des Banques Suisses* in their respective countries and guide Italy along the road of industrial expansion – industrial output rose by over 150 per cent between 1947 and 1961. The Bank has become so successful that big businessmen were claiming in 1970 that 'it is quite possible to run the economy without the government provided that the machinery for handing out funds and the Bank of Italy, one of the most modern central banks with an excellent research staff, runs the credit policy.' The efficiency, despatch and realism of the Bank's action contrasted with the 'archaic, centralized, over manned, slow-moving and legalistic' activity of ministerial departments. Thus, when rumours of the departure of the Bank's Governor, Guido Carli, appeared in the press in Spring 1970, the Milan Stock Exchange fell; and the press commented significantly : 'There has to be somebody at the helm somewhere.'

It is not that the government has abdicated all responsibility, but too often, when faced with opposition within its own ranks, its measures become a case of too little too late. For instance, the government provisions intended to relaunch the economy after the 'hot autumn' of 1969 were elaborated immediately after the renewal of the labour contracts and wage rises. As a result of two cabinet crises and a long parliamentary battle forced more by government supporters than the opposition, they were not applied until over a year later when the economic situation was very different. In general, for much of the postwar period Italian society has

operated on the basis of a division of labour between politicians, and businessmen and bankers : the former interesting themselves in the *minutiae* of partisan politics; and the latter being left
to look after the economy. Yet the government was active in promoting a number of measures designed to strengthen the
advanced part of the economy (creation of ENI, withdrawal of
State employers from *Confindustria*, creations of Ministry of State
Holdings, nationalization of electrical supply industry, setting up
planning machinery, etc.) In fact, there was even a confused
attempt by politicians to take a lead in the economic sphere
through control of public enterprise, but in face of the violent reactions of private business, they became more circumspect.
Government reforming intentions have, therefore, been sporadic;
and often allowed to get bogged down in administrative detail.

The prime reason for the politicians' preoccupation with partisan politics is the Namier-style party system. Political fragmentation nourishes instability which in turn feeds immobilism. The
causes of political fragmentation are much debated. One of its
bases is the dualistic nature of the economy (both structural and
geographic). Another is the poverty of civil society which favours
the dispersion of partisan loyalty. Finally, it has been encouraged
by the activity of the parties. Once established in power and its
external unity assured thanks to the Church, the Christian Democrat Party's interest has been to dominate the party system by
ensuring as far as possible that its rivals remained divided or excluded from power (as in the case of the Communist Party). Moreover, government policy consciously cultivated social fragmentation by favouring through tax policies, subsidies and patronage,
the emergence and growth of a whole host of parasitic intermediary strata to offset the loss of support of the working class
when it expelled the Communist and Socialist Parties from the
government in 1947. Ideologically this action was justified by the
theme of '*interclassismo*' (all class) which was the basis of the
Christian Democrats' appeal in the decade 1950–60.

The effect on government action is slow and inadequate
decision-making. Important decisions requiring legislation or
cabinet approval need long and painful negotiations between
government partners and are always likely to be thrown into
question by one party or faction. Long negotiations in a rapidly
changing social and economic environment often mean that the

measures finally agreed upon are irrelevant when introduced. As many decisions as possible are taken informally inside single ministries or directorates, or simply not taken at all. Unfortunately there is a limit to this type of activity because of the need for coalitions, not only in Parliament but also in relation to civil society groups to ensure acceptance. Further, as a result of Fascist abuse of decree laws and administrative regulations, the Constitution made parliamentary approval necessary for most kinds of administrative decision or regulation.

In the fifties a division of labour between the economy and political affairs was just about possible. The operation of the political system was just adequate partly because weaknesses in the articulation of civil society permitted the manipulation of the subordinate classes in the traditional ways, and partly because the running of the economy could safely be left to the businessmen and bankers. Relations between the economic leaders and the government were mediated by the Bank of Italy. The result was that the Italian entrepreneur was able to live for almost fifteen years, as even *The Economist* was forced to admit, 'in a capitalist's dream'.

The growth of the Italian economy and the development of civil society allied to the social problems which the former brought in its wake and which the latter was able to articulate more coherently, put the balance of the system in jeopardy. It was not just a case of the massive rural exodus and archaic social amenities, but rather that the Neo-capitalist economy that Italy had been developing in the North was becoming less compatible with existing political institutions because it required a global intervention in, and control of, society. The old instruments of political manipulation were no longer sufficient. Ensuring social peace was not enough to ensure economic growth : it required active government intervention. But the state machinery was inadequate for the task : 'Our state is weak', one Minister confessed in private, 'our administration meddles impotently, months and months are required for any reform, however urgent.'

The centre-left was, in the minds of its promoters, an attempt to remedy this situation; and economic planning was its chosen instrument. It was based on the assumption that the support of the Socialist Party would make the reformers and technocrats stronger than the conservatives and jurists. Already in the forties, De

Gasperi had thought along similar lines : the creation of the special administrative agencies (*Cassa*, ENI, land reform agencies, etc.) had represented his attempt to give the reformers their head over the conservatives. However the type of economic growth that the Einaudi-line promoted in Italy required strengthening the conservatives by favouring the emergence and consolidation of the parasitic intermediary strata (*Federconsorzi*, urban speculation, etc.) to give it a larger social basis. The Socialist Party, in trying to represent the interests of all the new groups that were emerging in the sixties, ended up by representing nobody, and was reduced to vassal status by the Christian Democrats. The incapacity of the political leaders to recast the state machinery set a definite limit to their reforming capacity.

Today big business, both public and private, the financial institutions and the special agencies can be said to be in the hands of the technocrats and managers while the ordinary administration, judiciary, small business and trade is in the hands of the conservatives and bureaucrats. So far the technocrats have promoted reforms and the conservatives have managed to block them. This is because the conservatives are still powerful enough in the state machine. However, higher wages for workers without corresponding social reforms has meant a profits squeeze in industry for most of the sixties and a drying up of private investment. Public investment was increased under the spur of the technocrats but it could only be a small fraction of government resources because the major part was absorbed by the continually growing bureaucracy, and subsidized parasitic activities. At the same time decision-making was becoming concentrated and rationalized in those sectors over which the technocrats had control. But this action could only be partial, given that the sectors controlled by the conservatives became increasingly disconnected, and so the economic system became increasingly dysfunctional. Economic depression was prolonged and even growth, which had continued throughout the late sixties thanks to the prompting of the public sector, came grinding to a halt in 1970.

In 1973 it is now believed that a recovery of growth is imminent as a result of changes in the structure of Italian industry imposed by the depression, which have made both big and small industry competitive once again in international markets. These changes (concentration by big industry and deconcentration by small industry) by making them no longer competitors for labour, are expected to fragment the working class, stop the rural exodus, and hence take the pressure off the urgency for reform. If they do not, or recovery fails to materialize, then the Italian ruling class will be forced to choose between its progressive and authoritarian faces. On the one hand, a new majority (including the Communist Party); on the other new (Presidential) institutions. The former is likely to unlock the party system and introduce welcome elements of political mobility and governmental stability. The latter is likely to cause large-scale political unrest, but that would not necessarily deter its supporters. In any event, the technocrats are likely to come out on top in either case, but in the first they would have a more progressive face, and in the second a more authoritarian one. Should the ruling class refuse, or find itself unable, to choose, then, and only then, would the present institutional system and the economic structure which supports it be in any danger. It was no coincidence that the so-called De Lorenzo *coup* was organized during the 1963–5 recession. For while it is true that the inefficiency of the present system represents a decline in hegemony of the ruling class that controls it, it is equally true that the decline has not, as yet, provoked the rise of the hegemony of an alternative class or coalition of classes. For this the international situation is responsible in no small measure since it is a feature common to all the countries of Western Europe.

Bibliography

The literature in Italian on government and politics is immense. It is chiefly of two kinds: treatises on constitutional or public law, like Costantino Mortati's *Istituzioni di diritto pubblico*, 8th edition (Padua, 1969) or Paolo Barile's *Istituzioni di diritto pubblico* (Padua, 1972) or polemical journalism. There is also an up and coming school of Italian political science which this book draws on extensively. Its most obvious monument to date is the five volume *Ricerche sulla partecipazione politica in Italia* carried out by the Cattaneo Institute of Bologna (4 volumes, 1967–9). The bibliography which follows has been confined to English and French works because they are likely to be more accessible to the average English reader.

Bibliographical Sources
F. S. Stych, *How to Find Out About Italy* (Oxford, 1970), Chapters 1 (bibliography), 2 (periodicals and newspapers) and 4 (social sciences)
J. Meyriat, 'Problèmes politiques de la république italienne, état des travaux' in *Revue Française de Science Politique* (March 1962)

General
M. Grindrod, *Italy* (London, 1968)
H. S. Hughes, *The United States and Italy* (Cambridge, Mass., 1965)
N. Jucker, *Italy* (London, 1970)
J. Nobécourt, *L'Italie à vif* (Paris, 1970)
Presidency of Council of Ministers, *Italy, Documents and Notes* (Italian government English language publication, appears every two months, but lacks the quality and range of the French equivalent, *La documentation française*)

Historical Background
L. Cafagna, *The Industrial Revolution in Italy, 1830–1914* (London, 1971)
S. B. Clough, *The Economic History of Italy* (New York, 1964)
B. Croce, *A History of Italy, 1871–1915* (Oxford, 1929)
H. Finer, *Mussolini's Italy* (New York, 2nd ed. 1965)
A. Gramsci, *Selections from the Prison Notebooks* (London, 1971)

251

Bibliography

D. Mack-Smith, *Italy: A Modern History* (Ann Arbor, 1959)
G. Salvemini, *The Fascist Dictatorship in Italy* (London, 1928)
G. Salvemini, *Under the Axe of Fascism* (London, 1936)
G. Salvemini and G. La Piana, *What to do with Italy* (London, 1943)
C. Seton-Watson, *Italy from Liberalism to Fascism* (London, 1967)
S. J. Woolf (ed.), *The Nature of Fascism* (London, 1967)

Postwar Period
F. R. Willis, *Italy Chooses Europe* (New York, 1971)
F. Chabod, *A History of Italian Fascism* (London, 1963)
N. Kogan, *A Political History of Postwar Italy* (London, 1966)
G. Mammarella, *Italy after Fascism* (Notre Dame, 1965)
S. J. Woolf (ed.), *The Rebirth of Italy, 1943–50* (London, 1972)

The Southern Question
G. Barbero, *Land Reform in Italy, Achievement and Perspectives* (Rome, 1961)
M. Carlyle, *The Awakening of Southern Italy* (London, 1962)
G. Schachter, *The Italian South, Economic Development in Mediterranean Europe* (New York, 1965)

The Economy
G. Hildebrande, *Growth and Structure in the Economy of Modern Italy* (Cambridge, Mass., 1965)
M. Kidron, *Western Capitalism Since the War* (London, 1970)
V. Lutz, *Italy – A Study in Economic Development* (London, 1962)
OECD, *Economic Survey, Italy* (Paris, annually since 1954)
M. Selvati, 'The Impasse of Italian Capitalism' in *New Left Review*, 76 (November–December 1972)
A. Shonfield, *Modern Capitalism* (London, 1965)

Emigration
J. Lopreato, *Peasants No More* (San Francisco, 1967)
J. S. and L. D. MacDonald, 'Italian Migration to Australia' in *Journal of Social History* (Spring 1970)

Class Structure
F. Alberoni, 'Classes and Generations' in *Social Science Information* (December 1971)
P. Ammassari, 'The Italian Blue-Collar Worker' in *International Journal of Comparative Sociology*, No. 1–2 (1969)
J. Anglade, *La vie quotidienne contemporaine en Italie* (Paris, 1973)
L. Gallino, 'Italy' in M. S. Archer and S. Giner (eds.), *Contemporary Europe: Class, Status, Power* (London, 1971)
L. Gallino and others, *Social Structure and Factory Structures in Italy: A Pilot Study* (Turin, 1969)

Bibliography

J. Lopreato, 'Upward Social Mobility and Political Orientation',
  American Journal of Sociology (Winter 1967)
S. J. Surace, *Ideology, Economic Change and the Working Class:
  The Case of Italy* (Berkeley, 1966)

Political Culture
P. A. Allum, *Politics and Society in Postwar Italy* (Cambridge, 1973)
E. C. Banfield, *The Moral Basis of a Backward Society* (New York,
  2nd ed. 1967)
M. Brandon-Albini, *Midi vivant* (Paris, 1963)
D. Dolci, *Poverty in Sicily* (London, 1966)
D. Dolci, *The Man who Plays Alone* (London, 1967)
H. S. Hughes, *Consciousness and Society* (New York, 1961)
J. LaPalombara, 'Italy, Fragmentation, Isolation and Alienation' in
  L. W. Pye and S. Verba (eds.), *Political Culture and Political
  Development* (Princeton, 1964)
J. Meyriat (ed.), *La Calabre* (Paris, 1960)
J. Meyriat (ed.), *Tradition et Changement en Toscane* (Paris, 1970)
A. Momigliano, 'Reconsidering B. Croce (1866–1952)' in *Durham
  University Journal* (December 1966)
M. Pantaleone, *Mafia and Politics* (London, 1966)
A. Pizzorno, 'Amoral Familism and Historical Marginality' in *Int.
  Review of Community Development* (1966)
School of Barbiana, *Letter to a Teacher* (London, 1970)
Various Authors, *Culture and Ideology in Post-war Italy*, 20th Cen-
  tury Studies No. 5 (September 1971)

The Catholic Church
D. A. Binchy, *Church and State in Fascist Italy* (London, 1970)
C. Falconi, *Pope John and His Council* (London, 1964)
A. C. Jemolo, *Church and State in Italy, 1850–1950* (Oxford, 1960)
P. Nichols, *The Politics of the Vatican* (London, 1968)
C. Pallenberg, *Vatican Finances* (London, 1971)
G-F. Poggi, *Catholic Action in Italy* (Stanford, 1967)
P. Vincent Bucci, *Chiesa e Stato* (The Hague, 1969)
L. C. Webb, *Church and State in Italy, 1947–1957* (Melbourne,
  1958)

Party System
P. A. Allum, 'Italy – Politics of Namier' in *New Society* (2 April
  1970)
P. A. Allum, 'Italy' in S. Henig and J. Pinder (eds.), *European
  Political Parties* (London, 1970)

Bibliography

G. Galli and A. Piandi, *Patterns of Political Participation in Italy* (New Haven, 1970)

J. Meynaud, *Les partis politiques en Italie* (Paris, 1965)

G. Sartori, 'European Political Parties : The Case of Polarized Pluralism' in J. LaPalombara and M. Weiner, *Political Parties and Political Development* (Princeton, 1966)

S. Tosi, 'Italy : Anti-System Opposition within System' in *Government and Opposition* (January 1967)

Christian Democrat Party

J-P. Chasseriaud, *Le parti démocrate chrétien en Italie* (Paris, 1965)

T. Godechot, *Le parti démocrat chrétien italien* (Paris, 1964)

R. A. Webster, *Christian Democracy in Italy, 1860–1960* (London, 1961)

R. Zariski, 'Intra-party Conflict in a Dominant Party : The Experience of Italian Christian Democracy' in *Journal of Politics* (February 1965)

Communist Party

P. A. Allum, *The PCI since 1945* (Reading, 1970)

D. L. M. Blackmer, *Unity in Diversity, Italian Communism and the Communist World* (Cambridge, Mass., 1968)

R. H. Evans, *Coexistence: Communism and its Practice in Bologna, 1945–1965* (Notre Dame, 1965)

M-A. Macciocchi, *Letters from inside the Communist Party to Louis Althusser* (London, 1973)

S. G. Tarrow, *Peasant Communism in Southern Italy* (New Haven, 1967)

S. White, 'Gramsci and Italian Communist Party' in *Government and Opposition* (Spring 1972)

Socialist Parties

S. H. Barnes, *Party Democracy, Politics in an Italian Socialist Federation* (New Haven, 1967)

V. Foa, *Social Democracy – Yesterday and Today* (Reading, 1968)

R. Zariski, 'The Italian Socialist Party : A Case Study in Factional Conflict' in *American Political Science Review* (June 1962)

Elections and Electoral Behaviour

P. A. Allum, 'The Italian Elections of 1963' in *Political Studies* (October 1965)

J. Besson, 'Les élections italiennes du 25 mai 1958' in *Revue Française de Science Politique* (Juin 1959)

M. Clark and R. E. M. Irving, 'The Italian Political Crisis and the General Elections of May 1972' in *Parliamentary Affairs* (Summer 1972)

M. Dogan, 'Le comportement politique des italiens' in *Revue Française de Science Politique* (Juin 1959)

M. Dogan, 'Comportement politique et condition sociale en Italie' in *Revue Française de Sociologie*, numéro spéciale (1966)

M. Dogan, 'Political Cleavage and Social Stratification in France and Italy' in S. M. Lipsett and S. Rokkan (eds.), *Party Systems and Voter Alignments* (London, 1967)

N. Edelman, 'Sources of Popular Support for the Italian Christian Democrat Party in the Postwar Decade' in *Midwest Journal of Politics* (May 1958)

N. Edelman, 'Causes of Fluctuations in the Popular Support for the Italian Communist Party' in *Journal of Politics* (August 1958)

R. C. Fried, 'Urbanization and Italian Politics', in *Journal of Politics* (August 1967)

J. LaPalombara, 'The Italian Elections and the Problem of Representation' in *American Political Science Review* (September 1953)

Party Finance

S. Passigli, 'Italy' in A. J. Heidenheimer and R. Rose, *Comparative Political Finance: A Symposium*, special number of *Journal of Politics* (1963)

Interest Groups

D. L. Horovitz, *The Italian Labour Movement* (Cambridge, Mass., 1963)

J. LaPalombara, Interest Groups in Italian Politics (Princeton, 1964)

M. F. Neufield, *Italy: School for Awakening Countries* (Ithaca, 1961)

Executive and Legislature

The text of the Constitution is in A. J. Peaslee, *The Constitutions of Nations*, Vol. 2 (The Hague, 2nd ed. 1965)

J. P. Adams and P. Barile, 'The Implementation of the Italian Constitution' in *American Political Science Review* (March 1953)

F. Cosentino, 'Parliamentary Committees in the Italian Political System' in *Journal of Constitutional and Parliamentary Studies* (Summer 1967)

U. Cosentino, *Legislative Power of Committees in Chamber of Deputies* (Geneva, 1950)

G. J. Dirienzo, *Personality, Power and Politics* (Notre Dame, 1967)

M. Duverger, *Institutions politiques et Droit constitutionnel* (Paris, 11th ed. 1970)

Bibliography

M. Einaudi, 'The Constitution of the Italian Republic' in *American Political Science Review* (August 1948)
P. Ferrari and H. Maisl, *Les groupes communistes aux assemblées parlementaires italiennes et françaises* (Paris, 1969)
R. Miliband, *The State in Capitalist Society* (London, 1970)
G. Sartori, 'Italian Parliamentarians' in *International Social Science Journal*, IV (1961)

Public Administration and Military
B. Chapman, *The Profession of Government* (London, 1959)
F. DeMarchi, *La bureaucratie italienne*, paper presented to IPSA Conference (1970)
S. Finer, *Man on Horseback* (London, 1964)
J. LaPalombara, *Italy: The Politics of Planning* (Syracuse, 1966)
E. Rossi, 'Italy' in M. Einaudi, *Nationalization in France and Italy* (Ithaca, 1955)
M. V. Posner and S. J. Woolf, *Italian Public Enterprise* (London, 1967)
S. Holland (ed.), *The State as Entrepreneur* (London, 1972)
G. Treves, 'Public Corporation in Italy' in *Government Enterprise* (London, 1970)
M. M. Watson, *Regional Development Policy and Administration in Italy*
N. Kogan, *The Politics of Italian Foreign Policy* (London, 1963)
L. Free and R. Sereno, *Italy: Dependent Ally or Independent Partner* (Princeton, 1957)
J. Wullus-Rudiger, 'Italy's Role Within NATO' in *Military Review* (February 1959)

Judiciary and Legal System
M. Cappelletti, J. H. Merryman and J. M. Perillo, *The Italian Legal System* (Stanford, 1967)
M. Cappelletti and J. M. Perillo, *Civil Procedure in Italy* (The Hague, 1965)
G. Cassandro, 'The Constitutional Court of Italy' in *American Journal of Comparative Law* (August 1959)
T. Cole, 'Three Constitutional Courts' in *American Political Science Review* (December 1959)
M. Evans, 'The Italian Constitutional Court' in *International and Comparative Law Quarterly* (July 1968)
R. P. Franchino, 'Some Observations on the Italian Constitutional System : Historical Development, General Characteristics and Individual Rights' in *Journal of Public Law* (Spring 1960)
G. Miele and others, 'Italian Administrative Law' in *International and Comparative Quarterly* (July 1954)

G. Treves, 'Judicial Review of Legislation in Italy' in *Journal of Public Law* (Fall 1958)

G. Treves, 'Judicial Review in Italian Administrative Law' in *Chicago Law Review* (Winter 1958)

J. Millner, 'Note on Italian Law' in *International and Comparative Law Quarterly* (December 1965)

G. Cardaci, 'The Status of Women in the World Today : Italy' in *Review of Contemporary Law*, Part 1 (1960)

L. Galeotti, *The Judicial Control of Public Authorities in England and Italy* (London, 1954)

E. Sereni, 'The Legal Profession in Italy' in *Harvard Law Review* (December 1950)

L. Del Russo, 'The Notary Public in the Civil Law of Italy' in *George Washington Law Review* (Summer 1952)

Local Government

L. Cappelletti, 'Local Government in Italy' in *Public Administration* (Winter 1963)

R. C. Fried, *The Italian Prefects* (New Haven, 1963)

R. C. Fried, 'Communism, Urban Budgets and the Two Italies', in *Journal of Politics* (November 1971)

R. C. Fried, *Planning the Eternal City* (New Haven, 1973)

G. Pianese, 'Local Finance' in *Economic Conditions in Italy*, I (1969)

R. Pryce, *The Italian Local Elections of 1956* (London, 1957)

The Regions

P. A. Allum and G. Amyot, 'Regionalism in Italy : New Wine in Old Bottles?' in *Parliamentary Affairs* (Winter 1970–1)

P. Ferrari, *Les regions italiennes* (Paris, 1972)

R. C. Fried, 'Administrative Pluralism and Italian Regional Planning' in *Public Administration* (Winter 1968)

C. Palazzolo, *Les regions italiennes* (Tunis, 1966)

G. Woodcock, 'Trentino – Alto Adige – Problems of an Autonomous Region' in *Il Politico* (March 1967)

G. Woodcock, 'Regional Government : The Italian Example' in *Public Administration* (Winter 1967)

G. Woodcock, 'Italy's New Regions' in *Il Politico* (March 1971)

Italian Ruling Class

P. Farneti, 'Problems and Analysis of the Italian Political Elite', paper presented to IPSA Conference (1970)

P. H. Frankel, *Mattei: Oil and Power Politics* (London, 1966)

J. Meynaud, *Rapport sur la classe dirigeante italienne* (Lausanne, 1964)

D. Votaw, *The Six-Legged Dog, Mattei and ENI, A Study in Power* (Berkeley, 1964)

Index

Acerbo Law, 7, 74, 77
Action Party, 17
Administration Courts, 186–90
  hierarchy of, 187
Administrative system, 140–53
  compartmentalization, 162
  dispersion of ministerial offices
    in, 145
  increased number of ministries
    in, 144
  lack of coherent legislation
    governing, 145
  lack of delegation of authority
    in, 145
  role of prefect in, 147
Andreotti, Giulio, 89, 103, 120,
    138, 234
  preference votes, 80, 89
Assolombarda (Association of
    Lombard Industrialists), 84
Avvocatura dello Stato, 201
Azzariti, Gaetano, 191

Badoglio, Marshal, 16
Bank of Italy, mediation between
    government and economic
    leaders, 248
  monetary and credit policy and,
    169, 246
  role in economic policy making,
    27
Basso, Lelio, 194
Bernabei, 163
Bicameralism, 125

Binchley, D. A., 49
Blocco storico, the, 22
Bonomi, Pietro, 98
Bosco, Giacinto, 121
Braibanti, 209
Bureaucratic intervention:
    clientela and *parentela*, 104–7
Burgalassi, Don Silvane, 53
Bustarella, the, 158

Cabinet instability, 119–20
  effects on policy-making, 121–4
  reasons for, 137
Cappelletti, Professor M.L., 184, 201
Cappelletti, Professor L., 215–6
Carabinieri, the, plan to take politi-
    cal powers, 178
  role of, 174
Cardona, Senator, 8
Carli, Guido, 246
Cassandro, Giovanni, 194
Cassa per il Mezzogiorno (Southern
    Development Fund), 23, 24,
    29, 152–3, 249
Casse Mutue (Small Farmers'
    Health Insurance Agency), 98
Catholic Action, 50, 54, 57
  and direct representation, 103
  hierarchy and clergy control
    over, 56
  intervention in administrative
    process, 107
Catholic Church, attitude towards
    Communist Party, 58–9

and educational system, 57
influence in Italian politics, 48
interference in the Administration, 60, 61
and Italian national life, 15
neutrality in party politics, 49
place in Italian society, 51–8, 244
political activity, 58–61
Catholic Union of Italian Secondary School Teachers (UCIIM), 55
Catholic University of the Sacred Heart, 57
Cattaneo Institute of Bologna, 79, 160
study of municipal budgetary policies, 220
Cavour, 3, 4, 9, 21, 22
Central Giunta, 56
'Centrist' coalition, 138
Chabod, Federico, 5, 7
Chamber of Deputies, electoral system, 75–6, 125–6
procedure, 129
Chapman, Professor B., 144, 156
Chefs de Cabinet, role in Ministry, 144–5, 162–3
Chiurco, 12
Christian Democrat Party, 56
absolute majority, 121
and the elections, 76, 79, 82
financial affairs, 83, 84
ideological tradition, 66
internal struggles, 137
organization, 68–74
and *parentela* relationship, 106
as a permanent government party, 62
power structure, 88–9, 91–2
relationship with the communists, 67
role in economic miracle, 28–9
use of IRI, 99
Church-State relations, 48–51
CIPE (Interministerial Committee for Economic Planning), 24, 152

Civic Committees, 55
Civil and political rights, 205
Civil rights, protection of, 204–11
Civil service, 155, 158
the four classes in, 151–2
Civil service: structure and recruitment, 153–61
Class structure, 36–40
Clientela, the, 22, 23, 79, 88, 105, 106
and factionalism, 106, 107
role in Civil Service posts, 155
CLN (Committee of National Liberation), 16, 17
liquidation, 242
Code of jurisdiction, 181
Coldiretti (National Confederation of Small Farmers), 55, 69, 82, 95, 97–8
and direct representation, 103
influence on the Christian Democrat Party, 98
relationship with administration, 105
Colombo, Emilio, 90, 120, 122, 161
Comitato dei Ministri per il Mezzogiorno, 152
Committee of the Heads of General Staff, 174–6
Commune, as basic unit of local government, 213–5
role of Mayor in, 215
Communist Party, as anti-system party, 62–3
attitude towards Church, 58, 61
discipline, 86–7
and the electorate, 79, 80–1
exclusion from party system, 163
financial affairs, 83–5
ideological tradition, 66
list system of PR, 75–6
power structure, 91–2
relationship with Christian Democrats, 67
relationship with Soviet Union, 85
restoration of parliamentary democracy, 243

Concordat, the, and Catholic
  Action, 49–50
Confapi (National Confederation of
  Small Industries), 95
Conference of the Italian Episcopacy (CEI), 59
Confindustria (General Confederation of Italian Industry), 30,
  84, 95–6, 244–5
  lobbying, 103
  relationship with administration,
  105–7
Confintesa, 100
Confragricoltura (General Confederation of Agriculture), 95
Conscription, 124
Constituent Assembly, the, and
  bicameral system, 124
  and the judicial system, 202
Constitutional Court, 132, 134,
  189, 190, 191–9, 233
  civil rights and conflicts of
  competence cases, 195–7
  conflict with Cassation Court,
  198
  selection of judges, 193
Control Committee on the Acts of
  Provinces and Communes,
  223–4, 234
Control Commission, 233
Co-option, 245
'Corporate State', 7
  and Fascism, 11–15
Corriere della Sera, and the
  Feltrinelli affair, 209
Corte dei Conti, the, 165
Council, local, 214–6
  regional, 227–8
Council of State, 141, 164, 188–90
  sections in, 188
Court of Exchequer, 141
  sections in, 189
Courts, organization of the, 182–90
Croce, Benedetto, 3

Dahrendorf, Rolf, 127
D'Annunzio's expedition, 178
Decision-making process, 161–7

role of the Committee of
  Director-Generals in, 164
De Gasperi, Alcide, 16, 26, 60, 88–9,
  115–6, 249
  four-party centrist coalition
  under, 123
  permanent parliamentary
  majority, 121
De Gasperi-Einaudi package, 246
De Lorenzo, General, 114, 178, 250
Demarchi, Professor D., 167
De Martino, Francesco, 121
De Mita, Ciriaco, 237
Democratic Popular Front (FDP),
  list system of PR, 75
Democratic Union of Italian
  Labour, 96
De Nicola, Enrico, 112, 113, 191
Denison, E., 29
Depretis, *transformismo*, 6
Destra storico, the, 5–6, 8
Diplomatic examination, 155
Direct representation in Parliament
  and lobbying, 101–4
Dissolution of Parliament, 137–8
District Council of Judges, 200
Divorce Bill, and the Christian
  Democrats, 134
  and the Church, 50
  and the Constitutional Court, 197
Divorce League, 95
Doroteo faction, 90–1
D'Orsi, A., 176–7
Dual system of jurisdiction,
  administrative courts, 186
  civil servants, 201
  hierarchy, 187
  ordinary courts, 182
  conciliatori, 182
  corte d'appello, 183
  corte di cassazione, 183, 188, 189
  pretori, 182, 183
  tribunali, 182, 183

Ecclesiastical structure, differences
  between North and South, 52
Economic and social rights, 204,
  206

Economic depressions, 30, 31, 249
Economic miracle, 25–33
Economic planning and develop-
    ment problems, 167–72
Edison Electrical Company, 104–5
'Einaudi Line', 26–7
    ambiguity in, 28
    influence on the economy, 246,
    249
Einaudi, Luigi, 26, 112–5, 194
Elections and the electorate, 74–82
Electoral system, 78
    proportional representation in,
    74, 77
ENEL (*Ente Nazionale di Energia
    Elletrica*), 150–1
ENI (*Ente Nazionale Idrocarburi*),
    24, 26, 149–51
    creation, 249
    and economic planning, 172
    Mattei direction, 151–2
    oil concessions in Morocco, 114
    as owner of *Il Giorno*, 100
    and patronage system, 84
European Charter of Human
    Rights, 207
European Social Charter, 207
Executive, 117–8
Executive-legislative relations,
    137–8

Factionalism, 90–2
Fanfani, Amintore, 89, 116, 120,
    131, 140, 158, 160–2
Farini, 9
Fascist Code of Public Security,
    1931, 211
Fascist Party, rise to power, 7
Fascist State, role of Prefect in, 14
Federconsorzii (Federation of Agri-
    cultural Syndicates), 98
Federterra (for agricultural
    labourers), 69
Ferrari, P., 231, 237
Fiat, decision to manufacture the
    '600', 27
    and economic planning, 172
    as interest group, 95

a owner of *La Stampa*, 100
Finer, Herman, 15
Five-year plans, 167–72
Forcella, Enzo, 101
Fried, Professor R., 222

Galli, G., 79, 80, 85, 87, 98, 160
Garibaldi, 1860 expedition, 3
    Naples liberation, 9
Gaspari Reform, 159, 161
Gaspari, Remo, 159, 161
Gazetta Ufficiale, 131, 164
Gemelli, Father, 57
General Confederation of Italian
    Labour (CGIC), 69, 95
    membership, 96
General Italian Petroleum Agency
    (AGIP), 150
General Presidency, 56
General Staffs, Heads of, 174, 176,
    178
Giolitti, Antonio, 7, 25, 148
Giornale d'Italia, 100
Government Commissioner, role in
    local government, 224, 234
Gramsci, A., 45
Gronchi, Giovanni, 112–6, 160
Grosser, Alfred, 124
Gui, Luigi, 120, 161, 173

High Court of Sicily, 182
Higher Council of the Armed
    Forces, 174
Higher Judicial Council (Con-
    siglie Superiore della Magis-
    tratura), 201
    and enabling legislation, 202–4
Hobbes, Sir Thomas, 47
Holy Consistorial Congregation,
    58

Il Giorno, 100
Il Manifesto, 101
ILO Convention on equal pay, 210
Il Roma, 100
Impegno democratico, 90
Iniziativa democratica movement, 161
Iniziativa popolare, 90

Institute for Workers' Compensation (INAIL), 95, 148
Institute of Studies on Economic Planning (ISPE), 169
Instituto Fomazione Addestramento Professionale, 160
Interest-group, activity, 93–4
and the decision-making process, 165–6
and direct representation in Parliament, 102
influence, 99
intervention in administration, 104–6
links with parties, 95
Interministerial committees, creation of, 123
Interministerial Committee on Economic Planning (CIPE), 169, 170
Interministerial Committee for Savings and Credit, 169
Interministerial Committee on Prices, 166
Internal migration, 33–6
consequences, 35–6
and the economic miracle, 33
Inter-Parliamentary Committee on Regional Problems, 235
Intersind (State-held company employers), 95, 96
Intra-departmental committees, role of, 163–4
IRI (*Instituto per la recostruzione industriale*), 14, 24, 149–51
and economic planning, 170, 172
as instrument of propaganda, 99
and managerial training school, 160
and patronage system, 84, 158
ISAP, 155
Italcementi, 84
as owner of *Giornale d'Italia*, 100
Italian Association of Christian Workers (ACLI), 55
Italian Confederation of Free Trade Unions (CISL), 69, 95
membership, 96

Italian justice, characteristics, 184–6
class biased, 186
Italian Labour Movement, 96–7
Italian Labour Union (UIL), 95
Italian Parliamentary Standing Committees' legislation, 102

Jervolino, Raffaele, 120
John XXIII, Pope, 54
and new orientation of Holy See, 59, 60
Judges, the, and the independence of the judiciary, 199–204
promotion, 201
recruitment, 199–200
selection, 200
Judicial system, the, and Italian legal culture, 181
Junta, the, role in relation to the local council, 214–6
role in relation to the regional council, 227–8

Kogan, Professor N., 112, 122, 155, 162, 163

'Labour Charter', 207
La Malfa, Ugo, 130, 140
LaPalombara, Professor J., 60, 94, 95, 101, 103, 104, 106, 146
La Pira, Giorgio, 114
La Stampa, 100
Lateran Pacts, 48–50, 54
attitude to the Church, 15, 210
Lauro, Achille, 190
as owner of *Il Roma*, 100
Law of Guarantees, 48
Lazarsfeld, Professor P., 99
League of Cooperatives, 69
Legge truffa (swindle law), 76
Legislation, judicial review of, 181, 191
Legislative activity, 132–3
Legislative power, 228–9
Leone, Giovanni, 112, 116, 125, 137
Liberal party, 62, 63
and the electorate, 82

financial affairs, 84
role in economic miracle, 28, 29
List system, proportionality of,
75–6
Local autonomy, 212–3
State Treasury intervention and,
220
Local finance, state of, 218–9
Local government, autonomy, 220
control of, 221–5
educational system in, 217
functions, 216–21
income, 217–21
role of Council in, 214–5
structure, 213–6
Lotta Continua, 101

Mafia trials, 186
Mancini, Giuseppe, 80
Marinetti, Francesco, 13
Marx, 22
Mass-media of communication, 99
Maszini, *chef de cabinet,* 162–3
Mazza, Crescenzo, 121
Merton, Professor R., 99
Merzagora, Carlo, 125
Metternich's 'geographical
expression', 3, 20
Meynaud, Professor J., 244
Middle classes, characteristics,
243–4
Military apparatus, organization
and recruitment, 172–9
Military budget, 173–4
Military recruitment, crisis in,
176–7
Ministerial *cabinets,* importance of,
162
Ministerial stability, 119–20
Ministry of Agriculture, Industry
and Commerce, 11
Ministry of the Budget, reorganiza-
tion, 141, 168–9
and economic planning, 167–8
Ministry of the Budget and
Economic Planning, 168
Ministry of Defence, 174, 176
Ministry of Posts, 11

Ministry of State Holdings,
creation of, 141, 150
Ministry of the Treasury, 11
Monarchist Party, 62, 63
and the electorate, 82
financial affairs, 84
list system of PR, 75–6
organization, 68–74
Montedison, 95
Moro, Aldo, 116, 120, 122
preference votes, 80
reform agency stronghold, 161
Movement for the Regional
Autonomy of Piedmont
(MARP), 35
Municipal self-government, election of communal council in,
213
Mussolini, attitude to the Church, 15
attitude towards elections, 74, 77
and the Bolshevik peril, 11, 12
early years, 7
speech before Fascist Assembly,
12, 13
and the *statuto albertino,* 191

Namier, Sir Lewis, 63–4
Napoleonic administrative system,
adoption of, 141–4
Natali, Aldo, 121
National Association of Magistrates,
203
National Committee of Atomic
Energy (CNEN), 104
National Committee for Economic
Planning (CNPE), 167, 168
National Council of Economy and
Labour, 146, 168, 169
National Federation of Small
Farmers, *see Coldiretti*
National Health Insurance
Institute (INAM), 148
National Institute for Social
Security (INPS), 95, 148–9
National Institute for Workers'
Compensation (INAIL), *see*
Institute for Workers'
Compensation

NATO, Italian military integration into, 172
loyalty to, 73
Nenni, Pietro, 88, 116, 121, 141
Nenni Socialist Party, 68, 69, 72
Neo-fascist Party, 62, 63
and the electorate, 82
financial affairs, 84
list system of PR, 75–6
organization, 68–74
Neo-fascist Union (CISNAL), 69
membership, 96
Nichols, Peter, 58
Nobécourt, Jacques, 134, 136, 165, 184
Northern bourgeoisie, economic influence, 244
Notte, 100
Nuova Sinistra faction, 91

OECD report, 170–2
Olivetti, 95
Ordinary courts, 182–6 and *see also* dual system of jurisdiction

Pacciardi, Rodolfo, 120
Pact of Rome, June 1944, 69
Parentela, the, 105
and factionalism, 106, 107
Pariticrazia, domination of, 138
Parliament, and the control of government, 135–7
dissolution, 137
factionalism in, 104
and legislative process, 130–5
organization and procedure, 128–30
power, 124–37
Parliamentarians, characteristics, 126–8
Party organization, 68–74
Party system, the, 62–8
cabinet instability in, 63
factionalism in, 104
financial aspect of, 83–92
Namierite form of, 92
Proportional Representation in, 66
Passigli, Professor S., 83, 84

Pasti, General, 173, 178
Pavolini, 85
Peasants' Alliance, 69
Pella, Giuseppe, 114, 120, 162
Pertini, Alessandro, 130
Pescatere, Gabriele, 153, 160
Pesenti, 100
Pirelli, 95
Pius IX, Pope, rejection of the Law of Guarantees, 48
Pius XI, Pope, 47
Pius XII, Pope, 50
determination to direct Italian affairs, 60
Planning procedure, law on, 170
Political culture, 40–4
and the 'Southern Question', 41
Political fragmentation, causes of, 247
Political hegemony, 68
Political rights, 205–6
Political system, interest groups' pressure in, 93
Popular Party, 6
programme, 10
Posner, M. V., 150–1
Prandi, A., 79–80, 85, 98, 160
Predieri, Alberto, 117, 134
Prefect, the, control exercised by central government over, 222
role in local government, 221–5
use of dissolution, 223
President of the Republic, the, functions, 111–7
personal intervention in political life, 113–4
political influence, 114–7
President of the Senate, the, as the second personage of the State, 125
Press, the, Catholic interests in, 101
freedom of, 208–9
influence on public opinion, 99–101
lack of readership, 101
limitation, 101
predominance of business in, 101

Proportional representation, 74
and dissolution, 137
in larger communes, 214
as the most stable of all electoral
systems, 77
Provinces, the, as the inter-
mediaries between communes
and regions, 215
Provincial governments, financial
situation, 221
powers, 220

RAI (the state-owned radio and
television service), and the
patronage system, 83-4
Rapporteurs, judges acting as, 194
Red provinces, Marxist framework
in, 42
Referendum, 134-5
Regional Administrative Judge,
224
Regional Administrative Tribunal,
187, 224
Regional autonomy, 213, 225
Regional Committees for Economic
Planning (CRPE), 169
Regional division, 5, 6
Regional Finance Act, 230
Regional Government, 213
control, 233
economic policy, 232
electoral system, 226-7
financial independence, 230
powers, 228-35
revenue, 230-1
structure, 225-8
Regional political autonomy, 236
Regional Reform, 238
Regional subcultures, institutionalization of, 41-3
Regions, the, 'complementary
legislative power' and
'limited exclusive legislative
power' of, 228-9
ordinary and special regions
among, 225-6
relationship with central government, 237, 238

Religious freedom, 210
Republican Constitution, resistance
responsibility in, 16
Republican Party, 62, 63
and the electoral system, 75-6
financial affairs, 84
organization, 68-74
Resistance, the, 15-17
Restivi, 120
Rocco Penal Code, 207-9
Rochat, Giorgio, 178
Roman Law, in legal system, 181
'Roman Question', the, 48-50
Romeo, Rosario, 4
Rossi, Ernesto, 166
Ruini, Meuccio, 235
Rumor, Mariano, 90-1, 97, 116,
122, 160

Salvemini, Gaetano, 9, 13
Sandulli, Aldo, 191, 196
Saraceno, Pasquale, 21
'Saraceno Plan', 168
Saragat, Giuseppe, 88, 112, 113,
116, 117, 121
personal intervention, 114
Saragat Social Democrats, the, and
the American Labour Unions,
85
organization, 72
Sardinian Action Party, 10, 62
Sartori, Professor G., 126
Scalfari, Eugenio, 27, 151-2
Scelba Law, 237
Scelba, Mario, 114, 120
School Teachers' Movement, 54
*Scuola Superiore della Publica
Amministrazione*, 156, 160
Secret vote, in legislative function,
130-1
Segni, Antonio, 112-7
Selvati, Michele, 32
Senate, the, electoral system,
75-6, 125
procedure, 129
Sex discrimination, 210
Simigaglia plan, 27
Sinistra storica, the, 5

Social Democrat Party, 62, 63
  financial affairs, 84, 85
  organization, 68–74
Socialist Party (PSIUP), 6, 62, 63,
  78, 249
  and the electoral system, 75–6
  financial affairs, 83
  organization, 71
Social Security, 148–9
Somogyi, Professor S., 128
Southern Development Fund,
  153, 160
Southern emigration, 23
Southern graduates, and the civil
  service, 157
Southern *jacqueries*, 23
Southern policy, and the EEC,
  24–5
'Southern Question', the, 8–11,
  20–5
Specialized agencies, and political
  patronage, 160
Speech, freedom of, 208
Spreafico, Professor A., 145
Standing committees, membership,
  129
  decision on bills, 130–1
State, the, civil servants' view of,
  158–9
State-citizen relations, 210
Statuto albertino, 1848, 4, 5
  and dictatorship, 12, 191
Student Movement, 68
Study Office, 168, 169
Sturzo, Luigi, 10
Sullo, Fiorentino, 91
Supreme Defence Council, 174
Sylos-Labini, P., 36, 40

Tambroni, Ferdinando, 91, 116
Tarrow, S. G., 82
Tasca, Angelo, 49
Taviani, Paolo Emilio, 90–1, 120
Terni steel works, 148
Togni, Giuseppe, 103
Trabucchi, Senator, 198
Trade unions, the, action on the
  Pensions Bill, 97

and industry, 29
and the reform of the Health
  Service, 97
relationship with the
  Administration, 105
role in the economic miracle,
  28, 29
strikes for housing reform, 97
Trade-union confederations, direct
  representation, 103
Treasury and State Accounting
  Office, 169
Trieste agreements, 114
Tupini Committee, 237

Unification, as a compromise, 3, 4
  leading to a strong centralized
  state, 7, 8
  and the 'Southern Question',
  20, 21
Union of Italian Labour (UIL), 69
Union of Italian Magistrates, 203
University Graduates' Movement,
  54
University Students' Movement
  (FUCI), 54
USA, Italy's loyalty to, 173
USA economy, link between
  Italian economy and, 25–6

Valpreda, Pietro, 208
Vanoni, Enzo, 120
'Vanoni Plan', 167
Vatican II, 54
Veterans' Associations, 98
  relationship with administration,
  105
Victor Emanuel II, 4
Vilipendio, cases of, 209

Weaponry, inadequacy of, 173, 177
White provinces, Catholic tradition
  in, 42
Wilson, Professor, 166
Woolf, S. J., 150–1
Working class, progressive
  embourgeoisement of, 43
Wright-Mills, C., 43

Zoli, Aldo, 125

Index